Performing Power in Zimbabwe

Focusing on political trials in Zimbabwe's Magistrates' Courts between 2000 and 2012, Susanne Verheul explores why the judiciary have remained a central site of contestation in post-independence Zimbabwe. Drawing on rich court observations and in-depth interviews, this book foregrounds law's potential to reproduce or transform social and political power through the narrative, material and sensory dimensions of court-room performances. Instead of viewing appeals to law as acts of resistance by marginalised orders for inclusion in dominant modes of rule, Susanne Verheul argues that it was not recognition *by* but *of* this formal, rule-bound ordering, and the form of citizenship it stood for, that was at stake in performative legal engagements. In this manner, law was much more than a mere instrument. Law was a site in which competing conceptions of political authority were given expression, and in which people's under-standings of themselves as citizens were formed and performed.

SUSANNE VERHEUL is a Research Fellow in International Development at the University of Oxford where her research focuses on questions of law and politics in southern Africa. She previously taught at University College Roosevelt, Utrecht University and holds a DPhil from the University of Oxford.

African Studies Series

The African Studies series, founded in 1968, is a prestigious series of mono-graphs, general surveys, and textbooks on Africa covering history, political science, anthropology, economics, and ecological and environmental issues. The series seeks to publish work by senior scholars as well as the best new research.

Editorial Board:

Other titles in the series are listed at the back of the book.

Performing Power in Zimbabwe

Politics, Law, and the Courts since 2000

SUSANNE VERHEUL
University of Oxford

CAMBRIDGE
UNIVERSITY PRESS

CAMBRIDGE
UNIVERSITY PRESS

Shaftesbury Road, Cambridge CB2 8EA, United Kingdom

One Liberty Plaza, 20th Floor, New York, NY 10006, USA

477 Williamstown Road, Port Melbourne, VIC 3207, Australia

314–321, 3rd Floor, Plot 3, Splendor Forum, Jasola District Centre, New Delhi – 110025, India

103 Penang Road, #05–06/07, Visioncrest Commercial, Singapore 238467

Cambridge University Press is part of Cambridge University Press & Assessment, a department of the University of Cambridge.

We share the University's mission to contribute to society through the pursuit of education, learning and research at the highest international levels of excellence.

www.cambridge.org
Information on this title: www.cambridge.org/9781009011792

DOI: 10.1017/9781009026826

First published 2021
First paperback edition 2023

A catalogue record for this publication is available from the British Library

Library of Congress Cataloging-in-Publication data
Names: Verheul, Susanne, 1986– author.
Title: Performing power in Zimbabwe : politics, law, and the courts since 2000 / Susanne Verheul, University of Oxford.
Description: Cambridge, United Kingdom ; New York, NY : Cambridge University Press, 2021. | Series: African studies | Based on author's thesis (doctoral - University of Oxford, 2017) issued under title: 'Government is a legal fiction' : performing political power in Zimbabwe's magistrates' courts after 2000. | Includes bibliographical references and index.
Identifiers: LCCN 2021024666 (print) | LCCN 2021024667 (ebook) | ISBN 9781316515860 (hardback) | ISBN 9781009011792 (paperback) | ISBN 9781009026826 (epub)
Subjects: LCSH: Political crimes and offenses–Zimbabwe. | Courts of first instance–Zimbabwe. | Zimbabwe–Politics and government–1980-
Classification: LCC KTZ441 .V47 2021 (print) | LCC KTZ441 (ebook) | DDC 345. 6981/0231–dc23
LC record available at https://lccn.loc.gov/2021024666
LC ebook record available at https://lccn.loc.gov/2021024667

ISBN   978-1-316-51586-0   Hardback
ISBN   978-1-009-01179-2   Paperback

Voor Oma

Contents

Figures

Acknowledgements

The seeds for this book were sown while I was sitting in the World Food Programme's office in Kampala, Uganda, following the news about the 2008 presidential and parliamentary elections in Zimbabwe. During my M.Phil and D.Phil in International Development at the University of Oxford, these seeds were able to grow into a research project, and, over the course of my Leverhulme Trust Early Career Fellowship, into a book.

Writing this book, then, was a lengthy process, during which I benefitted from immeasurable opportunities and support. First and foremost, I am indebted to all those who shared their lives, experiences and thoughts with me during my time in Zimbabwe. I am not able to name everyone here, but I hope I have done justice to our exchanges. Among the select few I can mention, I wish to thank Zimbabwe Lawyers for Human Rights for facilitating my access to the courts in Harare and Bulawayo, to the Royal Netherlands Embassy in Harare for their support, to Ushehwedu Kufakurinani, Phillan Zamchiya, Innocent Kasiyano, Cleto Manjova and Eddson Chakuma for showing me new sides of Harare on a regular basis, and to Rodrick Fayayo, Delta Mbonisi and Philani Mpofu at the Bulawayo Progressive Residents Association for sharing their wisdom and their office space. For their continued assistance in Zimbabwe and following my return to Oxford, I am especially indebted to David Hofisi, Hopewell Gumbo, Jeremiah Bamu, and Kucaca Phulu. Owen Maseko created this book's cover image, beautifully capturing both the form and atmosphere of Zimbabwe's courtrooms.

My research trips to Zimbabwe were generously supported by the Prins Bernhard Cultuur Fonds, the Oxford Department of International Development and the Leverhulme Trust. With funding from Point Sud and the Deutsche Forschungsgemeinschaft I was also given the opportunity to attend a series of thought-provoking international workshops on Courts in Africa in Niamey, Niger (December

2014) and Ouagadougou, Burkina Faso (February 2016). I am further grateful for my time at the University College Roosevelt, The Netherlands: teaching at an undergraduate level showed me another side of academia and highlighted the importance of strong academic role models.

In that vein, my heartfelt thanks go to Jocelyn Alexander, whose thoughtful and thorough supervision guided me during my postgraduate years, and whose commitment to scholarship and to Zimbabwean history and politics continue to be an inspiration, encouraging me to think more critically, to work more methodically and to persevere. For igniting the spark of academic research during my undergraduate studies, and for their continued support along the way, I am indebted to John Friedman and Fatima Mueller-Friedman. In their positive feedback and encouragement to transform my thesis into a book, my examiners Jonny Steinberg and Sara Rich Dorman were further invaluable guides. For their generous support throughout the publication process, I thank Maria Marsh, Daniel Brown, Atifa Jiwa, Natasha Whelan, Dhivyabharathi Elavazhagan, Dan Harding and the entire Cambridge University Press African Studies series team, as well as the two anonymous reviewers for their encouraging feedback on an early draft of this book

Many of the ideas in this book grew out of exchanges with the dynamic academic community in Oxford, particularly with the members of Tuesday's Southern Africa Discussion Group, the Loft community and the Womyn's Discussion Group. Alex Löwe, Andy Emmerich, Carolin Fischer, Chloé Lewis, Dan Hodgkinson, George Karekwaivanane, Georgia Cole, Hannah Hoechner, Hannah Waddilove, Luisa Enria, Miles Tendi, Shrochis Karki and Taylor St John – thank you for listening to or reading various drafts of this work, and offering me an intellectual home where we could share research advice, coffee, wine and the occasional much-needed rant. To everyone who had to suffer living with me through all this, but especially the Cranham 'girls' – Andrea Kölbel, Andrea Ruediger, Eveliina Lyytinen and Nora Stappert – thank you for making our house such a warm and welcoming home, and for our continued friendship. I am immensely grateful also for our friendship: Alex Barnard, Cole Paulson, Fauzia Jamal, Sasha Romary and Sophia Mann.

Most of all, I am grateful for my parents Gonnie Biemold and Jeroen Verheul, my brother Bart and my Opa Eppie and Oma Willie. I would never had started this journey if they hadn't pushed me to finish high school, and I probably would not have completed it without their unwavering support, the occasionally necessary constructive criticism and the many calls to bridge the physical distance between us. Last but certainly not least, I want to thank my new-found family, Laelia Dard-Dascot, for not only putting up with my imperfections, but for reminding me often that it is precisely through this crack in everything that the light gets in.

Earlier versions of Chapter 2 and Chapter 3 were published as articles in the *Journal of Southern African Studies*[1] and *Africa*[2] respectively. In addition, I drew on empirical material from Chapter 5 for an article in *Political and Legal Anthropology Review*,[3] and on parts of the historical review from Chapter 1 for a chapter in an edited volume on Zimbabwean politics for Oxford University Press.[4]

[1] Susanne Verheul, '"Rebels" and "Good Boys": Patronage, Intimidation, and Resistance in Zimbabwe's Attorney General's Office Post-2000', *Journal of Southern African Studies*, 39, 4, 2013, pp. 765–82.

[2] Susanne Verheul, '"Zimbabweans Are Foolishly Litigious": Exploring the Internal Logics for Appeals to a Politicised Legal System', *Africa*, 86, 1, 2016, pp. 78–97.

[3] Susanne Verheul, '"Rotten Row Is Rotten to the Core": The Material and Sensory Politics of Harare's Magistrates Courts after 2000', *PoLAR: Political and Legal Anthropology Review*, 43, 2, 2020, pp. 262–79.

[4] Susanne Verheul, 'Land, Law and the Courts in Zimbabwe', in Jocelyn Alexander, JoAnn McGregor and Miles Tendi (eds), *Handbook of Zimbabwean Politics*, July 2020, retrieved from https://www.oxfordhandbooks.com/view/10.1093/oxfordhb/9780198805472.001.0001/oxfordhb-9780198805472-e-4.

Abbreviations

CCJP	Catholic Commission for Justice and Peace
CFU	Commercial Farmers Union
CIO	Central Intelligence Organisation
GNU	Government of National Unity
GPA	Global Political Agreement
ICTR	International Criminal Tribunal for Rwanda
ISO	International Socialist Organisation
ISO-Z	International Socialist Organisation in Zimbabwe
LOMA	Law and Order Maintenance Act
LRF	Legal Resources Foundation
MDC	Movement for Democratic Change
MLF	Mthwakazi Liberation Front
MP	Member of Parliament
POSA	Public Order and Security Act
SPT	Solidarity Peace Trust
ZANLA	Zimbabwe African National Liberation Army
ZANU	Zimbabwe African National Union
ZANU-PF	Zimbabwe African National Union-Patriotic Front
ZAPU	Zimbabwe African People's Union
ZINASU	Zimbabwe National Students Union
ZIPRA	Zimbabwe People's Revolutionary Army
ZLHR	Zimbabwe Lawyers for Human Rights
ZLP	Zimbabwe Liberators Platform
ZNLWVA	Zimbabwe National Liberation War Veterans' Association
ZRP	Zimbabwe Republic Police

Introduction
Law, State Authority and the Courts

If you are going to be fair in your analysis of the Zimbabwean judiciary, you need to look at it from that perspective. Where it all crumbled. Why an executive, which in itself is a creature of law, decides then to say 'ignore law', because that is risky for any government. Because once you say that you yourself do not respect law, what it means is that you yourself are attacking the very legitimacy that you've got. Government itself is a legal fiction.[1]

In September 2001, a month after resigning from the bench, Zimbabwe High Court Judge Michael Gillespie published his review of a case involving a supporter of the country's ruling party, the Zimbabwe African National Union-Patriotic Front (ZANU-PF), who was convicted of attempting to extort $3,000 from his former employer, a white Zimbabwean, but had, in Justice Gillespie's opinion, received an unjustifiably lenient sentence in the Magistrates' Courts. In his review, Justice Gillespie tied his commentary on the man's sentence to his reasons for leaving the bench. The political and judicial context in which this sentence was passed, he argued, posed a 'challenge to his conscience'.[2] As a result of partisan packing of the bench, selective prosecution and the manipulation of court rolls, he could no longer consider himself 'an independent Judge in an impartial Court'. Instead, he found 'himself in the position where he is called upon to administer the law only as against political opponents of the government and not against government supporters'.[3] In the state media, Professor Jonathan Moyo, then minister of information for ZANU-PF, dismissed Justice Gillespie's remarks as those of 'an unrepentant racist', whose

---

[1] Interview, Tawanda Zhuwarara, human rights lawyer, Harare, 7 September 2010.
[2] From Judgment HH 148-2001, at pp. 5–6 (issued on 26 September 2001 by Justice Gillespie in *State v. Humbarume*).
[3] Ibid.

resignation from the bench and departure from Zimbabwe were 'really good riddance to bad rubbish'.[4]

A multitude of national and international human rights reports published on the state of the judiciary in Zimbabwe echoed Justice Gillespie's conclusion that the ruling party had mastered the 'techniques which provide a government determined to do so with the opportunity to subvert the law while at the same time appearing to respects its institutions'.[5] These reports drew particular attention to the seemingly paradoxical manner in which the government maintained a rhetorical commitment to judicial due process while relying on the Zimbabwe Republic Police (ZRP) force and the courts to harass and intimidate political opponents through violent arrests, physical and psychological abuse in custody, prolonged detentions often in inhumane conditions and artificially drawn-out trials.

In Zimbabwe, legal processes appeared to be simply a façade to mask the violence of ZANU-PF's rule. In this book, I argue that this approach obfuscates myriad ways that state authority, and the notions of citizenship that are tied to this authority, can be consistently negotiated and (per)formed through law. Both Justice Gillespie's reasoning and Jonathan Moyo's response suggest that judicial institutions and practitioners, as well as ideas about the law, occupied a more complex position in Zimbabwe's political debates. Jonathan Moyo's attack on Justice Gillespie as 'the unrepentant racist', for instance, turned not to

---

[4] 'Top Former Judge Says Mugabe "Engineered Lawlessness"', *Deutsche Presse-Agentur*, 6 October 2011, accessed on 5 December 2015 at www.iol.co.za/news/africa/mugabe-engineered-lawlessness-says-top-judge-74776.

[5] From Judgment HH 148-2001, at pp. 5–6 (issued on 26 September 2001 by Justice Gillespie in *State v. Humbarume*). Key human rights reports include: International Bar Association (IBA), *Report of IBA Zimbabwe Mission 2001* (London, IBA, 2001); Solidarity Peace Trust (SPT), *'Subverting Justice': The Role of the Judiciary in Denying the Will of the Zimbabwean Electorate since 2000* (Johannesburg, SPT, March 2005); IBA Human Rights Institute, *Partisan Policing: An Obstacle to Human Rights and Democracy in Zimbabwe* (London, IBA, October 2007); Human Rights Watch (HRW), *'Our Hands Are Tied': Erosion of the Rule of Law in Zimbabwe* (New York, HRW, November 2008); Bar Human Rights Committee (BHRC), *'A Place in the Sun', Zimbabwe: A Report of the State of the Rule of Law in Zimbabwe after the Global Political Agreement of September 2008* (London, BHRC, June 2008); HRW, *False Dawn: The Zimbabwe Power-Sharing Government's Failure to Deliver Human Rights Improvements* (New York, HRW, August 2009); and SPT, *Walking a Thin Line: The Political and Humanitarian Challenges Facing Zimbabwe's GPA Leadership – and Its Ordinary Citizens* (Johannesburg, SPT, June 2009).

the language of law, but to the country's history of colonial domination to dismiss Justice Gillespie's critique of ZANU-PF's governance as illegitimate. In turn, Justice Gillespie's reference to the ways his work conditions challenged his 'conscience' tied his decision to leave the bench to a commonly shared interpretation of his profession, and of the law, as ethical, procedural and proper only when these were not infringed upon by politics. His judgement and resignation, and Moyo's response, suggest that there were cracks in the regime's control over its judicial institutions, and the normative understanding of law that the members of these institutions should propound.

This book expands the study of the law beyond the idea of a façade or a mask for political repression by focusing on the trials, highlighted in human rights reports, of individuals accused of political offences in Harare and Bulawayo's Magistrates' Courts between 2000 and 2012. I ask: Why is the judiciary a central site of contestation in post-independence Zimbabwe? How is this contestation performed in political trials? And what does this contestation tell us about the making of political power? In posing these questions, the book places particular emphasis on the work courtroom performances do, foregrounding law's potential to reproduce or transform social and political power through the narrative, material and sensory dimensions of these performances. Contrary to studies which examine appeals to law as acts of resistance by marginalised orders for inclusion in dominant modes of rule, I argue that it was not recognition *by* but *of* this formal, rule-bound ordering, and the form of citizenship it stood for, that was at stake in performative legal engagements. In this manner, law was much more than a mere instrument. Law was a site in which competing conceptions of political authority were given expression, and in which people's understandings of themselves as citizens were formed and performed.

In this introduction, I situate the book within the conceptual framework that it expands on. I then briefly state why Zimbabwe offers an important case study to examine the questions raised by this framework, and describe the methodologies used to conduct the study. Finally, I set out the structure of the book's remaining chapters.

Law's Legitimacy and State Authority

The relationships between law, state and society are long-standing areas of examination for historians, anthropologists and socio-legal studies scholars. Although each discipline varies in its approach to the study of law, they are compatible in their conceptualisation of law as both a set of institutions and an idea(l) through which the power and authority of states and their citizens can be constructed, negotiated or undermined.[6] This approach enables scholars to distinguish between the practice of law within the state's judicial institutions, and the role of law within the political imaginations of a diverse range of actors. It further allows them to highlight the law's 'Janus-faced' workings.[7] Law, they argue, works as a double-edged sword that both legitimises the legal categories and rules through which states control their populations, and aids those marginalised by this form of state control to resist it.

Through this interplay between repression and resistance, law simultaneously reproduces social hierarchies and constitutes new categorisations.[8] The historian E. P. Thompson's examination of the Black Act in eighteenth-century England was influential in recognising that, through this dynamic, a government's reliance on legal processes as a mechanism for repression need not undermine the law's legitimacy.[9] Conceptualising of the law as both an ideology and a set of social norms that can be studied 'in terms of its own logic, rules, and procedures',[10] Thompson concludes that law's legitimacy stems from the possibility of justice:

[6] Kamari Maxine Clarke and Mark Goodale (eds), *Mirrors of Justice: Law and Power in the Post-Cold War Era* (Cambridge, Cambridge University Press, 2010); Mark Goodale, *Anthropology and Law: A Critical Introduction* (New York, New York University Press, 2017).

[7] John L. Comaroff, 'Colonialism, Culture and the Law: A Foreword', *Law and Social Inquiry*, 26, 2, 2001, p. 306. The understanding of law as a double-edged sword was further developed in the study of colonial governance and resistance: Martin Chanock, *Law, Custom and Social Order: The Colonial Experience in Malawi and Zambia* (Cambridge, Cambridge University Press, 1985); Sally Falk Moore, *Social Facts and Fabrications: Customary Law on Kilimanjaro, 1880–1980* (Cambridge, Cambridge University Press, 1986); Kirsten Mann and Richard Roberts (eds), *Law in Colonial Africa* (London, James Currey, 1991); Sally Engle Merry, 'Legal Pluralism', *Law and Society Review*, 22, 5, 1988, pp. 869–96.

[8] Mindie Lazarus-Black and Susan F. Hirsch (eds), *Contested States: Law, Hegemony and Resistance* (London, Routledge, 1994).

[9] E. P. Thompson, *Whigs and Hunters: The Origin of the Black Act* (New York, Pantheon Books, 1975).

[10] Ibid., p. 260.

The essential precondition for the effectiveness of the law, in its function as ideology, is that it shall display an independence from gross manipulation and shall seem to be just. It cannot seem so without upholding its own logic and criteria of equity; indeed, on occasion, by actually being just.[11]

Arguing for the law's propensity for justice, Thompson recognises that all members of society may relate to multiple, at times contradictory understandings of law. By locating the legitimacy of law primarily in its ability to bring about occasional 'just' outcomes, however, he limits the practical and ideological degree to which those repressed by law may invoke it.

In her ambitious historical analysis of law and colonial rule, Lauren Benton moves beyond the focus on law's outcomes to foreground citizens' expectations of the law.[12] She demonstrates how those repressed under the law in colonial states had no expectations of its equal application, but granted it legitimacy because it provided a forum through which they could engage with, or challenge, the political, economic and social agendas promoted by the state. While the law's outcomes featured in determining its legitimacy, it was the process through which law was understood, defined and related to that mattered more. Susan Hirsch and Mindie Lazarus-Black similarly suggest that, when examining the place of law in 'contested' colonial and postcolonial states, we should ask not whether citizens' engagement with the law yielded successful outcomes, but rather how and why law was invoked and to what effect.[13]

Through its invocations law can work hegemonically, as a mode of governance that shapes, and is shaped through, interactions in all spheres of society and encompasses both coercion and consent. By turning to law, it becomes 'naturalised', normalised and firmly rooted as a legitimate form of governance in the imagination of states and their citizens. This process of naturalisation obscures the fact that law's legitimacy is in fact 'the consequence of particular historical actors,

---

[11] Ibid., p. 263.
[12] Lauren Benton, *Law and Colonial Cultures: Legal Regimes in World History, 1400–1900* (Cambridge, Cambridge University Press, 2002).
[13] Susan F. Hirsch and Mindie Lazarus-Black, 'Introduction – Performance and Paradox: Exploring Law's Role in Hegemony and Resistance', in Mindie Lazarus-Black and Susan F. Hirsch (eds), *Contested States: Law, Hegemony and Resistance* (London, Routledge, 1994), pp. 1–34.

classes, and events'.[14] Moreover, law's power frequently does remain debated, rather than naturalised. Law's hegemony may thus be fragmented, as Sally Engle Merry contends in her study on domestic conflict mediation in Hawaii's lower courts.[15]

When citizens invoke law as a form of resistance against the state, this works through consciousness of precisely this fragmented hegemony, and of the plurality of orders that can be invoked. By incorporating the notion of consciousness, law works ideologically rather than hegemonically. Distinguishing between hegemony and ideology, Jean Comaroff and John L. Comaroff observe that '[w]hereas the first consists of constructs and conventions that have come to be shared and naturalized throughout a political community, the second is the expression and ultimately the possession of a particular social group ... Hegemony homogenizes, ideology articulates.'[16] To capture the role of consciousness in creating spaces for resistance through the articulation of the law, Merry speaks of 'legal consciousness'.[17] In her account of legal consciousness among working-class Americans, she argues that law has the 'capacity to construct authoritative images of social relationships and actions'.[18] The legal ideology of those who may be repressed through it is therefore 'a negotiated, constructed reality developed in local social settings through repeated interactions, not a faithful replica of the dominant ideology'.[19]

Merry concludes, however, that the outcomes of citizens' legal consciousness remained marked by a paradox: in their attempt to break free from the dominant ideology through their legal engagements, citizens increased their reliance on the ways law ordered and

---

[14] Hirsch and Lazarus-Black, 'Introduction', p. 7.
[15] Sally Engle Merry, 'Courts as Performances: Domestic Violence Hearings in a Hawai'i Family Court', in Mindie Lazarus-Black and Susan Hirsch (eds), *Contested States: Law, Hegemony, and Resistance* (London, Routledge, 1994), p. 54.
[16] Jean Comaroff and John L. Comaroff, *Of Revelation and Revolution: Christianity, Colonialism and Consciousness in South Africa* (London, University of Chicago Press, 1991), p. 24.
[17] Sally Engle Merry, *Getting Justice and Getting Even: Legal Consciousness among Working-Class Americans* (London, University of Chicago Press, 1990); Sally Engle Merry, 'Everyday Understandings of the Law in Working-Class America', *American Ethnologist*, 13, 2, 1986, pp. 253–70.
[18] Merry, *Getting Justice and Getting Even*, p. 8.
[19] Merry, 'Everyday Understandings of the Law', p. 255.

categorised them.[20] More recently, particular attention has been paid to how this paradox plays out in claims to citizenship by populations excluded from, or on the margins of, the modern state and its normative structures of accountability, such as stateless populations, migrants and refugees, who often have to turn to the language of human rights to be 'heard' and so remain bound to the state categories that marginalise them.[21] Mobilisations of law within citizenship struggles remain highly diverse, however, reflecting a range of ideas about citizenship itself.[22] Citizenship, Catherine Neveu argues, 'is a socially and politically constructed, and thus arbitrary, notion' which has very real practical, political, legal and institutional effects.[23]

'Legal consciousness' and the understanding of law as ideology that shapes state and society relations push us to examine the creation, circulation and impact of multiple articulations of, and claims made on, the law. Throughout this book, I argue that the recognition of a variety of engagements with law, and the study of their interactions and effects, is essential for examining the judiciary as a site for political contestation, and for identifying the productive place of law in manufacturing state authority and notions of citizenship. In doing so, I challenge the manner in which scholars of authoritarian or postcolonial states continue to frame the use of law as a paradox of repression and resistance.

The binary of repression and resistance is evident in the work of scholars studying the role of courts and judicial activism in semi-democratic and authoritarian regimes,[24] and scholars examining the place of law within postcolonial contexts. They caution that, despite the persistence of discourses of rights within postcolonial society, law

[20] Merry, *Getting Justice and Getting Even.*
[21] See, for example: Ilana Feldman, 'Difficult Distinctions: Refugee Law, Humanitarian Practice, and Political Identification in Gaza', *Cultural Anthropology*, 22, 1, 2007, pp. 129–69; Ramah McKay, 'Afterlives: Humanitarian Histories and Critical Subjects in Mozambique', *Cultural Anthropology*, 27, 2, 2012, pp. 286–309.
[22] Nandini Sundar, 'The Rule of Law and Citizenship in Central India: Postcolonial Dilemmas', *Citizenship Studies* 15, 3–4, 2011, p. 422.
[23] Catherine Neveu, 'Discussion: Anthropology and Citizenship', *Social Anthropology*, 13, 2, 2005, p. 200.
[24] Tamir Moustafa and Tom Ginsburg, 'Introduction: The Function of Courts in Authoritarian Politics', in Tom Ginsburg and Tamir Moustafa (eds), *Rule by Law: The Politics of Courts in Authoritarian Regimes* (Cambridge, Cambridge University Press, 2008), p. 2.

remains a conservative force, reproducing rather than reforming existing power relations and modes of governance. Comaroff and Comaroff, for example, argue that the postcolonial polity is marked by a paradox of increased crime, violence and disorder on the one hand, and growing democratisation and a commitment to the law on the other.[25] Within, and as a result of, this dynamic, the law is 'fetishized'. Almost all dimensions of the postcolony, they contend, 'exist ... in the shadow of the law'.[26] The prevailing, almost religious, adoration for the law, the Comaroffs argue, turns it into the central framework around which communities, including the state, are formed.[27] Within the postcolony, they further argue that this 'fetishi zation of law', and the underlying interaction between law and disorder, gives rise to 'lawfare' as a primary mode of governance, defined as 'the resort to legal instruments, to the violence inherent in the law, to commit acts of political coercion, even erasure'.[28] 'Lawfare' may be mobilised as a 'weapon of the weak'; however, the Comaroffs observe that 'ultimately it is neither the weak nor the meek nor the marginal who predominate in such things. It is those equipped to play most potently inside the dialectic of law and disorder.'[29]

While the Comaroffs argue that 'lawfare' is not the most effective mode for resistance within the postcolonial polity, anthropological accounts of African politics have highlighted that those best equipped to play with the law's power need not be located within the state's institutions. Ethnographies of governance within the postcolony argue for the workings of multiple, complementary or competing centres of power. The existence of this multitude of actors both contributes to the disorder that characterises the postcolony, and ensures that the forms and functions of the law may be appropriated and mobilised by forces beyond the state.[30]

---

[25] John L. Comaroff and Jean Comaroff, 'Law and Disorder in the Postcolony: An Introduction', in Jean Comaroff and John L. Comaroff (eds), *Law and Disorder in the Postcolony* (London, University of Chicago Press, 2006), pp. 1–56.
[26] Comaroff and Comaroff, 'Law and Disorder in the Postcolony', p. 34.
[27] Ibid. See also, Jean Comaroff and John L. Comaroff, 'Criminal Justice, Cultural Justice: The Limits of Liberalism and the Pragmatics of Difference in the New South Africa', *American Ethnologist*, 31, 2, 2004, pp. 188–204.
[28] Comaroff and Comaroff, 'Law and Disorder in the Postcolony', p. 30.
[29] Ibid., p. 31.
[30] Thomas Bierschenk and Jean-Pierre Olivier de Sardan (eds), *States at Work: Dynamics of African Bureaucracies* (Boston, Brill, 2014); Christian Lund,

As important as it is to recognise the workings of multiple forms of governance, and to study the relationship between law's legitimacy, state authority and society, through the production and circulation of legal consciousness 'from the margins', I argue throughout this book that we should return to the idea of the state as tied to its institutions and actors to explain the persistence of the authority of law. In essence, I combine E. P. Thompson's understanding of the effect of occasional 'just' outcomes in legal institutions on the legitimacy of states[31] with Lauren Benton's recognition of law as a language and practice through which citizens can express their expectations of the state,[32] and to take this combined approach into the postcolonial setting. By so doing, I build on Thomas Hansen and Finn Stepputat's ethnographic explorations of the postcolonial state. Hansen and Stepputat demonstrate that law not only accords legitimacy to the ruling regime, but also shapes our idea of the state.[33] With its symbolism the law grants the state authority. This authority is closely tied to an understanding of 'the state' as standing above 'society' as a guarantor of rights, and as a means of ensuring justice.[34] Hansen and Stepputat allow for law to work alongside multiple 'languages of stateness', and call for ethnographic explorations of the role of law in maintaining particular state–society relations.

I argue that, in order to conduct such ethnographic explorations, scholars should empirically disentangle law from repressive rule and examine instead the ideas about state authority and citizenship that are embodied, enacted and debated through it. When we dichotomise law as either a mode of, or a tool for, repressive governance within postcolonial regimes, or a language of resistance to this governance, we run the risk of relating all engagements with the law and its forums directly to opposition to the state (defined both as a set of institutions and an imaginary), and judging the meaning of such engagements with law by the space they create for citizens to break out of the state's categorisations. This does not allow us to ask what understandings of the state, and one's political belonging to it, are authorised and contested

'Twilight Institutions: Public Authority and Local Politics in Africa', *Development and Change*, 37, 4, 2006, pp. 685–705.
[31] Thompson, *Whigs and Hunters*.   [32] Benton, *Law and Colonial Cultures*.
[33] Thomas Blom Hansen and Finn Stepputat, *States of Imagination: Ethnographic Explorations of the Postcolonial State* (London, Duke University Press, 2001).
[34] Hansen and Stepputat, *States of Imagination*, p. 15.

through interactions with the law – or what 'myth of the state' is being articulated.[35]

Rather than reducing the debates that take place within legal institutions in postcolonial polities to symptoms of the 'fetishisation' of law, in this book I ask instead how dynamic performances engaging, or taking place within, these institutions generate and contest a 'state consciousness', a concept which links peoples' mobilisations of 'legal consciousness' to the ideas of the state that are at stake in their contestations.[36] I argue that, in the case of Zimbabwe, civil servants and citizens may engage the law not only as an attempt to reform or reject the modes of governance used against them, but also to reaffirm their ideal of the state and their understanding of citizenship within this state, demanding that their government engage with and be held accountable to this ideal.

In this book, I therefore foreground interactions within judicial institutions, and argue that we should move questions of what law as a language of 'stateness' authorises back into our study of the dynamics of meaning-making within the state's institutions specifically. As Lazarus-Black and Hirsch show, the judicial system, and particularly the courts, are 'complex sites' within which a range of hierarchies and power relations can be contested and restructured.[37] To capture these dynamics, I study trials in the Zimbabwean courts as spaces of performance. In the following section I lay out why this is a useful approach in relation to political trials.

Courts as Spaces of Performance

Scholars have derived important insights into the dynamics of state formation and contestation by studying courtrooms as spaces of

---

[35] Philip Abrams, 'Notes on the Difficulty of Studying the State', *Journal of Historical Sociology*, 1, 1, 1988, pp. 58–89; Timothy Mitchell, 'Society, Economy and the State Effect', in G. Steinmetz (ed.), *State/Culture: State-Formation after the Cultural Turn* (London, Cornell University Press, 1999), pp. 76–97.

[36] In developing the notion of 'state consciousness', my conversations with, and engagement with the work of, Dr Sophie Andreetta have been hugely beneficial. See Sophie Andreetta, 'Pourquoi Aller au Tribunal si l'On n'Exécute Pas la Décision du Juge? Conflits d'Héritage et Usages du Droit à Cotonou', *Politique Africaine* 141, 1, 2016, pp. 147–68.

[37] Lazarus-Black and Hirsch, *Contested States*.

performance.[38] This approach incorporates Judith Butler's influential notion of 'performativity', which accommodates both repressive and productive aspects of power that are performed in the actions and demeanour of social agents.[39] Applied to the court, the metaphor of theatre allows scholars to examine how actors within the courtroom employ certain scripts, execute specific actions and make use of the court as a 'stage' on which to perform and challenge (state) power.

The cosmetic similarities between courtrooms and theatres emerge in early accounts from legal practitioners, who identified similarities between courts and the theatre in the symbolism of the courtroom, the practice of costuming, the use of props and ritual procession and the creation of space for an audience. These accounts are divided on the value of considering courts as theatres, however, as some point to the potentially corruptive elements of theatricality in court[40] while others valorise it.[41] Written from the perspective of legal practitioners, this debate captures the diverse views actors within the courtroom

---

[38] Academic interest in the use of the metaphor of theatre can in part be traced back to the performative turn in the social sciences. Influential works include Erving Goffman, *The Presentation of Self in Everyday Life* (New York, Anchor Books, 1959); Victor Turner, *The Anthropology of Performance* (New York, PAJ Publications, 1986); Richard Schechner, *Performance Theory* (New York, Drama Books Specialists, 1988).

[39] Judith Butler, *Gender Trouble: Feminism and the Subversion of Identity* (New York, Routledge, 1990); Judith Butler, *Bodies That Matter: On the Discursive Limits of 'Sex'* (New York, Routledge, 1993); Judith Butler, *Excitable Speech: A Politics of the Performance* (New York, Routledge, 1997).

[40] Allan Greenberg, 'Selecting a Courtroom Design', *Judicature*, 59, 9, 1976, pp. 422–8; Adi Parush, 'The Courtroom as a Theater and the Theater as Courtroom in Ancient Athens', *Israeli Law Review*, 35, 2001, pp. 118–37; Larry Geller and Peter Hemenway, 'Argument and Courtroom Theatrics', *National Association of Administrative Law Judges*, 16, 2, 1996, pp. 175–84; Peter Murphy, '"There's No Business Like . . . ?," Some Thoughts on the Ethics of Acting in the Courtroom', *South Texas Law Review*, 44, 1, 2002, pp. 111–25.

[41] Milner Ball, 'All the Law's a Stage', *Law and Literature*, 11, 2, 1999, pp. 215–21. See also, Richard Harbinger, 'Trial by Drama', *Judicature*, 55, 3, 1971, pp. 122–8; Mark I. Milstein and Laurence R. Bernstein, 'Trial as Theater', *Trial*, 33, 10, 1997, pp. 64–9; John Gillespie, 'Theatrical Justice (Criminal Trial as a Morality Play)', *Northern Ireland Legal Quarterly*, 31, 1, 1980, pp. 67–72; Julie Stone Peters, 'Theatricality, Legalism and the Scenography of Suffering: The Trial of Warren Hastings and Richard Brinsley Seridan's "Pizarro"', *Law and Literature*, 18, 1, 2006, pp. 15–45; Allan Tow, 'Teaching Trial Practice and Dramatic Technique', *Journal of Paralegal Education and Practice*, 13, 1, 1997, pp. 59–96.

may hold over how theatrical behaviour fits into their norms of justice. They do not inform us, however, of how trials work as social processes.

To examine the meaning of performance within trials we must turn instead to the work of legal anthropologists, historians and sociologists. Within these accounts the meaning of legal performances is not linked to the idea of whether or not the court is undermined. Instead, legal performances are examined for the ways in which they encompass actors' efforts to affirm their political or social belonging, or their attempts to challenge this belonging if it results in their exclusion. The courtroom provides a stage on which its actors can construct and contest identities, practices and institutions. What is being upheld or challenged on this stage could be fundamentally different.

Situated in a broader debate on capital punishment, for example, studies on trial and punishment identify rule-based legal performances as central to preserving the legitimacy of states.[42] In such trials, defendants may try to disrupt the trial proceedings with the aim of exposing legal procedures as a mask for state violence.[43] The co-defendants in Saddam Hussein's trial, for instance, aimed to question the very legitimacy of the court in which they were tried, and the state that authorised their trial, through disruptive improvisation.[44] Studies of African colonial courts, in turn, demonstrate that disruptive improvisation was not the only performance defendants and litigants could engage in. In an effort to challenge the legitimacy of the courts, or to get what they wanted, some actors would conform to, and play on, the stereotypes or prejudices colonial judges held.[45] Examining cases

---

[42] Thought-provoking discussions on trial and punishment as law-preserving violence include: Dwight Conquergood, 'Lethal Theatre: Performance, Punishment and the Death Penalty', *Theatre Journal*, 54, 3, 2002, pp. 339–67; Austin Sarat, *When the State Kills: Capital Punishment and the American Condition* (Princeton, Princeton University Press, 2001); and Nicole Rogers, 'Violence and Play in Saddam's Trial', *Melbourne Journal of International Law*, 8, 2, 2007, pp. 428–42. See also, Roger Caillois, *Man, Play, and Games* (Urbana, University of Illinois Press, 2001) [Translation of *Les Jeux et Les Hommes*, 1961, by Meyer Barash].

[43] Rogers, 'Violence and Play'; Susan Coutin, 'The Chicago Seven and the Sanctuary Eleven: Conspiracy and Spectacle in U.S. Courts', *Political and Legal Anthropology Review*, 16, 3, 1993, pp. 1–28.

[44] Rogers, 'Violence and Play'.

[45] Stacey Hynd, 'Deadlier Than the Male? Women and the Death Penalty in Colonial Kenya and Nyasaland, c. 1920–57', *Stichproben*, 12, 2007, pp. 13–33;

brought against African women in colonial Zimbabwe's High Court between 1900 and 1952, for example, Tapiwa Zimudzi casts them as agents who were legally aware. He writes that to conform to the traditional gender roles held by colonial judges, 'violent African female offenders consciously used courtroom demeanour'.[46] Taken together, such diverse performances affirm Hirsch and Lazarus-Black's point that 'the focus on performance illuminates instances when legal struggles crystallize in infamous trials and also capture how routine encounters with law shape social processes less dramatically, but more pervasively'.[47]

In part, law can shape social processes through the (re)production of historical and political narratives. Kim Lane Scheppele observes that the defence and the prosecution within the court tell competing stories, aimed at producing competing 'truths'.[48] Some African litigants and defendants, for example, reproduced and played into colonial narrative structures to 'reframe arguments . . . in their favour'.[49] Rather than subverting legal rules and the norms and morals these rules prescribed, litigants stayed within them in order to exploit the spaces for social change opened up by these rules. In this way, historians, anthropologists and sociologists can read court records as scripts which tell us about how defendants and litigants expressed themselves as agents, not only subjects, before the law. The interaction between different legal narratives, in turn, shapes and creates our understanding of the social

---

Derek R. Peterson, 'Morality Plays, Marriage, Church Courts and Colonial Agency in Central Tanganyika, ca. 1876–1928', *American Historical Review*, 111, 4, 2006, pp. 983–1010.

[46] Tapiwa B. Zimudzi, 'African Women, Violent Crime and the Criminal Law in Colonial Zimbabwe, 1900–1952', *Journal of Southern African Studies*, 30, 3, 2004, p. 502.

[47] Hirsch and Lazarus-Black, 'Introduction', p. 14.

[48] Kim Lane Scheppele, 'Foreword: Telling Stories', *Michigan Law Review*, 87, 8, 1989, pp. 2073–98. See also, Robert A. Ferguson, 'The Judicial Opinion as Literary Genre', *Yale Journal of Law & the Humanities*, 2, 1, 1990, pp. 201–19; Bernard S. Jackson, 'Narrative Theories and Legal Discourse', in Cristopher Nash (ed.), *Narrative in Culture: The Uses of Storytelling in the Sciences, Philosophy, and Literature* (London, Routledge, 1990), pp. 23–50; Jane B. Baron and Julia Epstein, 'Is Law Narrative?', *Buffalo Law Review*, 41, 1997, pp. 141–87; Steven Cammiss, '"He Goes Off and I Think He Took the Child": Narrative (Re)Production in the Courtroom', *King's Law Journal*, 17, 1, 2006, pp. 71–95.

[49] Peterson, 'Morality Plays', p. 988.

and political categorisations of law. As Pierre Bourdieu reminds us, law not only names but actively creates the things it names.[50]

Law's narrative creation extends to incorporate history. Austin Sarat and Thomas Kearns observe that law's legitimacy is to some degree the result of its history. Either by framing judicial decisions within a long continuum, or by explicitly noting how they break with history, decisions are granted authority.[51] Law not only uses history. Law also constructs historical narratives, with courts working as a site of memory and commemoration, and constructing judicial narratives that play an important role in building, or 'writing', the state.[52] Courts also 'write history' in a literal sense, creating a material record through court documents, transcripts and written judgements or opinions. Through recordings of the narrative actions of trials, 'courts can become archives in which that record serves as the materialization of memory'.[53] Legal narratives are therefore not only expressed before courtroom actors, such as the magistrate, judge, defence council or prosecution, but they remain available as an archive to be accessed by an audience in the future.

Trials also incorporate audiences in the present. The members of the public seated in the gallery play a central part in shaping law's legitimacy. Following Antoine Garapon, Nigel Eltringham suggests that it is through their entrance into the courtroom that visitors are 'transformed' to take on 'a new *temporary*, liminal status as a spectator'.[54] Reflecting on his own observations during hearings of the International Criminal Tribunal for Rwanda (ICTR) in Arusha, Tanzania, he observes how processes that check and control the visitors' conduct create a 'public' for trials. Trials, Eltringham argues, are highly speech-oriented proceedings aimed at producing a permanent record, within

---

[50] Pierre Bourdieu, 'The Force of Law: Towards a Sociology of the Juridical Field', *Hastings Law Journal*, 38, 1987, p. 831.

[51] Austin Sarat and Thomas R. Kearns (eds), *History, Memory and the Law* (Ann Arbor, University of Michigan Press, 1999).

[52] Sarat and Kearns, *History, Memory and the Law*; Daphne Barak-Erez, 'Collective Memory and Judicial Legitimacy: The Historical Narrative of the Israeli Supreme Court', *Canadian Journal of Law and Society*, 16, 1, 2001, pp. 93–112.

[53] Sarat and Kearns, *History, Memory and the Law*, p. 13.

[54] Nigel Eltringham, 'Spectators to the Spectacle of Law: The Formation of a "Validating Public" at the International Criminal Tribunal for Rwanda', *Ethnos*, 77, 3, 2012, p. 431 (emphasis in original).

which the 'noise' produced by lawyers, prosecutors and judges needs to be contrasted with, and validated by, the presence of a 'silent public'.[55] As visitors are asked to surrender their passports, are given an ID badge and pass by guards as they move through security checks, the process of transformation from an individual visitor into a member of the 'silent' and 'validating' public is set into motion. These checks are 'normalised' through their 'redundant repetition', and serve to make visitors legible, uniform and anonymous. Once led into the courtroom, this 'validating public' is further silenced through the lack of information they receive about the proceedings or meaning of the trial, and through the enforcement of rules governing the public's behaviour, rules different from those that apply to the lawyers, prosecutors and judges.

Eltringham concludes that the material processes through which visitors were brought into the court, and continued to be observed within the courtroom, allowed their silent observations to validate the power of the law and the judicial actors' speeches.[56] Linda Mulcahy adds that such controls on the public exist not only to validate the trial, but to avoid the engagement of the public in 'uncharted or unscripted performance[s]', which could signal the public's full inclusion in the public ritual and thus allow them to call the legal system to account.[57] These discussions of the public dimensions of the courtroom not only draw our attention to the role of audiences, but further highlight the links between trials, the production of historical and political narratives and the performance of social rituals.

In recent years the focus on performances within the courtroom has been extended to include not only the study of the architectural and material dimensions of this theatre and its stages, but also its 'atmospheres'.[58] In these studies the material and infrastructural are just one of three dimensions along which the courtrooms atmosphere emerges,

---

[55] Eltringham, 'Spectators to the Spectacle of Law', p. 429.   [56] Ibid.
[57] Linda Mulcahy, *Legal Architecture: Justice, Due Process and the Place of Law* (Oxford, Routledge, 2011), p. 10.
[58] Aina Backman, *Courtroom Atmospheres: Affective Dynamics in Courts, Sessions of Criminal Matter in Vienna* (unpublished Masters' thesis, Stockholm University, 2017); Jonas Bens, 'The Courtroom as an Affective Arrangement: Analysing Atmospheres in Courtroom Ethnography', *The Journal of Legal Pluralism and Unofficial Law*, 50, 3, 2018, pp. 336–55.

with the visual a second and sound a third dimension that warrant ethnographic inquiry. Although the study of courts as spaces for performance has taken diverse forms, I argue throughout this book that approaching trials through the lens of these multiple dimensions to examine a trials' narrative and ritual productions is particularly illuminating as it allows us to reveal diverse forms of authority and drives us to examine how forms of authority are manufactured by, and debated within, this performance.

Relating these performances to the construction of, and contestations over, state consciousness as I do in this book, however, also raises a set of questions that push us beyond existing approaches in two ways. First, courtroom performances should be contextualised within a longer chain of interactions with the law, including experiences of arrest and detention prior to the trial, as these all constitute essential steps in the debate over, and formation of, ideas concerning law and the authority they grant to the state. Second, this consciousness is negotiated through more than the narrative elements of the courtroom performance, driving us to expand our lens to look at the interaction between state-making and the material and sensory conditions within the courtroom as well. As a whole, this takes us beyond the binary purpose of trials as either enabling state repression or facilitating resistance, to examining the negotiated authority that emerges out of the performances of the state consciousness that marks the relationship between law, the state and its citizens in the run-up to and during the trial.

In the remainder of this chapter I outline why Zimbabwe offers a fascinating case through which to examine these questions, expand on the methods used to address them and outline the book's chapters.

The Case for Zimbabwe

Zimbabwe offers an informative and challenging case study to examine the relationship between law, state and society through courtroom performances. Throughout its colonial and postcolonial history the authority that law granted the government, and the ideal of the state, was dramatically contested by a wide range of actors, including government officials, judges, lawyers, nationalists, guerrillas, political activists and citizens. The persistence of the judiciary as a site of political contestation in Zimbabwe after 2000 is rooted in the country's precolonial political systems,[59] in the formation and often violent maintenance of colonial political and legal structures between 1880 and 1980,[60] in the models of authority and governance on which the nationalist parties in the struggle for liberation in the 1970s were founded[61] and in practices of nation-building, state-making and political contestation after independence.[62] In Chapter 1, I examine Zimbabwe's colonial and postcolonial history more closely to demonstrate how we can historically locate and situate 'legal consciousness', negotiations over state authority and citizenship, and the political performance of these debates through the law. To adequately introduce the significance of the post-2000 period it is necessary, however, to briefly outline these different historical periods in Zimbabwe.

Zimbabwe was known as Rhodesia when it was a British colony until 1965, when the Rhodesian Front party unilaterally declared independence and extended and expanded repressive white minority rule until independence in 1980. Independence was won through a

---

[59] See, for example, Ngwabi Bhebe and Terence Ranger (eds), *The Historical Dimensions of Democracy and Human Rights in Zimbabwe. Volume One: Pre-Colonial and Colonial Legacies* (Harare, University of Zimbabwe Publications, 2001); Sabelo Ndlovu-Gatsheni, 'Who Ruled by the Spear? Rethinking the Form of Governance in the Ndebele State', *African Studies Quarterly*, 10, 2–3, 2008, pp. 71–94.

[60] See, for example, Welshman Ncube, 'The Courts of Law in Rhodesia and Zimbabwe: Guardians of Civilisation, Human Rights and Justice or Purveyors of Repression', in Ngwabi Bhebe and Terence Ranger (eds), *The Historical Dimensions of Democracy and Human Rights in Zimbabwe. Volume One: Pre-Colonial and Colonial Legacies* (Harare, University of Zimbabwe Publications, 2001), pp. 99–123; Ndlovu-Gatsheni, 'Who Ruled by the Spear?'; Brian Raftopoulos and Alois Mlambo (eds), *Becoming Zimbabwe: A History from the Pre-colonial Period to 2008* (Harare, Weaver Press, 2009); George Hamandishe Karekwaivanane, *The Struggle over State Power in Zimbabwe: Law and Politics since 1950* (Cambridge, Cambridge University Press, 2017).

[61] See, for example, Terence Ranger, 'Democracy and Traditional Political Structures in Zimbabwe, 1890–1999', in Ngwabi Bhebe and Terence Ranger (eds), *The Historical Dimensions of Democracy and Human Rights in Zimbabwe. Volume One: Pre-Colonial and Colonial Legacies* (Harare, University of Zimbabwe Publications, 2001), pp. 31–52; Norma Kriger, *Guerrilla Veterans in Post-War Zimbabwe: Symbolic and Violent Politics, 1980–1987* (Cambridge, Cambridge University Press, 2003); Sara Rich Dorman, *Understanding Zimbabwe: From Liberation to Authoritarianism* (London, Hurst and Company, 2016).

[62] See, for example, Dorman, *Understanding Zimbabwe*.

violent struggle for liberation in the 1970s, the Second *Chimurenga*,[63] fought by two major nationalist parties, the Zimbabwe African People's Union (ZAPU) and the Zimbabwe African National Union (ZANU). Under the leadership of Robert Mugabe, ZANU won the country's first elections. The first years of independence were marked by a 'politics of inclusion',[64] with the ZANU-PF government promoting unity, nationalism, development and modernisation in areas in which it enjoyed support. At the same time, in the Matabeleland and Midlands provinces where ZAPU had strong support, these early years of independence were marked by the *Gukurahundi*, a violent, government-sanctioned onslaught against ZAPU and its supporters, and against the predominantly Ndebele-speaking population of the western regions more generally. Under the guise of protecting the newly established nation from a looming 'dissident threat', between 10,000 and 20,000 people were killed, beaten, tortured, detained or 'disappeared'.[65] In 1987, ZANU-PF and ZAPU signed the Unity Accord, ending the violence and absorbing ZAPU into ZANU-PF and some of its leaders into government against a backdrop of growing economic weakness.

Sara Rich Dorman characterises the period between 1987 and 1997 as marked by the 'politics of durability'.[66] Often described as a phase of neoliberalism and minimal repression by the state, she asks how ZANU-PF's regime maintained its power in a time when the rhetoric of development and modernisation from which the party drew authority came under increased criticism as a result of the country's economic decline and eventual collapse. Corruption scandals and growing urban

---

[63] The Second *Chimurenga* is framed as a continuation of Zimbabwe's struggle for liberation, following the First *Chimurenga*, which refers to the Shona and Ndebele uprisings against the British South Africa Company in the 1890s.

[64] Sara Rich Dorman usefully and accurately periodises Zimbabwe's post-independence politics in the following sequence: the politics of inclusion (1980–7), the politics of durability (1987–97), the politics of polarization (1998–2000), the politics of exclusion (2000–8) and the politics of 'winner takes all' (2008–14). See Dorman, *Understanding Zimbabwe*.

[65] Catholic Commission for Justice and Peace (CCJP) and Legal Resources Foundation (LRF), *Breaking the Silence, Building True Peace: A Report into the Disturbances in Matabeleland and the Midlands 1980–1988* (Harare, CCJP and LRF, 1997); Jocelyn Alexander, Joann McGregor and Terence Ranger, *Violence and Memory: One Hundred Years in the 'Dark Forests' of Matabeleland* (Oxford, James Currey, 2000), especially chapters 8 and 9.

[66] Dorman, *Understanding Zimbabwe*, pp. 71–113.

poverty led the early disaffection with ZANU-PF's governance, primarily among Zimbabwean citizens who experienced the *Gukurahundi*, to spread in the 1990s. Civil society organisations, trade unions, residents' associations and student movements gained traction, organising strikes and mobilising a range of political and economic grievances, some of which were framed around rights and the law. Until the late 1990s, however, civil society remained reluctant 'to criticize government, or move outside the regime's framing discourses of unity and development'.[67] In addition, civil society's efforts were weakened by the regime's '[s]trategic use of government institutions and law-making'.[68]

To remain in power and to maintain a semblance of legitimacy, ZANU-PF mobilised its state institutions, extending its control over the Electoral Supervisory Commission and appointing and supporting partisan judges who would rule in favour of the party's agenda, and against members of the political opposition who brought electoral challenges to the courts. Particularly in urban spaces, where strikes and demonstrations were concentrated, ZANU-PF deployed the state's security apparatus to respond violently to these protests, tear-gassing and arresting citizens. Indicative of a shift in ZANU-PF's sources of authority, the government re-engaged traditional authorities, such as the chiefs and headmen.[69]

As the failing economy and accusations of corruption undermined the legitimacy of the government's rhetoric of development and modernisation, ZANU-PF also increasingly attempted to capitalise on its liberation war credentials. In the 1990s this was perhaps most evident in the party's response to the members of the Zimbabwe National Liberation War Veterans Association (ZNLWVA), an organisation formed in 1990 to advocate for liberation war fighters, many of whom were marginalised and impoverished, and to claim compensation. Members of ZNLWVA were able to organise demonstrations without meeting the government's heavy-handed response. Through their public demonstrations for compensation payments, war veterans emphasised that the government had failed to meet its liberation promises. Suggestive of their symbolic power, the war veterans were granted

[67] Ibid., p. 113.   [68] Ibid.
[69] Jocelyn Alexander, *The Unsettled Land: State-making and Politics of Land in Zimbabwe 1893–2003* (Oxford, James Currey, 2006).

compensation in 1997. Subsequently they were rapidly aligned to ZANU-PF, and proved willing to act on its behalf.[70] In this same period political differences rapidly polarised, and in 1999 the growing civic and union movements formed an opposition political party, the Movement for Democratic Change (MDC).

The politics of the 1990s set the scene for the period of heightened political contestation and polarisation between 2000 and 2012, on which this book concentrates. In addition to being a period of political contestation, I chose this period as it was marked by a public shift in ZANU-PF's strategy towards the law, when the party more explicitly than ever before placed political interests above safeguarding the rule of law. This shift was perhaps most dramatically evident when the government refused to condemn the invasion of the Supreme Court by a group of some 200 war veterans on 24 November 2000. Led by Joseph Chinotimba, an outspoken ally of ZANU-PF and a central figure in the violent invasions of predominantly white-owned commercial farms that were being contested by the Commercial Farmers Union (CFU) in the courts at the time, the 'mob … stood on chairs, benches and tables in a show of absolute contempt', shouting political slogans, and calling for judges to be killed.[71] In the months leading up to this dramatic physical and symbolic attack on the authority of the courts and the sanctity of the rule of law, the High and Supreme Courts had ruled against the government to declare individuals' violent actions, and the land occupations themselves, illegal. Despite the protestations of Chief Justice Anthony Gubbay, the invasion was not condemned and the war veterans were not prosecuted. Subsequently, Chief Justice Gubbay was forced to 'retire'.

At the opening of this chapter I quoted Tawanda Zhuwarara, a lawyer working for Zimbabwe Lawyers for Human Rights (ZLHR), a leading non-profit organisation that seeks to promote human rights and the rule of law. He argued that the war veterans' attack on the Supreme Court was 'where it all crumbled'. Through its verbal and

---

[70] Jocelyn Alexander and JoAnn McGregor, 'Elections, Land and the Politics of Opposition in Matabeleland', *Journal of Agrarian Change*, 1, 4, 2001, p. 513; Erin McCandless, *Polarization and Transformation in Zimbabwe: Social Movements, Strategy Dilemmas, and Change* (Plymouth, Lexington Books, 2011); Dorman, *Understanding Zimbabwe*, pp. 81–3.

[71] Anthony Gubbay, 'The Plight of Successive Chief Justices of Zimbabwe in Seeking to Protect Human Rights and the Rule of Law', *Rothschild Lecture* (unpublished lecture, 2001), p. 16, accessed on 11 March 2012 at www .rothschildfostertrust.com/materials/lecture_gubbay.pdf.

physical attacks on the judiciary, ZANU-PF exposed its lack of respect for the rule of law.[72] Human rights reports have similarly identified the attack on Chief Justice Gubbay as a critical turning point in the Zimbabwean regime's respect for the rule of law.[73] Zhuwarara continued that ZANU-PF's approach to law was fundamentally an attack on the government's legitimacy.[74] Conversely, scholars of the 'fetishisation of law' in the postcolony, such as John and Jean Comaroff, point to the ways that ZANU-PF attempted to gain control over the judiciary. This, they argue, makes Zimbabwe, under ZANU-PF's governance, an 'infamously contemporary' example of the workings of 'lawfare', in which acts of political coercion are masked in legal language and practice, enabling the party 'to launder brute power in a wash of legitimacy, ethics, [and] propriety'.[75]

Empirically rich examinations of the dynamics between the ruling party and society in Zimbabwe after 2000, however, paint a more complex picture.[76] Examining a range of governance techniques – from intimidation through violent urban demolition campaigns like Operation *Murambatsvina*,[77] to establishing narrative control through the production of jingles and media reports,[78] and citizens' responses to these – points to the ways ZANU-PF's power, and the authority of the state, were rooted in an interplay between 'professional', ordered, bureaucratic and technocratic governance on the one hand, and 'illegitimate', disordered and uncontrolled violence on the other. The dramatic political contestations through the law in Zimbabwe also raise

---

[72] Interview, Tawanda Zhuwarara, human rights lawyer, Harare, 7 September 2010.
[73] See, for example, BHRC, '*A Place in the Sun*', p. 16; International Bar Association Human Rights Institute (IBAHRI), *Zimbabwe: Time for a New Approach* (London, IBA, September 2011), pp. 24–7; and Sokwanele, '*I Can Arrest You': The Zimbabwe Republic Police and Your Rights* (Harare, Sokwanele, July 2012).
[74] Interview, Tawanda Zhuwarara, human rights lawyer, Harare, 7 September 2010.
[75] Comaroff and Comaroff, 'Law and Disorder in the Postcolony', pp. 30–1.
[76] See, for example, Joseph Chaumba, Ian Scoones and William Wolmer, 'From *Jambanja* to Planning: The Reassertion of Technocracy in Land Reform in South-Eastern Zimbabwe?', *Journal of Modern African Studies*, 41, 4, 2003, pp. 533–54; Joost Fontein, 'Anticipating the *Tsunami*: Rumours, Planning and the Arbitrary State in Zimbabwe', *Africa*, 79, 3, 2009, pp. 369–98; Jeremy Jones, 'Freeze! Movement, Narrative and the Disciplining of Price in Hyperinflationary Zimbabwe', *Social Dynamics*, 36, 2, 2010, pp. 338–51.
[77] Fontein, 'Anticipating the *Tsunami*'.
[78] Chaumba et al., 'From *Jambanja* to Planning'; Jones, 'Freeze!'.

the question of what role law plays within these dynamics, and make it an important case study for research into how courtroom performances and narratives shape, and are shaped by, the relationship between law, state and society. In the following section I discuss the methodologies I used to examine these contestations.

Motivations and Methods

To address the question of how the law was, and remained, a central site of political contestation in Zimbabwe, and to examine how this contestation was performed in political trials, I used three main methods: observation, interviewing and document analysis. Working with these three methods I aimed to ascertain how citizens, lawyers and judicial officials engaged with the law and legal procedure prior to, and within, politicised criminal trials, and how, in doing so, they were engaged in a political and social performance of their commitment to a particular kind of state and their belonging to it.

All of my courtroom observations and the majority of my interviews were conducted during two three-month visits to Zimbabwe. I first lived in Harare between July and September 2010, a period when the country was under the Government of National Unity (GNU), which was formed in 2009 to combine ZANU-PF and the two factions of the opposition MDC after the violent parliamentary and presidential elections of March 2008, and the economic collapse of that period. In these elections, for the first time since independence, ZANU-PF lost its parliamentary majority. The results of the presidential elections were contested. The Electoral Supervisory Commission released the results in May 2008, concluding that Morgan Tsvangirai received more votes than President Mugabe, but had not gained the required 50 per cent plus-one vote.[79] In the period preceding the presidential run-off of June 2008, politically targeted violence reached levels not seen since *Gukurahundi* in the 1980s.[80] Tsvangirai was arrested twice, and decided to pull out of the elections.[81] Mugabe won the presidential run-off unopposed.[82]

---

[79] Eldred V. Masunungure, *Defying the Winds of Change: Zimbabwe's 2008 Elections* (Harare, Weaver Press, 2008).
[80] SPT, *Walking a Thin Line*.
[81] Morgan Tsvangirai was arrested in October 2000, June 2003, March 2007 and June 2008.
[82] SPT, *Walking a Thin Line*.

In response to national, regional and international criticism, economic decline and, for the MDC, political repression, ZANU-PF and the MDC engaged in negotiations following the 2008 elections. The GNU was formed under the Global Political Agreement (GPA), which was signed in September 2008. In February of 2009 the GNU took office.[83] However, the political expectations of the power-sharing government were not met. Initial expectations gave way to the view that the GNU was hampered by 'the continued failure of the new government to create a situation in Zimbabwe where there is total respect for human rights and the rule of law'.[84] The GNU incorporated both ZANU-PF and the MDC, but human rights lawyers and political activists continued to view the judiciary (the courts, police and prisons) as a set of institutions driven by ZANU-PF's political agenda.

The GNU, however, also facilitated openness to political debate and discussion. In this period, my access to the Magistrates' Courts was not restricted. In October 2011, my contacts in Zimbabwe expressed their concern that the political situation was shifting against a backdrop of increased discussion around the new constitution and upcoming elections. I therefore travelled to Bulawayo and Harare to continue researching between November 2011 and February 2012.

To unpack the performative dimensions of interactions with the law I chose to conduct courtroom ethnography, rather than relying primarily on written court records. My observations allowed me to examine not only the scripts employed during courtroom performances, but also to study demeanour and interpersonal dynamics, and the spatial, material and sensory dimensions of these performances. By expanding the use of the theatre metaphor, highlighting which scripts, demeanours, appearances and actions actors adopt and adapt, and for which purposes, we can ask how the interpretation and use of law shapes, and is shaped by, social and political power relations.

For these observations I focused on the trials of individuals accused of political offences in Harare and Bulawayo's Magistrates' Courts. I identified 'political' trials through a combination of three factors: the law under which the defendant was charged, the defendant's social and political position and the self-identification of their lawyers as human rights lawyers. Specifically, defendants whose cases I followed were

---

[83] IBA, *Report of IBA Zimbabwe Mission 2001.*
[84] SPT, *Walking a Thin Line*, p. 5.

charged under the Public Order and Security Act (POSA), the Access to Information and Protection of Privacy Act, or particular sections of the Criminal Law (Codification and Reform) Act that were marked out as 'crimes against the state'. The majority of the defendants were either members of the opposition political party, the MDC, student and political activists, or members of civil society movements. Their lawyers were most frequently associated with ZLHR.

I initially intended to observe cases meeting these criteria in both the High and Magistrates' Courts. The first case I attended in July 2010 took place in the High Court. This experience, however, narrowed my focus down to trials taking place in Magistrates' Courts for two reasons. The first related to access, the second the connections between ongoing cases and my research focus. During my visit to the High Court, I was informed by the lawyers on the case I was observing that most of the real drama in the matter had occurred previously, in the Magistrates' Courts. The case at hand involved Farai Maguwu, the director of the Centre for Research and Development in Mutare.[85] In June 2010, Maguwu was arrested and charged with publishing false statements prejudicial to the state, under Section 31 of the Criminal Law (Codification and Reform) Act.[86] The chief investigating officer, Detective Inspector Henry Dowa, who was notorious among lawyers and activists as his involvement in human rights violations perpetrated by the Law and Order division of the ZRP had gained him a 'reputation for brutality',[87] dramatically argued in the Magistrates' Court that he felt Maguwu must be charged for 'demonising Zimbabwe'.[88] When the magistrate strayed from his script at Maguwu's third bail hearing in the same court by granting a request from the defence counsel, the prosecutor 'lost her temper and scribbled on a paper: "These Guys are Mad!"'.[89] Earlier in the case, the prosecutor had also lost her temper with the lawyers, informing the

[85] In this hearing, five defence lawyers successfully appealed the Magistrates' Court's decision to refuse bail and the High Court ordered Maguwu's release from custody. On 22 October 2010, the state dropped the charges against Maguwu before the plea.
[86] Government of Zimbabwe, *Criminal Law (Codification and Reform) Act* (Harare, Government Printer, 2005), s. 31.
[87] The REDRESS Trust, *The Case of Henry Dowa: The United Nations and Zimbabwe Under the Spotlight* (Harare, REDRESS, January 2004), p. 4.
[88] Tinoziva Bere, human rights lawyer, in email to author, 23 June 2010.
[89] Ibid.

lawyers that for all she cared, Maguwu could 'rot in jail'.[90] To understand how things such as the presence of the notorious Henry Dowa
and the dramatics of the prosecutor were important elements in the
political performances in the courtroom, and so shaped ideas about
law, state authority and citizenship, I turned my attention to the
Magistrates' Courts.

Between July 2010 and February 2012, I observed a total of fifty-
nine court sessions, thirty-seven of which were at the Magistrates'
Courts in Harare, eighteen in Bulawayo and one in Hwange. Many
of the cases I observed took place in the mornings, when the courts
began their sessions. Some cases ran all day, but most sessions lasted
between half an hour and two hours. I followed particular cases closely
and interviewed both the accused and human rights lawyers involved.
During my first visit to Zimbabwe this was possible with five cases, all
of which were in court at least four times during the research period. In
the second fieldwork period this was possible for three cases, two of
which took place in Bulawayo and were in court for three sessions, and
one in Harare, of which I observed five sessions.

As I was interested in understanding not just what happened inside the
courtroom, but how the various actors in political trials understood their
engagement with the law and the Zimbabwean state, I supplemented my
observations with extended interviews. I interviewed seventy-six judicial
officials, human rights lawyers and their clients, political and student
activists, and academics and political analysts. To facilitate access to the
human rights community I had established contact with two lawyers
within ZLHR, David Hofisi and Jeremiah Bamu in Harare. Through
contacts with the National Constitutional Assembly, Crisis Coalition
Zimbabwe, Student Solidarity Trust and Heal Zimbabwe Trust, I also
established contact with political and student activists who had been
arrested, detained and tried prior to my courtroom observations in
2010 and 2012. On my second visit I also spent two months in
Bulawayo, to offer the comparative perspective on court cases in the
two major cities that informs Chapters 7 and 8. In Bulawayo I worked
with ZLHR, Abammeli Lawyers Network, Solidarity Peace Trust, the
Legal Resources Foundation and Bulawayo Progressive Residents
Organisation. Building on these connections I was able to interview a
diverse range of actors. Due to the political restrictions surrounding my

---

[90] Ibid.

research topic I was, however, not able to obtain a broad view from ZANU-PF actors.

I had planned to return after my visit in February 2012, but the run-up to the constitutional referendum in March 2013, the campaign period and ZANU-PF's victory in the parliamentary and presidential elections of July 2013 closed the space for research on the interaction between law and politics. To address this I altered my approach by focusing on cases I had been able to observe already, conducting further interviews on Skype and relying more heavily on document analysis, including court records I obtained. I began analysing material gained from media and human rights reports for the ways they might substantially supplement my research. While this detracted from my initial aim to capture and assess performances beyond what is revealed from the written court records, it allowed me to build a deeper under-standing of the cases I discuss throughout the book. Many of the reports I draw on in this book are freely accessible online, such as those published by Solidarity Peace Trust, Human Rights Watch, Amnesty International and the International Bar Association. I also gathered materials from ZLHR's and Legal Resources Foundation's (LRF) libraries, and examined court records at the offices of Mbidzo, Muchadehama & Makoni. When it became clear that it was no longer possible for me to return to Zimbabwe to continue the research, David Hofisi, Lizwe Jamela and Jeremiah Bamu assisted by scanning court records. Unfortunately these records remained sparse as most court proceedings were not recorded and hand-written notes were not tran-scribed. Dramatic exchanges in the courts, however, were frequently reported in news coverage by the independent media and in ZLHR's weekly newsletter, the *Legal Monitor*.

Many these reports, as well as most of the interviews I conducted, detail experiences with politically motivated violence, including hor-rific conditions in police detention, the loss of friends or family members through torture, organised abductions and continual restric-tion on freedom of movement and expression, social and economic mobility and mental and physical well-being. These narratives were distressing and at times traumatic, and pushed me to confront the question of how to incorporate rather than diminish the humanity of such harrowing experiences within an academic text. Throughout my research, and in my analysis of the material derived from all three methodologies used, I hoped to address this by striking a balance between allowing space for recounting people's complex, at times contradictory, recollections of the violence they experienced through law, and interpreting how these accounts inform us of the place of law within negotiations over the state and one's relationship to it within the postcolony.

The majority of the activists and lawyers I interviewed asked to have their experiences recounted in detail, and to be identified by name in this book. I have attempted to balance such requests against an awareness that their accounts might reveal information that heightens threats to their safety at the time of writing, or possibly at a later date. For the majority of student activists, rank-and-file MDC supporters and political activists whose cases were not discussed at length in the national or international media, I have chosen to change their names to protect their anonymity. In the high-profile cases I discuss in later chapters, and for human rights lawyers who frequently articulated their views in court and in the media, this degree of anonymity was neither possible nor desired.

Working through these methodologies, I realised that, in contrast to the literature discussed in the earlier section on courts as spaces of performance, which focuses primarily on interactions between different actors within the courtroom, a narrow discussion of such exchanges within the courtroom alone failed to address the question of why and how the judiciary remained a central site of political contestation in Zimbabwe. Through my interviews and in my courtroom observations it became clear that the earlier interactions with the police on the stages of arrest and detention fundamentally shaped understandings of law, discussions around state authority and the content and interpretations of courtroom performances and narratives. The content and structure of the remainder of this book, discussed in the next section, reflect this broader focus.

Chapter Outline

I expand on the relationship between history, law and politics in Zimbabwe in Chapter 1. I trace historical trends in the mobilisation of law's coercive power by consecutive colonial and postcolonial governments, locate the development of legal consciousness in citizens' relations to the colonial legal system and examine debates over 'professionalism' and 'justice' between the executive and the judiciary, and within the judiciary itself. I then situate the attacks on members of the judiciary and the rule of law after 2000 in the context of ZANU-PF's increased mobilisation of a selective historical narrative, its 'patriotic history', to argue that conceptualisations of justice took on fundamentally new forms which shape the understandings of the legitimacy of law and its relation to state authority explored within this book, but which are rooted in this larger history.

In Chapter 2, I move from questions about the relationship between law's legitimacy and state authority into a discussion of how (the practice of) law was debated, understood and defined in a specific state institution, the attorney general's office. I demonstrate how, after 2000, the party extended its political control over the judiciary by staffing its institutions with political appointees. Within the attorney general's office, such political interference ran from the attorney general himself down to prosecutors working on ZANU-PF's 'instructions'. I argue, however, that when we look at the working conditions in the attorney general's office more closely, the fragmented hegemony of law within the Zimbabwean state becomes evident. ZANU-PF-instructed prosecutors – the 'good boys' – who were willing to set aside their professional conduct to toe the party political line, sat side by side with 'rebel' prosecutors, individuals who conducted themselves impartially, and did their job 'professionally', in an effort to safeguard 'substantive justice'. In its attempts to exert political control over the attorney general's office, the ZANU-PF-led government had to contend with historical debates over state professionalism, which rooted law's legitimacy in legal institutions' capacity to deliver justice, and tied state authority to the protection of this capacity. In their performances, 'rebel' prosecutors positioned themselves as actors within a wider community of judicial officials, human rights lawyers, activists and citizens that shared this consciousness of the value of professionalism.

Chapter 3 turns to look at how citizens articulated and mobilised their legal and state consciousness when they engaged with Zimbabwe's politicised legal institutions. Through the selective application of the law, ZANU-PF could endanger the safety of individuals reporting crimes to the police or taking cases to court. Citizens like Patrick and Father Mkandla situated themselves against these practices, demanding that the police and the courts 'follow the rules' by interacting with these institutions as if they were rule-bound. In these expressions of their legal consciousness, both men played upon the divisions within state institutions identified in Chapter 2 to achieve occasional 'successes' through the law. Their commitment to rule-bound behaviour was also an expression of their state consciousness. By 'remaining on the right side of law' themselves, these men could make claims to a particular kind of citizenship that demanded an extension of the authority of the state beyond its ability to guarantee 'rights', to a broader responsibility to safeguard citizens' human dignity, civility and morality.

In these ways, both within the Zimbabwean state's judicial institutions and among its citizens, the law was understood and engaged with not simply as a system of rules but as a moral and professional code of conduct. Chapter 4 examines the experiences of young, black, urban-based and predominantly male civic and political activists, who were pervasively persecuted by the ZRP through violent arrests and inhumane conditions in detention. For ZANU-PF, the stages of arrest and detention offered a public platform on which to perform the party's portrayal of activists as 'criminals'. Framing the physical violence, mental torment and isolation that marked their treatment at the hands of the ZRP as an experience which would not occur in a 'normal', 'rule-bound' and 'democratic' society, activists in turn refused to accept these efforts to criminalise them. ZANU-PF's use of the law, activists argued, could not grant it authority. Activists were confronted, however, with the fact that their understandings of their arrest and detention as 'illegitimate' were not universally shared. In the eyes of certain family members they were still 'criminalised', despite the fact that they were targeted for arrest due to their political activities, rather than for, for example, committing petty theft. This highlights the existence of multiple legal consciousnesses in Zimbabwe, some of which are built less on notions of how the law *should* work and more on a recognition of the power of law itself.

These complex dynamics came together during the activists' trials. Chapter 5 focuses on the material and sensory conditions of one space in which such trials took place, Harare's Magistrates' Courts at Rotten Row. I ask how human rights lawyers and their clients incorporated the material and sensory conditions in these courts into their courtroom performances. Their performances drew attention to the shortcomings of the courts as spaces in which to display state authority. I show that while the Magistrates' Courts were full of spatial and symbolic trademarks that aimed to highlight the power of the law, the political and economic situation in Zimbabwe after 2000 had severely damaged the courts' material condition. The real and symbolic effects of this material decline undermined law's authority, which lawyers tied to a widespread loss of professionalism within the judiciary, and argued negatively impacted their courtroom performances. At the same time, they argued that these conditions were indicative of the government's preoccupation with law's coercive rather than legitimating utility. This shift was evident in the sensory experiences of all those present in court. Through the visual, olfactory and auditory reminders of the horrific conditions in police detention, ZANU-PF demonstrated its control over activists' and lawyers' bodies and minds prior to their appearance in the courtroom. Lawyers and their clients, however, also used these sensory dimensions to contest the state's authority. By calling attention to their dirty, damaged and smelly bodies in the dock, lawyers and defendants aimed to expose the decline in moral and professional conduct they observed within Zimbabwe's judicial and police services.

In Chapter 6, I move away from the focus on performances by human rights lawyers and defendants to look at the narratives state prosecutors told in the court. I focus on the trial of Munyaradzi Gwisai, leader of the International Socialist Organisation in Zimbabwe (ISO-Z) and his five co-defendants. Against the backdrop of the Arab Spring uprisings, ZANU-PF used its courtroom narratives to delineate the limits to the party's tolerance for political protest, and articulated the consequences faced by those who were thought to be testing these limits. Two state prosecutors, Michael Reza and Edmore Nyazamba, and their star witness, Jonathan Shoko, reminded the court, and the public within and beyond its wall, of ZANU-PF's responsibility for upholding the security of the nation against local manifestations of 'foreign' and 'imperialist' influences.

Chapters 7 and 8 shift our focus to the region of Matabeleland. I examine how the historical narratives connected to the violent government repression of the 1980s shaped understandings of the legitimacy of law, the authority of the state and the dynamics of citizenship in a way that differed from other regions that did not share their history. In Chapter 7, I situate the founding of the Mthwakazi Liberation Front (MLF) within regional and ethnic politics to examine the formation of a local human rights network, Abammeli. When the MLF leaders were charged with treason, ZLHR lawyers based in Harare rejected the MLF case, despite the fact that it was working as the leading defence council in the Gwisai treason trial at that time. Formed as a response to ZLHR's refusal to defend the MLF leaders, Abammeli's formation highlights how the historical place of law shaped legal and state consciousness in Matabeleland. Abammeli's lawyers positioned themselves first and foremost as residents in, and citizens of, Matabeleland, and they articulated an understanding of citizenship that granted legitimacy to law if it protected a shared humanity, rather than a specific political agenda.

In Chapter 8, I examine a second interaction between *Gukurahundi* history, law and citizenship by looking at the trial of visual artist Owen Maseko. For his exhibition on the experiences of *Gukurahundi*, Maseko stood accused of 'inciting tribal hatred'. In their courtroom narratives, prosecutors elaborated on this accusation to communicate ZANU-PF's continued control over instruments of coercion to a 'Matabele' audience. Maseko and his defence team, in turn, performed in a rule-bound manner to draw attention to Maseko as a citizen with the freedom to express his interpretations of history, and to put these in the public domain for debate, rather than as a 'criminal' for failing to align with ZANU-PF's historical narrative. These different forms of courtroom performance highlight how the *Gukurahundi* as a violent historical event continued to inform negotiations over citizenship, and the understandings of law's legitimacy and state authority that they encompassed, in this region.

Together, these chapters examine how Zimbabweans within and outside of the state's institutions articulated varied, at times competing, forms of legal and state consciousness, which allowed them to situate themselves in the debates on what granted law legitimacy, and how this legitimacy worked to authorise the Zimbabwean state. I argue that, for certain judicial officials, human rights lawyers, activists and members of ZANU-PF's political opposition, legal consciousness encompassed specific understandings of professional and moral conduct, and 'substantive justice', which in turn safeguarded forms of citizenship based on human dignity, civility and humanity. Emotional, bodily, material and sensory experiences all shaped how this commitment to the law was performed in the courtroom. These performances were aimed at exposing the illegalities and illegitimacy of ZANU-PF's rule. In this way, legal consciousness was aligned to expressions of state consciousness. State consciousness not only encompassed critiques of ZANU-PF's rule, but also incorporated alternative imaginings of law's legitimacy and state authority. These understandings recognised the fragmented hegemony of law within the state's intuitions, making law more generally, and the courtroom specifically, productive sites of political contestation.

1 | History, Authority and the Law in Zimbabwe, 1950–2002

[T]he existing body of law in society at any point in time is a reflection of present political power and the surviving enactments of past political power.[1]

[B]y thinking historically we are able to observe the ways in which the new ruling class in Zimbabwe has drawn from the lessons of a repressive colonial past, to constrain the citizens of an independent Zimbabwe.[2]

In the Introduction, I posited that, with its long history of negotiation and contestation over the authority that law granted to ruling regimes and to an ideal of the state, Zimbabwe offers a particularly insightful case study through which to examine the relationship between the law, political contestation, state-making and citizenship. In this chapter, I substantiate this claim by situating three arguments made in the Introduction in Zimbabwe's colonial and postcolonial history.

First, I argued for supplementing our study of 'legal consciousness'[3] within society with research into the expectations of 'the state' (understood as an idea and a set of institutions) that were tied up with engaging the law, that is, 'state consciousness'. In this chapter, I contend that law has historically constituted an important 'language of stateness'.[4] It has worked as a language of legitimation, as a tool for state repression, discrimination and coercion, and as a mechanism through which citizens could articulate expectations, perform politics and challenge various regimes' (ab)use of legal institutions. Locating

---

[1] Claire Palley, 'Law and the Unequal Society: Discriminatory Legislation in Rhodesia under the Rhodesian Front from 1963 to 1969', *Race*, 12, 1, 1970, p. 17.

[2] Brian Raftopoulos, 'Lest We Forget: From LOMA to POSA', address at public meeting commemorating the 1960 protests, 24 July 2003, accessed on 5 July 2012 at http://archive.kubatana.net/html/archive/cact/030724ciz.asp?sector=CACT.

[3] Merry, *Getting Justice and Getting Even*, p. 8.

[4] Hansen and Stepputat, *States of Imagination*, p. 5.

the roots of this 'state consciousness' in Zimbabwe's colonial era is essential for our understanding of the production of the relationship between the legitimacy of law, state authority and notions of citizenship after 2000.

Second, when situating the relationship between law and state authority in postcolonial contexts, I argued for the necessity of examining the understandings of law held not only in relation to but *within* state institutions. By examining debates within Zimbabwe's judicial institutions over time we can trace the emergence of understandings of 'professional' conduct. These understandings were linked to the ethical and impartial practice of law, were aimed at the delivery of 'substantive justice' and, as we explore later, were tied into claims to citizenship. This understanding of 'professionalism' was frequently contrasted with illegitimate forms of support, by commission or omission, for successive ruling regimes. To assess the place of law in political contestations after 2000 we need to incorporate not only the history of legal and state consciousness, but also the emergence of notions of 'professionalism' and 'justice'.

To conclude this chapter, I turn not to history proper but to an examination of the historical narratives that were articulated in the very public debates between the judiciary and the executive over law and justice in early 2000. I show that the uses of these historical narratives reflect a qualitative shift in claims to, and contestations over, the legitimacy of law. This shift was linked to a broader change in ZANU-PF's political and historical narrative, in which it attempted to lay claim to authority by invoking the country's colonial history and the party's role in the liberation war. At the same time, historically rooted notions of 'professionalism' and 'justice' persisted, and were used, by the different actors in the debate. These interactions set the scene for the political contestations over law that this book examines.

'Legal' and 'State' Consciousness in Rhodesia

The establishment of a legal system was a central priority for the British South Africa Company following the laying of claims to the territory that would become Zimbabwe in late 1889. In colonial Rhodesia, a social and political order founded on racial segregation and the economic exploitation of Africans was enforced and maintained through law, repressive state institutions and legislation, and

through structures of customary authority.[5] Early legislation policed a
very wide range of matters, from freedom of movement and access to
urban areas to interracial sexual relations, and from workplace conduct to 'subversive' behaviour and etiquette.[6] As the colonial state
relied on the legal system to expand its authority across its territory,
it was central that within this system the courts were viewed as the final
arbiters of justice.[7]

There is some debate on how, in the early years of colonial rule,
Africans responded to this expanding legal system. In her study of
courtroom interactions in the Melsetter District during the early
1900s, Diana Jeater proposes that while Africans and white settlers
frequently met in the legal arena, legal narratives and practices could
not be effectively translated between the two, so that 'white adjudi-
cators and African litigants largely ended up talking at cross purposes'.[8] In contrast, writing about this same period, Elizabeth
Schmidt finds that women were aware of the purposes and powers of
new laws, and used the legal system to, among other things, challenge
patriarchal authority.[9] Writing about later decades, Tapiwa Zimudzi,
whose work on female African defendants in the High Court was
discussed in the Introduction, argued that 'violent African female
offenders consciously used courtroom demeanour together with specific explanations and rationalisations of their crimes as legally aware
strategies aimed at gaining favourable treatment from colonial
judges'.[10] Their legal awareness was sufficiently acute that they shifted
strategies with time when judges stopped responding positively to

[5] See, for example: Brian Raftopoulos and Ian R. Phimister, *Keep on Knocking:
A History of the Labour Movement in Zimbabwe* (Harare, Baobab, 1997);
Jocelyn Alexander, *The Unsettled Land*, pp. 20–41.
[6] See, for example: Jock McCulloch, *Black Peril, White Virtue: Sexual Crime in
Southern Rhodesia, 1902–1935* (Bloomington, Indiana University Press, 2000);
Allison K. Shutt, '"The Natives Are Getting Out of Hand": Legislating Manners,
Insolence and Contemptuous Behaviour in Southern Rhodesia, c. 1910–1963',
Journal of Southern African Studies, 33, 3, 2007, pp. 653–72.
[7] Karekwaivanane, *The Struggle over State Power*.
[8] Diana Jeater, *Law, Language and Science: The Invention of the "Native Mind"
in Southern Rhodesia, 1890–1930* (Portsmouth, Heinemann, 2007), p. 77.
[9] Elizabeth Schmidt, 'Negotiated Spaces and Contested Terrain: Men, Women,
and the Law in Colonial Zimbabwe, 1890–1939', *Journal of Southern African
Studies*, 16, 4, 1990, pp. 622–48.
[10] Zimudzi, 'African Women, Violent Crime and the Criminal Law in Colonial
Zimbabwe', p. 502.

certain of their courtroom performances.[11] Studying cases of sexual assault in Bulawayo between 1946 and 1956, Koni Benson and Joyce Chadya also found evidence of African women's understandings of the law, locating them in the ways they challenged definitions of prostitution in court. Through these challenges, women defended their status in a rapidly shifting, urbanising environment, and defended a particular understanding of morality.[12]

There were likely discrepancies in the degree to which Africans were legally aware, and able to perform and use this awareness effectively in their interactions with law. Jeater's conclusion that Africans fundamentally miscommunicated with the white settler state in the legal arena, however, radically minimises African agency in the legal arena. As Sally Engle Merry argues, 'the ability to interpret or apply meaning to an event confers power'.[13] Taken together, Zimudzi, Benson and Chadya, and Schmidt provide examples of how African women found meaning, and so power, in their interactions with the colonial legal system. To fight for favourable outcomes and to renegotiate their position within existing and emerging social and colonial orders, African women engaged their legal consciousness. These legal engagements produced a particular subjectivity, one in which expectations of the state were tied to the courts. In enacting their 'legally aware strategies', Africans were also expressing their 'state consciousness'. Such expressions of 'state consciousness' would further play an important role in the political cases that became pervasive in the later stages of colonial rule.

Following the Second World War, and the spread of independence across the African continent, nationalism boomed. In response, the Southern Rhodesian government passed a series of repressive laws aimed at controlling African political engagement. These laws included the Subversive Activities Act of 1950 and the Public Order Act of 1955. In February 1959, then Prime Minister Edgar Whitehead declared a month-long national state of emergency, which increased executive control while limiting the power of the judiciary. The state of emergency was extended in March, facilitating the introduction of two

[11] Ibid.
[12] Koni Benson and Joyce M. Chadya, 'Ukubhinya: Gender and Sexual Violence in Bulawayo, Colonial Zimbabwe, 1946–1956', *Journal of Southern African Studies*, 31, 3, 2005, pp. 587–610.
[13] Merry, 'Everyday Understandings', p. 254.

more laws aimed at quashing African political militancy: the Unlawful Organisations Act and the Preventive Detention Act. The Acts expanded government powers to ban African nationalist parties, prohibit organisations deemed likely to disturb the public order and issue detention orders without relying on the state of emergency. In 1960, the Law and Order Maintenance Act (LOMA) and the Emergency Powers Act were passed. Taken together this legislation greatly expanded state powers over the political sphere: nationalist parties were banned and hundreds of their leaders and supporters were arrested, imprisoned and detained.

Examining the role of law in legitimation and coercion in Zimbabwe between 1950 and 1990, George Karekwaivanane details how the Rhodesian government orchestrated the trials of its political enemies with the assistance of this repressive legislation. These trials allowed the state to assert its power, and to undermine the credibility and effectiveness of nationalism.[14] Within Rhodesian government and society these measures were contentious.[15] Members of the settler community, white opposition parties and journalists expressed their concerns that the repressive measures contained in the legislation would extend to their activities, while nationalists played on the way legislation was framed as defending liberties, but only defended the liberties of the settler community, 'mock[ing] the state's democratic pretensions'.[16] As we will see, repressive legislation also divided the state itself.

Playing on these debates, nationalists and guerrillas invoked the law and its legitimacy in their trials and used them as places in which to perform for nationalist audiences. Karekwaivanane observes that 'there was some room for nationalists to exercise agency within the courtroom in ways that caused great anxiety amongst state officials'.[17] In 1963, for example, Joshua Nkomo, the president of the ZAPU,[18] was tried in Rusape under LOMA. His trial drew a large audience of ZAPU members, many of whom gathered outside the courts wearing

[14] Karekwaivanane, *The Struggle over State Power*.   [15] Ibid., pp. 87–97.
[16] Ibid.; also see George Hamandishe Karekwaivanane, *Legal Encounters: Law, State and Society in Zimbabwe, c. 1950–1980* (D.Phil thesis, University of Oxford, 2012), p. 116.
[17] Karekwaivanane, *The Struggle over State Power*, p. 133.
[18] Under Joshua Nkomo's leadership the Zimbabwe African People's Union (ZAPU) was founded in 1961. In 1963, the party split and the Zimbabwe African National Union (ZANU) formed, led by Ndabaningi Sithole.

fur hats, well-known symbols of nationalism.[19] Inside the court the hats served as emblems of the imagined nation, and challenged the legitimacy of the state's legal rituals. Nkomo's trial also challenged racial barriers, as he was represented by Rhodesia's first African lawyer, Herbert Chitepo, a formidable presence in the courts. Karekwaivanane illustrates how, through Nkomo's case, the nationalist cause drew local and international attention and how, ultimately, the colonial government 'failed to stamp its authority on the proceedings. For the crowds that thronged the court dressed in party regalia, the trial was generally not seen as a performance of state power: this was Nkomo's "meeting".'[20]

African nationalists thus challenged the authority of the Rhodesian state, and contested the coercive use of law through their performances in court. From these performances emerged a legal consciousness that was rooted in nationalists' commitment to rights-bearing citizenship and the rule of law, and a state consciousness that tied the use of law to safeguarding these rights.[21] Following the Rhodesian Front's electoral victory in 1963, and the passing of the Unilateral Declaration of Independence in 1965, which cut ties with Great Britain and protected white minority governance, nationalists adapted their legal strategies to an increase in state coercion.[22] In the context of the liberation struggle, guerrillas fighting under ZAPU and ZANU's respective armed wings, the Zimbabwe People's Revolutionary Army (ZIPRA) and the Zimbabwe African National Liberation Army (ZANLA), their suspected supporters, and civilians very widely, were targets of government violence. To legitimise this violence the Rhodesian Front government dramatically intensified its reliance on martial law. The discourse around the government's response to African nationalism also shifted. Previously, African political prisoners were cast primarily as errant children temporarily detained in the interest of national security. Under the Rhodesian Front, nationalists were increasingly

---

[19] For details on symbolism of fur hats, see Sabelo Ndlovu-Gatsheni and Wendy Willems, 'Making Sense of Cultural Nationalism and the Politics of Commemoration under the Third Chimurenga in Zimbabwe', *Journal of Southern African Studies*, 35, 4, 2009, pp. 945–65; and Terence Ranger, *Voices from the Rocks: Nature, Culture and History in the Matopos Hills of Zimbabwe* (Oxford, James Currey, 1999).
[20] Karekwaivanane, *The Struggle over State Power*, p. 107.   [21] Ibid.
[22] Ibid., pp. 122–30.

criminalised, with political prisoners portrayed as 'thugs' and 'terrorists' deserving of isolation and, ultimately, death.

Jocelyn Alexander demonstrates how ideas of the law and citizenship were mobilised by political prisoners under Rhodesian Front rule.[23] Against their criminalisation, the imprisoned nationalists articulated their visions of social and political order through the lens of the law.[24] They created an idealised version of the state's judicial system inside detention, which was used to maintain law and order among detainees and to counter 'the "lawlessness" of the Rhodesian state and its construction of nationalists'.[25] Alexander observes that these political prisoners 'did not think of law as a means to political victory. ... The rule of law came to serve instead as a standard against which the Rhodesian Front could be held up and found wanting.'[26] In this manner, interactions with the law remained closely connected to Africans' expressions of expectations of the state, and their disappointment that the colonial state failed to meet these expectations.

Disappointment with, and objections to, the colonial state were also performed within the court. In his examination of political prisoners under Rhodesian rule, Munyaradzi Munochiveyi describes the security force's harrowing treatment of civilians in detention, and observes that despite this treatment, defendants found the space to challenge 'the repressive colonial judicial authorities by speaking out against their incarceration' from the dock.[27] Through legal petitions and verbal insults they drew attention to the extra-legal or illegal nature of their arrest, and 'creatively worked the judicial system themselves in order to escape prosecution, evade being charged for serious offences, or negotiate for reduced sentences'.[28] Nationalists now in exile also worked to critique the abuses of the war years, publishing critiques that drew attention to the state's inability and unwillingness to deliver

---

[23] Jocelyn Alexander, 'Nationalism and Self-Government in Rhodesian Detention: Gonakudzingwa, 1964–1974', *Journal of Southern African Studies*, 37, 3, 2011, pp. 551–69. See also, Jocelyn Alexander, 'The Political Imaginaries and Social Lives of Political Prisoners in Post 2000 Zimbabwe', *Journal of Southern African Studies*, 36, 2, 2010, pp. 483–503; and Jocelyn Alexander, 'Rethinking the State and Political Opposition through the Prism of the Prison', *Critical African Studies*, 4, 6, 2011, pp. 69–83.

[24] Alexander, 'Nationalism and Self-Government in Rhodesian Detention', p. 569.

[25] Ibid.   [26] Ibid., pp. 555–6.

[27] Munyaradzi Munochiveyi, *Prisoners of Rhodesia: Inmates and Detainees in the Struggle for Zimbabwean Liberation 1960–1980* (Basingstoke, Palgrave Macmillan, 2014), p. 112.

[28] Ibid., p. 112.

'substantive justice', thereby 'successfully unmask[ing] the legalistic pretences of the Rhodesian legal system'.[29]

Demonstrating the productive power of such articulations of legal and state consciousness, colonial officials felt compelled to respond to nationalists' performances. Among colonial officials there was a sense that nationalists were 'making a mockery of the Courts', which in turn prompted the Rhodesian Front government to rethink how it engaged with the law to rule.[30] To avoid being confronted with courtroom performances that challenged the authority of the colonial state, such as the performances at 'Nkomo's meeting' in 1963, many leading political leaders were tried in secret or simply detained without trial. Despite this shift in government tactics, Karekwaivanane shows how guerrillas on trial for their lives rejected entirely the legitimacy of the law. They 'assert[ed] their political convictions and put the settler state on trial'.[31] Speaking from the dock, guerrillas insisted on a substantive conception of justice, and 'dismissed the courts on the grounds that they were biased and were playing a part in holding up the Smith regime'.[32]

Law thus remained a negotiated and contested 'language of stateness',[33] if in different ways. Successive Rhodesian regimes drew on it as a mechanism of racial and economic discrimination, a language of legitimation, and increasingly as a tool of coercion. African litigants and defendants displayed their legal consciousness, invoking colonial stereotypes and understandings of law in the space of the court as an avenue of resistance to the state, and a tool for engagement with wider social and political struggles. Law was linked to Africans' subjectivity and to their claims to rights-based citizenship.

Displays of legal and state consciousness were not confined to non-state actors. With the increase in repressive uses of law, divisions within the state grew and were centred on debates over professional conduct and the substance of justice.

Debating 'Justice' and Judicial 'Professionalism'

When examining the relationship between the legitimacy of law and state authority we need to account for different uses of law by the state,

---

[29] Karekwaivanane, *The Struggle over State Power*, p. 123.   [30] Ibid., p. 108.
[31] Ibid., p. 246.   [32] Karekwaivanane, *Legal Encounters,* pp. 168–9.
[33] Hansen and Stepputat, *States of Imagination*, p. 5.

and debates over these uses and what they authorise within its institutions. As shown in the previous section, debates around the Rhodesian government's repressive legislation in the late 1950s opened up spaces for African nationalists as well as white constituents to critique the state. Such criticisms were, however, not confined to actors located outside of the state's institutions. Within the judiciary debates on the Law and Order Maintenance Bill proved particularly controversial. Federal Chief Justice Robert Tredgold argued that the Bill trampled on the ideal of the rule of law, and that '[i]t was the sacrifice of justice that the legislation made inevitable to which [he] was utterly opposed'.[34] Describing it as an 'anthology of horrors', the chief justice threatened to resign in protest.[35] The Bill passed in 1960, and Chief Justice Tredgold duly resigned.

Chief Justice Tredgold's resignation was bound up with an understanding of 'professional' conduct within the legal profession and judicial institutions that was tied to the ethical and impartial practice of law as a means of ensuring substantively 'just' outcomes. Under colonial rule such expressions of 'professionalism' were limited, however. Within the Rhodesian legal profession, Geoff Feltoe and George Karekwaivanane both identify a trend of 'formalism', a procedural commitment to the rule of law void of concern for 'substantive justice'.[36] Formalism, they argued, worked as a mask for the legal profession's and the judiciary's support for the Smith government, and thus did little to challenge the implementation of repressive legislation. There were, however, some exceptions, particularly among the black lawyers newly admitted to the bar. Facing high barriers to entering the profession, these lawyers were critical of formalism and articulated political ideas around law and, like Chief Justice Tredgold, were unwilling to 'sacrifice justice'.[37]

Diverging uses of law and debates between the judiciary and the executive can also be identified after independence. The Lancaster House constitutional negotiations, and the ceasefire of 21 December

---

[34] Robert Tredgold, *The Rhodesia That Was My Life* (London, George Allen and Unwin, 1968), p. 233.

[35] Tredgold, *The Rhodesia That Was My Life*, p. 229.

[36] Geoff Feltoe, 'Law, Ideology and Coercion in Southern Rhodesia' (M.Phil thesis, University of Kent, 1978), p. 81; Karekwaivanane, *The Struggle over State Power*, p. 152.

[37] See Karekwaivanane, *The Struggle over State Power*, chapter 5.

1979, brought an end to Zimbabwe's liberation war and paved the way for general elections in February 1980. ZANU-PF won these elections, and Robert Mugabe was installed as prime minister. Adopting a policy of 'developmental nationalism', the newly formed ZANU-PF majority government vowed to address the country's long history of repressive and racist rule, and to stimulate peace and economic prosperity.[38] The judiciary was identified as an important institution in achieving ZANU-PF's agenda of promoting modernisation and desegregation.[39]

This judicial system, set out in the Lancaster House Constitution of 1979, built on the system established under colonial rule. Predominantly uncodified, law was derived from multiple sources including legislation, common law, customary law and authoritative texts. In 2006, sections of the criminal law were codified under the Criminal Law (Codification and Reform) Act. The hierarchy of criminal courts and the trial process followed by state prosecutors[40] and defence lawyers in the Magistrates' Courts, however, continued to reflect colonial structures (see Figures 1.1 and 1.2).

At independence, ZANU-PF inherited a set of state institutions that remained both staffed by experienced and highly qualified officials and defined by racial division and violence. In order for the judiciary to work as the intended instrument for change, these colonial legacies needed to be addressed. According to Karekwaivanane, the most noteworthy changes made by the government occurred in three areas: judicial institutions were Africanised; the chief's and headmen's courts were restructured to move away from their focus on 'customary law' to

---

[38] For the government's early and shifting policies, see Government of Zimbabwe, *Transitional National Development Plan: 1982/3–1984–5, Volume One* (Harare, Government Printer, 1982); Lloyd Sachikonye, '"From Growth with Equity" to "Fast-Track" Reform: Zimbabwe's Land Question', *Review of African Political Economy*, 96, 2003, pp. 227–40. For a discussion of 'developmental nationalism' promoted by ZANU-PF see Ndlovu-Gatsheni and Willems, 'Making Sense of Cultural Nationalism'.

[39] See Karekwaivanane, *The Struggle over State Power*, chapter 6.

[40] Under Zimbabwe's pre-2013 constitution state prosecutors were public officials representing the attorney general (expanded upon in Chapter 2). Prosecutors were appointed to serve within a magisterial province or regional division. They did not have to be registered as legal practitioners but must have knowledge of, and adhere to, legal ethics and procedures. For further details, see Lovemore Madhuku, *An Introduction to Zimbabwean Law* (Harare, Weaver Press and Friedrich-Ebert-Stiftung, 2010), chapters 6 and 7.

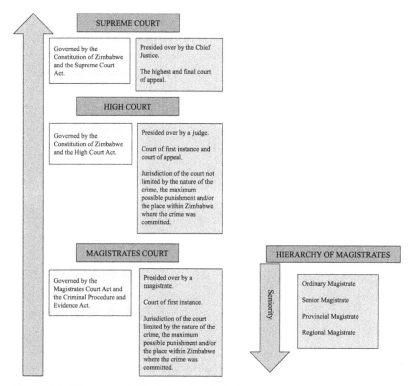

Figure 1.1 Hierarchy of Zimbabwe's criminal courts
Note: For further details on the composition and jurisdiction of these courts, see Madhuku, *An Introduction Zimbabwean Law,* chapter 5 and Otto Saki and Tatenda Chiware, *The Law in Zimbabwe,* GlobalLex, February 2007, available at www.nyulawglobal.org/globalex/Zimbabwe.html.

incorporate the symbolism and practices of 'state law'; and legislation concerning women's rights was updated in order to protect and expand these rights.[41] In this manner, the new government placed the desegregation and modernisation of its judicial institutions high on its agenda, working to deliver justice and to promote a variety of progressive social agendas.

Alongside these uses of law the government continued to rely on the law's coercive capacity, holding on to key repressive colonial laws. Much as in the era of the liberation struggle ZANU-PF justified this measure by arguing that these laws were necessary to uphold peace and

---

[41] Karekwaivanane, *The Struggle over State Power.*

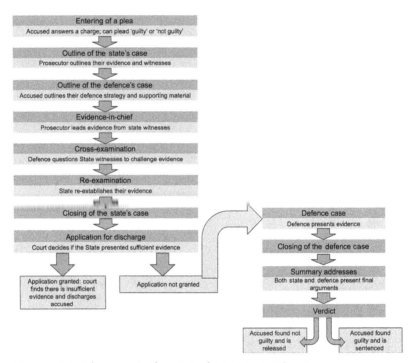

Figure 1.2 Trial process in the criminal Magistrates' Courts
Note: For further details on trial procedures in Zimbabwe, see Madhuku, *An Introduction to Zimbabwean Law,* chapter 7.

security. As discussed in the Introduction, from 1980 to 1990 a state of emergency was maintained with the intent of suppressing ZAPU, its supporters and civilians in the party's strongholds in Matabeleland and the Midlands. Divisions resulting from liberation war patterns of recruitment and operation along ethnic and regional lines, and animosity between ZAPU and ZANU, contributed to hostility between former guerrillas of the two liberation armies.[42] Claiming that ZIPRA guerrillas – dubbed 'dissidents' – threatened to undermine the newly installed government, ZANU-PF responded with 'massive force and draconian measures against civilians, dissidents, and ZAPU' between 1983 and 1987, a period referred to as the *Gukurahundi.*[43]

---

[42] Alexander et al., *Violence and Memory,* p. 181.
[43] Kriger, *Guerrilla Veterans in Post-War Zimbabwe,* p. 30.

During this period, the North Korean-trained Fifth Brigade, a unit of the Zimbabwe National Army unique in its set-up, its tactics and in its targets, was deployed in Matabeleland and the Midlands provinces. Under the command of Colonel Perence Shiri, 'the Fifth Brigade introduced a qualitatively new and more horrific kind of war. For those civilians who bore its brunt, all preceding armies paled in comparison.'[44] In addition to the widespread military violence against civilians, the government's tactics also included systematic detentions and torture, and the 'disappearances' of ZAPU officials, a strategy employed primarily by members of the Central Intelligence Organisation (CIO) and the Police Internal Security Intelligence unit.[45] In their detailed report on the *Gukurahundi*, the Catholic Commission for Justice and Peace (CCJP) and the LRF estimated that from 1983 to 1987 between ten and twenty thousand people lost their lives, the vast majority at the hands of government forces.[46]

The government justified this violence as necessary for the protection of the newly established nation. In line with this reasoning they continued to rely on Rhodesian-era state of emergency legislation, particularly LOMA and the Emergency Powers Act. This prompted the CCJP and LRF to conclude that 'the Zimbabwean Government used them [LOMA and the Emergency Powers Act] in the same way the Rhodesian Government did, to silence political opponents'.[47] In addition, Karekwaivanane shows that the newly established government was unwilling 'to be hindered by the law from taking any actions they deemed to be necessary in the political sphere'.[48]

Despite the indisputable uses and abuses of law for partisan and repressive ends, the judiciary itself was left remarkably untouched in the 1980s. This was a result of a combination of ZANU-PF's concern for its legitimacy, its attempts to promote a progressive social agenda and development through law, and a significant commitment to the rule of law and a belief in a professional judiciary among ZANU-PF

---

[44] Jocelyn Alexander, 'Dissident Perspectives on Zimbabwe's Post-independence War', *African: Journal of the International African Institute*, 68, 2, 1998, p. 159.

[45] 'Disappearing' was a strategy, employed particularly by the CIO, whereby people were taken from their homes in the middle of the night in mysterious circumstances, after which they could not be tracked at detention centres or police stations and remained classified as 'missing' as their deaths had not been witnessed and their bodies not found. See CCJP and LRF, *Breaking the Silence*.

[46] CCJP and LRF, *Breaking the Silence*.   [47] Ibid., p. 6.

[48] Karekwaivanane, *Legal Encounters*, p. 278.

leaders and civil servants. Ronald Weitzer commented in 1990 that 'much to the Government's credit, it has not attempted to pack the bench with political appointees tied to the ruling party'.[49] Despite the fact that its rulings were regularly ignored, this judiciary challenged ZANU-PF's reliance on the state of emergency and ruled against the executive to acquit individuals accused of breaching security law.[50]

The judiciary's actions were tied to an understanding of judicial professionalism, established in the Rhodesian period, which saw it as bound up with the ethical, impartial application of law and the delivery of 'substantive justice'. In the early years of independence, when the bench remained staffed by judges appointed by Ian Smith under Rhodesian Front rule, the judiciary's challenges to the executive could be read as resulting from the 'misalignment' between political elites in these two branches of government.[51] After 1984, when the government had appointed a new generation of black judges, there was a shift towards expressions of professionalism that invoked rights in new ways. By the late 1980s, judges were 'moving away from a rigid commitment to formalism and orienting themselves towards human rights'.[52]

Between 1987 and 2001, the guidance of Chief Justices Enoch Dumbutshena and Anthony Gubbay helped promote the reputation and practice of judicial institutions as independent and professional. In 1989, for instance, Dumbutshena observed that although experienced magistrates had left the country following independence, newer magistrates had upheld and even strengthened the standards of the judiciary. He held that magistrates, 'handled sensitive cases without fear or favour. They have tried powerful politicians with admirable courage

---

[49] Ronald Weitzer, *Transforming Settler States: Communal Conflict and Internal Security in Northern Ireland and Zimbabwe* (Oxford, University of California Press, 1990), p. 153.

[50] Weitzer, *Transforming Settler States*; and Adrian de Bourbon, 'Human Rights and the Independent Bar', *Advocate*, December 2002, pp. 18–20. See also, James Muzondidya, 'From Buoyancy to Crisis: 1980–1997', in Brian Raftopoulos and Alois Mlambo (eds), *Becoming Zimbabwe: A History from the Pre- colonial Period to 2008* (Harare, Weaver Press, 2009), pp. 167–200.

[51] Karekwaivanane, *The Struggle over State Power*; Martin Chanock, 'Writing South African Legal History: A Prospectus', *Journal of African History*, 30, 2, 1989, pp. 265–88.

[52] Karekwaivanane, *The Struggle over State Power*, p. 210.

and integrity.'[53] In line with this view, Adrian de Bourbon, a former Supreme Court judge, noted in 2002 that 'whenever possible the courts did rule in favour of the citizen against the state'.[54] Through such rulings the judiciary communicated its understanding of 'professional' conduct as it was connected to the delivery of 'substantive justice', to be contrasted with the rule-following behaviour of judges who had adhered to 'formalism' in the colonial era.[55]

In the early 1990s there were few political challenges to the judiciary's ability to maintain their professional conduct. Land emerged as a contentious issue, however, and one around which ZANU-PF could mobilise strategic law-making practices.[56] The Zimbabwean government inherited a highly unequal system of land settlement at independence. Half the agricultural land, and much of the best land, was designated for whites. The Lancaster House Agreement of 1979 provided a framework for land redistribution, as land distribution had been an issue at the centre of nationalism, along with demands for equal rights. The scope of reform under the Lancaster House Agreement was, however, limited. The agreement allowed only for exchange between 'willing sellers' and 'willing buyers' until 1990, restricting compulsory land acquisition and redistribution during this time. Land came to the political forefront in the 1990 elections, against the backdrop of emerging opposition movements and growing rural disillusionment.[57] To address this, the ZANU-PF government passed laws, such as the Land Acquisition Act of 1992, to facilitate land redistribution, ushering in a phase marked by compulsory acquisition with fair compensation.

The Land Acquisition Act was passed under the Constitution of Zimbabwe Amendment Act of 1990, Section 16(2) which attempted to 'oust the jurisdiction of the courts' in judging the fairness of

---

[53] Enoch Dumbutshena, 'Address to the Harare Magistrates and Prosecutors Forum, 15 September 1989', *Legal Forum*, 1, 6, 1989, p. 4.

[54] De Bourbon, 'Human Rights and the Independent Bar', p. 18.

[55] See, Karekwaivanane, *The Struggle over State Power* for a detailed analysis of this distinction over time.

[56] See discussion of 1990s in the Introduction; Dorman, *Understanding Zimbabwe*.

[57] Lovemore Madhuku, 'Law, Politics and the Land Reform Process in Zimbabwe', in Medicine Masiiwa (ed.), *Post-Independence Land Reform in Zimbabwe: Controversies and Impact on the Economy* (Harare, Friedrich Ebert Stiftung and Institute of Development Studies and University of Zimbabwe, 2004), pp. 124–47.

compensation arrangements.[58] Senior members of the judiciary criticised this provision. Former Chief Justice Enoch Dumbutshena, for
instance, 'described Parliament's powers to fix the price for land as
"regressive" and added that the measures were repugnant to "all
accepted norms of modern society and the rule of law"'.[59] The recently
appointed Chief Justice Anthony Gubbay in turn criticised the amendment in his speech to mark the opening of the legal year in 1991. Chief
Justice Gubbay argued that amendments had the potential to 'destroy
the very foundation or structure of the Constitution'.[60] More amendments to the constitution were to follow, in part in response to these
critiques from the upper echelons of the judiciary. Under the
Constitution of Zimbabwe Amendment Act of 1993, for example,
the provision for ousting the courts was removed and disputes over
compensation were referred to the Administrative Court.

Rather than generating an environment for smooth land redistribution, however, the numerous amendments, as well as the Land
Acquisition Act, increased public discontent.[61] Indeed, 'owing to fierce
opposition to this legal framework, the next few years were to witness
unending legal battles'.[62] The legal framework was predominantly
challenged by white commercial landowners, who objected to the
guidelines for land designation and acquisition (the prelude to state
land redistribution), and the prices set for their farms, in court. In July
1994, for example, the *Davies* case started in the High Court with five
white commercial farmers testing the constitutionality of the Land Act
of 1992 following the designation of their land for acquisition. The
farmers lost their case: their arguments were rejected and the case
dismissed with costs for the farmers.[63] In his ruling, then High Court
Judge Chidyausiku noted that 'once upon a time all the land in
Zimbabwe belonged to the African people of this country. By some
means foul or fair, depending on who you are in Zimbabwe, about half
that land ended up in the hands of a very small minority of

---

[58] Gino J. Naldi, 'Land Reform in Zimbabwe: Some Legal Aspects', *The Journal of Modern African Studies*, 31, 4, 1993, pp. 588.

[59] Naldi, 'Land Reform in Zimbabwe', p. 588.

[60] Madhuku, 'Law, Politics and the Land Reform Process', p. 133.

[61] Naldi, 'Land Reform in Zimbabwe', p. 600.

[62] Madhuku, 'Law, Politics and the Land Reform Process', p. 135; Gino J. Naldi, 'Constitutional Challenge to Land Reform in Zimbabwe', *Comparative and International Law Journal of Southern Africa*, 1998, pp. 78–91.

[63] Madhuku, 'Law, Politics and the Land Reform Process', p. 135.

Zimbabweans of European descent.' He concluded that land redistribution was in the 'public interest' because 'Africans ... see no merit in having to pay for land that was taken from them without compensation in the first place'.[64]

The commercial farmers appealed, and their case was heard by a full Supreme Court bench, under Chief Justice Gubbay's leadership, in May 1996. The Supreme Court unanimously upheld Justice Chidyausiku's decision. Examining the decision, Gino Naldi argued that the Supreme Court was aware its actions threatened the delicate balance it sought to maintain between honouring its 'robust history of defence of human rights and fundamental freedoms', and avoiding accusations of 'judicial activism'. In this sense the court was 'alive to the disappointment its ruling was likely to cause in certain circles', that is, among white farmers.[65] In Lovemore Madhuku's assessment, 'this decision dealt a decisive blow to white commercial farmers who had hoped that the courts would eventually come to their rescue. More fundamentally it demonstrated the readiness of the courts to support the thrust of the land reform process.'[66]

Although it had the Supreme Court on side, the government responded with a further amendment. The Constitution of Zimbabwe Amendment Act of 1996 was targeted at avoiding future court challenges, but passed within a context of spreading general disaffection with ZANU-PF's governance. Marred by corruption scandals, rising urban poverty, very little actual land redistribution and growing opposition among trade unions and civic organisations, ZANU-PF faced public criticism, and the party's efforts to pass the amendment reflected concern that the courts would stopping ruling in their favour. Despite these efforts, ZANU-PF's hold on power came under particular pressure following formation of the MDC, a political party that united members of the growing opposition groups in 1999, and was further tested in the constitutional referendum in February 2000. In the referendum the majority of voters rejected ZANU-PF's proposed constitution, supporting instead the National Constitutional Assembly and the MDC's campaign for the 'no' vote. ZANU-PF's defeat in the constitutional referendum was followed by a close race

[64] Zimbabwe Law Reports (ZLR), *Davies and Others v Minister of Lands, Agriculture and Water Development* (Harare, ZLR, 1994) p. 308.
[65] Naldi, 'Constitutional Challenge to Land Reform', p. 90.
[66] Madhuku, 'Law, Politics and the Land Reform Process', p. 136.

in the parliamentary elections of June 2000, in which the party won sixty-two seats to fifty-seven seats for the MDC.[67]

In response to this growing opposition, ZANU-PF looked to law to legalise its coercive practices and to land to gain political support. The Fast Track Land Reform Programme (FTLRP) was formally announced in July 2000, with the government setting a target of acquiring 3,000 farms for redistribution.[68] Under FTLRP, the at times violent 'occupation' of white farms by war veterans, ZANU-PF party activists, youth militias and black farmers was widespread. The CFU, made up of predominantly white farmers, contested the acquisition of their farms in the courts. For ZANU-PF, however, reclaiming Zimbabwe's land from the former 'colonial occupiers' was but the first step in arguing for the importance of protecting the sovereignty of the nation. After 2000, it was the interplay between sovereignty, rights and history that shaped the expectations and behaviour of the courts and government.

Narrating History through the Law after 2000

By placing the protection of the nation's sovereignty above the safe-guarding of citizens' rights as the central purpose of the party's rule, ZANU-PF began to promote a particular, narrow account of Zimbabwean history as of the late 1990s.[69] Understood in opposition to the globalised notion of human rights, ZANU-PF's notion of sover-eignty was based around defending the nation from a return to white, British colonial rule.[70] ZANU-PF's efforts to propound this view were evident in, for example, the manner in which the party levied its 'patriotic history' narrative against civic activists, opposition polit-icians and members of the judiciary. These actors stood accused of being 'Western puppets', using the 'a-historical' and 'universalising' discourse of human rights to promote and precipitate 'imperial'

---

[67] Dorman, *Understanding Zimbabwe*, p. 158.

[68] Human Rights Watch (HRW), *Fast Track Land Reform in Zimbabwe* (New York, HRW, 2002).

[69] Terence Ranger, 'Nationalist Historiography, Patriotic History and the History of the Nation: The Struggle over the Past in Zimbabwe', *Journal of Southern African Studies*, 30, 2, 2004, pp. 215–34.

[70] Blessing Miles Tendi, *Making History in Mugabe's Zimbabwe: Politics, Intellectuals and the Media* (Oxford, Peter Lang, 2010).

domination and regime change. Arnold Tsunga, a prominent Zimbabwean human rights lawyer, identified this narrative as 'psychological warfare', aimed at undermining the MDC's focus on the law as central in restoring Zimbabwean society.[71] In 2006, for example, an article in the state-owned newspaper, *The Herald*, identified Tsunga as 'the bellwether of imperialism', while the Law Society of Zimbabwe, of which Tsunga was secretary from 2005 to 2007, was represented as one of the 'institutions designed to defend and propagate white settlerism ... pushing for a neo-colonial model state'.[72] In this manner, ZANU-PF's political narrative also worked to delegitimise the rule of law, and challenged historically formed ideas about law's legitimacy that linked it not to colonial exploitation but to a defence of citizenship and 'substantive justice'.

ZANU-PF critiqued the law for its repressive role in the colonial period. As shown above, however, ZANU-PF had relied on precisely the coercive power of law to maintain its political dominance, even preserving or adapting pieces of repressive colonial legislation. In line with the judiciary's actions in the 1980s, certain of its members critiqued the government's behaviour after 2000, working to uphold their hard-fought reputation of independence and professionalism instead. These interactions between the judiciary and the executive were also shaped by a qualitative shift in ZANU-PF's techniques of governance. As shown in the Introduction, against the backdrop of a collapsing economy, professionalism and bureaucratic practices sat side by side with violence and disorder as mechanisms of rule.[73] The party thus looked to law to enable its coercive practices, but also sought to capitalise on the judiciary's reputation for independence to argue for its authority. As I show in the remainder of this chapter, in early 2000 this resulted in a shift in the way that debates about 'justice' were invoked to claim political legitimacy. This shift, in turn, shaped the ideas about, and contestations over, legal and state consciousness, professionalism and citizenship that run through this book.

---

[71] Arnold Tsunga, 'The Professional Trajectory of a Human Rights Lawyer in Zimbabwe between 2000 and 2008', *Journal of Southern African Studies*, 35, 4, 2009, p. 984.

[72] Quoted in Tsunga, 'Professional Trajectory of a Human Rights Lawyer', p. 985.

[73] See, for example, Chaumba et al., 'From *Jambanja* to Planning'; Fontein, 'Anticipating the *Tsunami*'; Jones, 'Freeze!'.

To explore the interaction between the judiciary and the executive in the early 2000s, I first turn to the invasion of the Supreme Court by approximately 200 war veterans on 24 November 2000, noted in the Introduction. The exchanges leading up to the attack on the Supreme Court and Chief Justice Anthony Gubbay began on 17 March 2000, when Justice Paddington Garwe ruled that the ZRP were responsible for evicting individuals who had illegally occupied farm land. As already mentioned, in the context of growing urban unrest, economic decline and the emergence of the MDC as a credible political opponent to ZANU-PF, the party looked to gain support by facilitating 'fast track' land resettlement. The police and government were 'frustrated' in their efforts to redistribute land, however, because of legal impediments.[74] Despite early successes, such as in the *Davies* case, it was the Land Acquisition Act of 1992 which ironically hampered the effective acquisition of land. Under the Act farm owners had been able to legally challenge farm occupations, and the courts had often ruled these invasions illegal 'because the procedures had not been followed'.[75] Tafadzwa Mugabe, a human rights lawyer in Harare, explained that in this way, 'the legal system actually became an impediment'. The courts' decisions were:

Very frustrating for the intended beneficiaries of the land reform programme, it was very frustrating for the government, which was saying, 'this is a policy we are going to pursue ... even the judges cannot reverse this, it is an unstoppable thing'.[76]

The frustration over the Act was indicative of the shift in the government's policies towards land reform, and divisions within ZANU-PF on whether to follow legal processes to achieve reform, or to support a 'revolutionary' change in ownership structures. On the one hand, the government passed new legislation to 'legalise processed that were formally illegal'.[77] On the other, it criticised the judiciary and condoned illegal occupations. Indeed, when Police Commissioner-General

[74] Interview, Tafadzwa Mugabe, human rights lawyer, Harare, 18 September 2010.
[75] Ibid. For an overview of the Supreme Court's decisions concerning the lawfulness of the land reform programme see IBA, *Report of IBA Zimbabwe Mission 2001*, pp. 42–5.
[76] Interview, Tafadzwa Mugabe, human rights lawyer, Harare, 18 September 2010.
[77] Ibid.

Augustine Chihuri, who had stated earlier that the invasions were 'a political issue' that was 'above the police', was tasked by the courts 'to deploy such manpower as is reasonably necessary' to ensure the order was complied with, the police took no action.[78] Chihuri instead launched an appeal before Justice Moses Chinhengo for a variation of the order, on the grounds both that the police did not have the resources to carry out the evictions, and that enforcing this order meant supporting an 'unjust and ethically iniquitous land ownership structure, through the application of brutal state power'.[79] This decision too was ironic, as ZANU-PF had in most of the 1980s and 1990s worked to protect property rights, evicting people who 'squatted' on farms.

In the contestations over land within the courtroom the notion of 'substantive justice', which had emerged among legal professionals and judicial officials in the 1960s, predominated.[80] Both the state and the judges dramatically tried to lay a claim to its defence, drawing on competing interpretations of 'professional' conduct and articulating diverging views of 'justice' in relation to narratives of history and the law. Attorney General Patrick Chinamasa, who chose to represent Commissioner Chihuri himself, invoked the country's colonial history to argue that 'the rule of law is a political concept. It is a tool which can be used from any political angle.' It was important, he continued, that the courts understood that 'a law which promotes injustice in society, a law which enforces unjust rights is not in compliance with the rule of law'.[81]

Justice Chinhengo rejected the state's application on 13 April. He articulated a different interpretation of 'just law' that also referred to the role of law under Rhodesian rule. He argued strongly for a different approach to law in independent Zimbabwe, stating, 'I would shudder to think that this perception of the rule of law could have been one of the reasons why the [commissioner] thought that he may not enforce the order'. He continued, clearly setting out that in his professional understanding, '[t]he rule of law means ... that everyone

---

[78] IBA, *Report of IBA Zimbabwe Mission 2001*, pp. 38–9.   [79] Ibid., p. 39.
[80] For a broader discussion on claims to 'substantive justice' in land cases, see Susanne Verheul, 'Land, Law and the Courts in Zimbabwe', in Jocelyn Alexander, JoAnn McGregor and Miles Tendi (eds), *Handbook of Zimbabwean Politics*, July 2020, retrieved from https://www.oxfordhandbooks.com/view/10 .1093/oxfordhb/9780198805472.001.0001/oxfordhb-9780198805472-e-4.
[81] Ibid.

must be subject to a shared set of rules that are applied universally and which deal even-handedly with people and which treat like cases alike'. He concluded that:

[t]he farm invasions are illegal and of a riotous nature. ... *In independent Zimbabwe, the law should no longer be viewed as being made for us, rather it must be viewed as our law.* We have the sovereign right to enact new laws, and repeal old laws which we find to be incompatible with the national interest.[82]

The drama moved from the High Court to the Supreme Court in September and October 2000, when the CFU, representing largely white commercial farm owners, launched two proceedings against the government. The first challenged the constitutionality of the land resettlement programme, and the second contested the legality of the procedures taken by the government to acquire land. On 10 November the Supreme Court, under the leadership of Chief Justice Anthony Gubbay, ruled on the second case. The Supreme Court ordered that the resettlement programme cease until the correct legal procedures were in place, and again tasked Commissioner Chihuri with removing all those who had 'unlawfully settled' on the land.

The police did not comply with the Supreme Court's order, and two weeks later war veterans invaded the Supreme Court. The invasion was not investigated, nor was it condemned by the government. Instead, members of the government argued that the judges had failed to understand the law in its appropriate historical context. Highlighting new, more pronounced divisions within the judiciary itself, Chief Justice Gubbay not only met verbal and physical threats from the attorney general, war veterans and ZANU-PF MPs, but was also critiqued by some of his fellow judges. At the opening of the legal year in January 2001, for example, then judge president of the High Court, Justice Chidyausiku, described the Supreme Court rulings as 'hardly tenable' and 'boggling the mind'.[83] Drawing on a speech Chief Justice Gubbay gave in 1991, Justice Chidyausiku accused him of racial bias and of failing to stand up for the lower economic classes in the country.[84] Following Chief Justice Gubbay's 'retirement' in March 2001, Justice Chidyausiku was appointed in his place.

[82] Ibid., pp. 39–40, emphasis added.   [83] Ibid., p. 41.   [84] Ibid., p. 41.

For many human rights lawyers, this blatant attack on the highest judge on the bench sent a warning signal that the ZANU-PF government would respond firmly and harshly to any opposition from within the legal arena. Tawanda Zhuwarara reflected, for example, that almost ten years on these events continued to 'define the whole judicial system in Zimbabwe': 'the ghost' of Chief Justice Gubbay's dismissal had 'never been exorcised'.[85] In the years that followed this fear was confirmed. Arnold Tsunga observed, for example, that 'members of the legal profession have been physically assaulted, manhandled, chased out of police stations, threatened with arrest, intimidated and generally harassed whilst executing their lawful mandates as provided for under the law'.[86] As we will see, these attacks impacted on the working environment of legal professionals working within and outside of the state's institutions, shaping their legal and state consciousness and informing the performative tactics human rights lawyers mobilised within the courts.

I briefly examine an early example of the repercussions that critical lawyers faced, looking at the attack on Sternford Moyo, then president of the Law Society of Zimbabwe. During the Law Society's annual meeting on 12 April 2002, Sternford Moyo had voiced concerns that the Supreme Court bench was staffed with ZANU-PF sympathisers, which called the independence of their decisions into question. He commented that the government's 'allegation that all white judges do not protect the rights of ordinary Zimbabweans' was 'unfair, defamatory and contemptuous', and had contributed to the resignation of numerous top judges.

On 18 April 2002, then minister of state for information and publicity, Professor Jonathan Moyo, published a statement in *The Herald*. In this statement Professor Moyo described the Law Society as 'an anti-Government, anti-black and pro-British sponsored opposition to African nationalism in Zimbabwe'.[87] He further cast the Law Society's president, Sternford Moyo, as a 'bad lawyer' whose

---

[85] Interview, Tawanda Zhuwarara, human rights lawyer, Harare, 7 September 2010.
[86] Tsunga, 'Professional Trajectory of a Human Rights Lawyer', p. 985.
[87] Legal Resources Foundation (LRF), *Justice in Zimbabwe* (Harare, LRF, September 2002), p. 107. See also, Jonathan Moyo, 'Zimbabwe: Bid to Dilute Sovereignty Slammed', *The Herald*, 18 April 2002, accessed on 15 September 2015 at http://allafrica.com/stories/200204180329.html.

expressions of concern that the bench was increasingly staffed with
ZANU-PF-aligned judges played to 'fictitious notions about judicial
independence' propounded by 'the British and the imperialist donors'
with the intent 'to dilute, if not destroy, Zimbabwe's sovereignty'.[88]
Sternford Moyo would be better suited working not as a 'bad lawyer'
but as a 'poor politician', Professor Moyo concluded.[89]

Less than two months after Professor Moyo's commentary the
'notorious Zimbabwean police torturer',[90] Detective Inspector Henry
Dowa, arrested Sternford Moyo.[91] On the basis of two letters, one
addressed to the British High Commission and a second to the secretary general of the country's leading opposition party the MDC,
Moyo and the Law Society's secretary Wilbert Mapombere were
arrested and accused of organising a meeting on 4 March 2002 to plan
a 'peaceful mass action' in support of the MDC. The men's arrest,
detention and appearance in court were marred by legal irregularities
that characterised many of the cases examined in this book. While the
men were moved between various police stations across Harare, their
lawyers appeared in the High Court to question the legality of their
arrest and to demand that they be given access to their clients.
Signalling divisions within the police force, the investigating officers
present in court were unable to provide the prosecution with the
reasons for the men's continued detention and 'had decided on two
separate occasions that [the men] ought to be released'.[92] The senior
police officers instructing the prosecution could not be contacted.
Sternford Moyo and Wilbert Mapombere only appeared in court on
Justice Paddington Garwe's orders, three days after their arrest.[93]

Once the men appeared, Justice Garwe found that the police were
attempting to charge them under a non-existent section of POSA.
Human rights lawyers and activists drew particular attention to
POSA as evidence that ZANU-PF had learned from the country's
colonial past in terms of formulating and utilising repressive legislation. Passed in 2002, POSA contained an array of powers for the police
to regulate public gatherings and demonstrations, and resembled

---

[88] Jonathan Moyo, 'Zimbabwe: Bid to Dilute Sovereignty Slammed', *The Herald*,
18 April 2002, accessed on 15 September 2015 at http://allafrica.com/stories/
200204180329.html.
[89] Ibid.   [90] REDRESS, 'The Case of Henry Dowa', p. 1.
[91] LRF, *Justice in Zimbabwe.*   [92] Ibid., p. 111.   [93] Ibid.

LOMA,[94] a fact that many members of the human rights community commented on, thereby highlighting their own historically rooted legal consciousness.[95] The Solidarity Peace Trust observed that 'laws such as POSA are not there to enforce law and order, but to undermine the rights of citizens to freedom of association, expression and movement'.[96] When Justice Garwe referred Moyo's case to the Magistrates' Courts, he suggested to the police which section of the Act they could turn to. The Magistrates' Courts released the men on bail pending their trial.[97] No trial date was set by the attorney general.

Underlining the contentious place of law in Zimbabwean politics, the case nonetheless remained a topic of public discussion within human rights reports and the state-owned media alike. In several reports published by leading national and international human rights organisations in the early 2000s, the case was cited as a clear and worrying example of the 'crude ... harassment and intimidation' that fit the trend in the government's often violent actions against any member of society who expressed criticism of the ruling party, ZANU-PF, its leader, President Robert Mugabe, and the tactics it relied on to govern. The government, on the other hand, cast Sternford Moyo as an unpatriotic traitor to his profession, who was defending white judges over his black peers. On 14 June 2002, Zimbabwe's government-run daily newspaper, *The Herald*, published an article accusing the Law Society of 'working to further white and British interests': 'instead of focusing on the defence of marginalised citizens', it was busy 'map[ping] out strategies against the sovereignty and hard-won independence of the country'.[98] The article asked what rule of law such lawyers could advocate for if they decided to 'agitat[e] for mass action, trading the courtroom for the streets and teargas'. Clearly, if they chose 'the tear smoke in place of the robe and genteel language of the courtroom', these lawyers were not fighting for the rule of law at all.[99]

---

[94] Institute of Justice and Reconciliation and Solidarity Peace Trust, *'Policing the State': An Evaluation of 1,981 Political Arrests in Zimbabwe 2000–2005* (Johannesburg, Solidarity Peace Trust, December 2006), p. 17.

[95] See, for example, Raftopoulos, 'Lest We Forget'.

[96] Institute of Justice and Reconciliation and Solidarity Peace Trust, *'Policing the State'*, p. 33.

[97] LRF, *Justice in Zimbabwe*, pp. 111–14.   [98] Ibid., p. 115.

[99] Ibid., p. 117.

In these contestations both sides voiced critiques that lay bare their competing understandings of what the law ought to protect – human rights or sovereignty – and the mutual allegations that, by expressing and acting upon these understandings, the other side was not acting 'professionally' or safeguarding justice and the rule of law. Both framed their actions as respectful of the rule of law and in the interest of 'justice', as actions taken in an effort to battle the other's contempt of these important aspects of government. This happened within a context where ZANU-PF's opposition, the MDC, also invoked the law and the language of international human rights in order to challenge ZANU-PF's narrow construction of citizenship in which it argued that not all Zimbabweans were protected under the law, specifically not the 'sell-outs' of the political opposition. As I explore through this book, not just lawyers, judges and political leaders but also activists and citizens displayed their legal and state consciousness through a commitment to a particular, historically rooted understanding of rights-based citizenship.

Conclusion

In this chapter I have traced the development and articulation of legal and state consciousness, and claims to 'professionalism' and 'substantive justice' over time. The Rhodesian government established a legal system which it used to enforce and maintain social and political order, entrench racial segregation and facilitate the economic exploitation of Africans. The legal system also opened up new avenues through which to engage the state, with African women performing legally aware strategies to defend their morality and dignity and restructure patriarchal relationships, and nationalists performing their politics from the dock. Over time the colonial government's increased reliance on coercive practices meant that the legal system lost legitimacy for guerrillas and nationalists. At the same time, Africans continued to display and deploy their legal and state consciousness. In prisons, in the courtroom and in the media they challenged members of the security forces, judicial officials and the Rhodesian government on the legality and justness of their actions. Civilians targeted under repressive legislation also continued to seek legal advice, indicating that an imaginary of rights-bearing citizenship persisted. In their engagements with law Africans held the view that their commitment to rule-bound behaviour did not necessarily legitimise the Rhodesian state, as this state's use and abuse of the law placed it beyond legitimation.

Within the Rhodesian state, and the Zimbabwean state after independence, there was also debate over the uses and meanings of law, justice and professional conduct. During the early years of independence the new government worked to desegregate and modernise the judiciary, and promoted numerous progressive social agendas. In parallel, to facilitate and legalise its violent strategies of repressing political opposition in the Matabeleland and Midlands provinces during the *Gukurahundi*, ZANU-PF maintained key repressive colonial laws. Mobilising understandings of judicial professionalism that were rooted in the Rhodesian era, members of the judiciary ruled against and criticised the executive's actions. Foreshadowing the dramatic accusations made against judicial officials after 2000, key members of ZANU-PF accused the judges of not practising 'fair' or 'just' law.

These debates took on new forms in the jurisprudential and political debates surrounding land cases after 2000, and in the attacks on members of the judicial profession more widely. In ZANU-PF's efforts to ground its legitimacy in a narrow retelling of liberation war history the use of law to rule against government policies was framed as 'illegitimate' and 'unfair'. Rather than erode actors' consciousness of the authority accorded by notions of 'professionalism' and 'justice', however, these ideas persisted among, and were mobilised by, a diverse range of actors. The coexistence of different interpretations of the relationship between law's legitimacy and state authority productively shapes political contestations over law, as I show in Chapter 2 with reference to a specific state institution, the attorney general's office.

2 | 'Rebels' and 'Good Boys'

Examining the Working Conditions in Zimbabwe's Attorney General's Office after 2000

Exploring legalism, as a way of thinking about and organizing the world, means examining law as rules, categories and argument; and it means examining what law promises, not just what it does [1]

On 22 October 2009, public prosecutor Andrew Kumire dramatically expressed his dissatisfaction with magistrate Chiwoniso Mutongi in her courtroom at Harare's Magistrates' Courts on Rotten Row. Calling her a 'maggot' and 'banging his hand on the desk and clicking his tongue', Kumire performed his contempt for the magistrate and his disagreement with her order that he stop putting leading questions to the state witness.[2] A prominent human rights lawyer, and the defendant in the case, Alec Muchadehama explained Kumire's 'click' as 'the height of contempt. It's like saying "ah, get away from me! Who do you think you are?"'[3] Responding to this insult, magistrate Mutongi sentenced Kumire to five days in prison for contempt of court.[4] Kumire turned around and walked out of the court.

By 'clicking' at magistrate Mutongi, and subsequently ignoring her decision and her authority by leaving the court, Andrew Kumire not only performed his frustration with the magistrate's efforts to restrain his behaviour in her courtroom, he also expressed his dissatisfaction with her failure to facilitate his efforts to prosecute Alec Muchadehama

---

[1] Fernanda Pirie, *The Anthropology of Law* (Oxford, Oxford University Press, 2013), p. 2.

[2] ZLHR, *The Legal Monitor*, edition 19, 26 October 2009, accessed on 9 June 2010 at http://archive.kubatana.net/html/archive/hr/091103zlhr.asp?sector=hr& year=2009&range_start=31; interview, Alec Muchadehama, human rights lawyer, Harare, 19 August 2010.

[3] Interview, Alec Muchadehama, human rights lawyer, Harare, 19 August 2010.

[4] ZLHR, *The Legal Monitor*, edition 19, 26 October 2009, accessed on 9 June 2010 at http://archive.kubatana.net/html/archive/hr/091103zlhr.asp?sector=hr& year=2009&range_start=31; interviews, Alec Muchadehama, human rights lawyer, Harare, 19 August 2010; Tafadzwa Mugabe, human rights lawyer, Harare, 18 September 2010.

on the 'instructions' from ZANU-PF.[5] Kumire was putting Muchadehama through the motions of a trial in an effort to harass him for defending several political activists and civil society members who were abducted and tortured by state agents between October and December 2008. Working with very limited evidence, Kumire continually and disruptively had to flout legal procedures to prosecute Muchadehama. While magistrate Mutongi attempted to curb Kumire's unruly behaviour, the prosecutor's conduct became increasingly contemptuous. Following his dramatic exit, Kumire returned to the court and further ignored magistrate Mutongi's authority as he applied to be released on bail in front of another magistrate, Mishrod Guvamombe, who granted it at US$30.[6]

In this chapter, I examine the working conditions within the state institution that employed and instructed Kumire, the attorney general's office, and ask what these working conditions can tell us about the practice and imagination of state-making and the law in Zimbabwe after 2000. As discussed in the Introduction, scholarship on the relationship between law's legitimacy, the making of state authority and society, particularly research focused on the production and circulation of legal consciousness as they structure state–citizen relations, does not directly address how these relationships are formed within state institutions. While these studies recognise the fragmented hegemony of law's legitimacy, they often remain silent on the fragmented hegemony of the state this law authorises. In scholarship of state authority in the postcolonial context I also observed that a number of scholars have argued for expanding our study of the spaces in which the state may be imagined, enacted, formed or contested beyond the institutions of government.[7] While such studies usefully draw our attention to the complexities of state-making beyond formal state

---

[5] Alec Muchadehama was charged with obstructing the course of justice under article 184 of the Criminal Law (Codification and Reform) Act; see 'Rights Lawyer Muchadehama Arrested', *The Zimbabwe Independent*, 14 May 2009, accessed on 27 June 2016 at www.theindependent.co.zw/2009/05/14/rights-lawyer-muchadehama-arrested.

[6] ZLHR, *The Legal Monitor*, edition 19, 26 October 2009, accessed on 9 June 2010 at http://archive.kubatana.net/html/archive/hr/091103zlhr.asp?sector=hr&year=2009&range_start=31.

[7] See, for example, Bierschenk and Olivier de Sardan (eds), *States at Work*; Thomas Bierschenk and Jean-Pierre Olivier de Sardan, 'Powers in the Village: Rural Benin between Democratisation and Decentralisation', *Africa: Journal of the International African Institute*, 73, 2, 2003, pp. 145–73. Lund, 'Twilight Institutions'.

institutions, here I argue that to productively observe the contested and fragmented hegemony of law within the state we should move questions of what law as a 'language of stateness'[8] authorises back into our study of the dynamics of meaning-making within the state's institutions.

By examining the imagination, articulation and practice of 'the law' from within through an in-depth study of one state institution, the attorney general's office, I shed light not only on how the ZANU-PF government sought to control this state institution to derive authority from the law. I also demonstrate the diverse ways civil servants working within it responded to, and mediated, their efforts. Tasked with representing 'the state' in court, prosecutors' responses to ZANU-PF's efforts to control their courtroom performances gave expression to varying interpretations of which practices of law would grant the state, and their professional place within it, authority.

First, I establish that the politics surrounding the appointment of attorney generals in post-2000 Zimbabwe were indicative of ZANU-PF's attempts to control the office's role as chief prosecutor. ZANU-PF sought to gain, and maintain, control over the prosecution services by influencing the position of the attorney general and the director of public prosecutions directly. In its efforts to capitalise on the authority of law, and to use the judiciary as an instrument of coercion and political repression, the attorney general had to be able to assign cases to prosecutors who were able and willing to apply repressive legislation selectively or to flout legal procedures to persecute ZANU-PF's critics. This form of partisan control was thus only really effective if it could be extended to incorporate a wider network of prosecutors.

To explore the conditions that facilitated the work of these politically partisan prosecutors, I turn to the accounts of two prosecutors, John and David, who joined the attorney general's office in 2008. They argued that partisan prosecutors worked on the basis of 'orders from above', that is, political directives issued by the attorney general and the director of public prosecutions. In a context of rapid economic deterioration, these 'orders from above' were enforced by a combination of enticement and intimidation. Extensive patronage networks born out of a broader system of corruption were reinforced by the

---

[8] See discussion in Introduction on law as a 'language of stateness'; Hansen and Stepputat, *States of Imagination*.

systematic coercion of prosecutors through threats, arrest, imprisonment or reassignment. The material and personal benefits of compliance, however, came at a price: in the eyes of the human rights community reporting on Muchadehama's case, for example, Kumire 'embarrassed' and 'humiliated' himself.[9] Not all prosecutors were willing to 'embarrass' themselves before this community by ignoring the correct legal procedures. As a result, ZANU-PF's tactics divided prosecutors into two categories: the 'good boys', who followed political instructions, and the 'rebels', who did not. At the heart of their debate were competing understandings of the relationship between the state's and the ruling party's authority, and the law's legitimacy. Through ZANU-PF's 'instructions', politically partisan prosecutors were tasked with maintaining the party's authority by acting in a manner that, some prosecutors argued, undermined the legitimacy of law.

In the final section of this chapter I expand on the position taken by 'rebel' prosecutors. Their defiance of ZANU-PF's political instructions tied them into a network of prosecutors, magistrates and lawyers who propagated an alternative understanding of 'good' prosecutors. Judicial actors who held this alternative understanding granted authority to prosecutors who behaved and performed ethically and 'professionally'. They articulated a belief that 'justice' and a fair trial were undermined by those prosecutors following political instructions, as the legitimacy of law and the authority of the state as a guarantor of justice depended on judicial actors' professional, rule-bound performances rather than on improvisation. From the interplay of these two registers, one of corruption and politicisation that explained the decision of the 'good boys' to follow 'political instructions' and improvise with the law, and another of professionalism and 'justice' that deterred the 'rebel' prosecutors from displaying such behaviour in court, there emerged a state institution that was marked by the fragmented hegemony of law.

Perceptions of Politicisation in the Attorney General's Office

ZANU-PF not only undermined the appearance that the party, and the government, would respect the rule of law through its spectacular

---

[9] Interviews, Alec Muchadehama, human rights lawyer, Harare, 19 August 2010 and Tafadzwa Mugabe, human rights lawyer, Harare, 18 September 2010.

verbal and physical attacks on the country's judiciary, as Chapter 1 showed. The party also aimed to draw on the authority law could grant its governance by controlling judicial institutions and by staffing them with politically loyal appointees. As ZANU-PF relied on the prosecution services to put members of the political opposition on trial, the office of the attorney general was particularly vulnerable to such political interference. In this section I examine the appointments made to the position after 2000, demonstrating that the office was increasingly politicised. Examining these appointments also shows fragmentation with ZANU-PF, as the party turned to judicial procedures not only to intimidate its political opposition but to keep their own political appointees in line.

Prior to the passing of Zimbabwe's new constitution in 2013 the attorney general was appointed by the president in consultation with the Judicial Services Commission and had three functions, namely to act as chief legal advisor to the government, as the main drafter of legislation and as the chief prosecutor, to whom the director of public prosecutions reported.[10] Through these three functions the post combined political and legal elements. In the function of chief prosecutor, however, human rights reports recommended that the attorney general ought to be the guided by law, not politics.[11] The independent national media regularly highlighted the politicisation of judicial officials following the war veterans' 'invasion' of the Supreme Court in 2000. In their reporting, the process of appointment of the attorney general was carefully scrutinised and explained in political terms. The media, human rights lawyers and (former) prosecutors linked the attorney general's security of tenure to the political, rather than legal, nature of decisions to prosecute individuals with ties to Zimbabwe's opposition political parties.

Owing to the party's reliance on the courts to harass its political opposition, it was particularly over the function of the attorney general

[10] Zimbabwe passed its new constitution in 2013. In the period under study, however, the constitution dating back to the Lancaster House agreements (with considerable amendments) was still in effect. It is this constitution that I refer to throughout this book. The appointment criteria were set out in the Zimbabwe Constitution (2005, amended), chapter 6, s. 76. The president similarly appointed the majority of the members of the Judicial Services Commission. See chapter 8, s. 90.
[11] IBAHRI, *Time for a New Approach*, pp. 27–8.

as chief prosecutor that human rights lawyers raised concerns. Tawanda Zhuwarara, a senior lawyer in ZLHR, remarked:

I really don't give a damn who is Attorney General, the position is a political position. You'll never get anyone who is not a politician to become Attorney General. The real problem is that the Attorney General and the prosecution department should be separate. The prosecution is too important to be entrusted in a political appointee.[12]

Zhuwarara held that it had become increasingly clear that the attorney general was a political appointee after Patrick Chinamasa, then attorney general, succeeded Emmerson Mnangagwa as ZANU-PF minister of justice in 2000. President Mugabe then appointed Chinamasa's deputy, Andrew Chigovera, as attorney general. Chigovera had worked as a lawyer and commissioner for the African Commission of Human and Peoples' Rights, and had no overt links with ZANU-PF. Both the independent and state media, however, scrutinised Chigovera's actions for displays of partisanship. In the independent media the attorney general was found to be accommodating to certain repressive reforms introduced by ZANU-PF, and simultaneously critical of the party's violent actions against MDC members and civil society activists in the run-up to the March 2002 presidential elections. Under Chigovera's reign, ZANU-PF's efforts to clamp down on political opposition were extended through repressive legislation such as POSA and the Access to Information and Protection of Privacy Act. In February 2002, however, Chigovera used POSA to argue that ZANU-PF's military-style 'terror bases'[13] were illegal if used for violent intimidation rather than peaceful political mobilisation.[14]

The ruling party, in turn, accused Attorney General Chigovera of bias in favour of the MDC. The state media had already raised concerns that the courts were too lenient in the context of MDC leader

---

[12] Interview, Tawanda Zhuwarara, human rights lawyer, Harare, 7 September 2010.

[13] Such 'terror bases' formed part of ZANU-PF's coercive strategies in the run-up to elections. Human rights reports document the abduction of MDC members by ZANU-PF supporters, youth militia members and war veterans to these bases, where they would be 'interrogated' and tortured. See, for example, SPT, *Subverting Justice*.

[14] Blessing Zulu, 'Terror Bases Unlawful Says Chigovera', *Zimbabwe Independent*, 8 February 2002, accessed on 4 October 2012 at http://allafrica.com/stories/200202080689.html.

Morgan Tsvangirai's treason trial, as Tsvangirai was quickly released despite the gravity of the charge against him.[15] Such accusations came to a head in November 2002, when Harare magistrate Caroline Chigumira[16] allowed two MDC legislators, Job Sikhala and Tafadzwa Musekiwa, who were charged with the mismanagement of government funds, out on bail. Their court appearance was delayed until the prosecution was able to present its case, and magistrate Chigumira acquitted the men. In response, Professor Jonathan Moyo, then ZANU-PF minister of information, attacked the attorney general's office:

There is something profoundly wrong and rotten between the AG's [attorney general's] Office and the Magistrates' Court because the wheels of justice have fallen off to a point where the police will be demoralised into inaction and where reasonable members of the public are concluding that MDC individuals have a license to commit all manner of crime with impunity.[17]

In the face of such high-powered political criticism, Attorney General Chigovera 'retired' in April 2003. His deputy, Bharat Patel, acted as attorney general until early 2005 when Sobusa Gula-Ndebele, a former colonel in ZANU's liberation army and chair of the Electoral Supervisory Commission during Zimbabwe's violent and contested presidential election in 2002, was appointed by President Mugabe. Gula-Ndebele was a staunch ZANU-PF supporter. Shortly after his appointment, however, he became entangled in the convoluted struggles over President Mugabe's succession. Gula-Ndebele reportedly backed a faction led by Vice President Joice Mujuru and her

---

[15] I discuss the trials against Morgan Tsvangirai in more detail in Chapter 6. For an overview of the state media coverage, see 'Weekly Media Update', *Media Monitoring Project Zimbabwe* (November 2002), accessed on 1 October 2012 at www.mmpz.org/sites/default/files/articles/2002–43.pdf; Brian Mangwende, 'Chigovera Forced to Retire', *Daily News*, 17 April 2003, accessed on 1 October 2012 at www.zimbabwesituation.com/apr17a_2003.html#link5.

[16] In 2004, magistrate Chigumira was herself arrested in her office, together with prosecutor Blessing Gorejena-Chinawa and a lawyer, Wilson Manase, 'for merely for doing their job in a manner, which caused dissatisfaction to some elements within the state'. See Zimbawe Lawyers for Human Rights (ZLHR), 'Arrest of Magistrate, Public Prosecutor and Senior Lawyer', *Kubatana*, 10 January 2004, accessed on 4 November 2013 at http://archive.kubatana.net/html/archive/hr/040110zlhr.asp?sector=lab&year=2004&range_start=31.

[17] 'Zanu PF's Final Blow on Judiciary?', *Financial Gazette*, 21 November 2002, accessed on 2 October 2012 at www.zimbabwesituation.com/nov22a_2002.html#link13.

husband, the retired military commander General Solomon Mujuru. They competed with a second faction led by then Minister of Housing Emmerson Mnangagwa, who had close ties to Minister of Justice Patrick Chinamasa. Gula-Ndebele's decision in 2006 to approve the trial of ZANU-PF heavyweight Minister of Justice Chinamasa specifically caused trouble, as ZANU-PF factionalism appeared to be at the heart of the controversial decision. Chinamasa was accused of defeating the course of justice by influencing state witnesses in a case of political violence involving then ZANU-PF State Security Minister Didymus Mutasa's supporters.[18] Given the highly political nature of the case against Chinamasa, and fearing the potential implications resulting from this, several magistrates in Manicaland province had refused to preside over the case. Eventually, Rusape Magistrate Phenias Chipopoteke came out of retirement to preside over the trial. He acquitted Chinamasa in September 2006.[19]

In December 2007, President Mugabe suspended Gula-Ndebele as attorney general. The previous month Gula-Ndebele had been arrested on charges of misconduct. It was alleged that he had met former National Merchant Bank of Zimbabwe Chief Executive James Mushore. Mushore had fled Zimbabwe in 2004 when he was accused of breaching foreign exchange laws. Gula-Ndebele, it was argued, had assured Mushore that he would not be prosecuted.[20] In the independent media Gula-Ndebele's arrest was interpreted as resulting from his

[18] Media coverage includes: Clemence Manyukwe, 'Chinamasa Under Probe', *Zimbabwe Independent*, 28 April 2006; Clemence Manyukwe, 'Chinamasa Trial in Doubt', *Zimbabwe Independent*, 30 June 2006; Clemence Manyukwe, 'Chinamasa Set to Deny Charges', *Zimbabwe Independent*, 28 July 2006; 'Retired Magistrate Takes Over Chinamasa Trial', *New Zimbabwe*, 4 August 2006; Tenda Maphosa, 'Zimbabwe Justice Minister's Trial Finally under Way', *Voice of America*, 9 August 2006, all accessed on 3 October 2012 at www .zimbabwesituation.com/.

[19] The attorney general's office initially appealed this judgment but then withdrew. See Lebo Nkatazo, 'AG Appeals against Chinamasa Acquittal', *New Zimbabwe*, 23 September 2006; Clemence Manyukwe, 'No Way out for Chinamasa, Says AG's Office', *Zimbabwe Independent*, 29 September 2006; Clemence Manyukwe, 'Chinamasa off the Hook', *Financial Gazette*, 16 February 2006, all accessed on 3 October 2012 at www.zimbabwesituation.com/.

[20] Transparency International, *Johannes Tomana's Reign as Attorney General of Zimbabwe: A Trail of Questionable Decisions* (Harare, Transparency International, 2011), p. 56; 'Zimbabwe: Police Arrest Attorney General Gula-Ndebele', *Financial Gazette*, 8 November 2007; Njabulo Ncube, 'More Woes for AG', *Financial Gazette*, 15 November 2007; Clemence Manyukwe,

willingness to try Chinamasa and his ties to the Mujuru faction in ZANU-PF's succession struggles.[21] Gula-Ndebele's suspension can, however, also be linked to his efforts to defend a prosecutor who fell victim of the politicisation of the office, Levison Chikafu. Working as the prosecutor in Patrick Chinamasa's case, Chikafu received threats from war veterans and his superiors in October 2006, causing him to resign from the case.[22] In April 2007, Chikafu was accused of soliciting a bribe in a murder trial. He held that the accusation was an extension of the victimisation he had experienced for prosecuting Chinamasa.[23] Chikafu was suspended pending the minister's inquiry into the charges, but Gula-Ndebele lifted his suspension before a decision had been made.

Shortly afterwards, Gula-Ndebele himself was suspended. A tribunal appointed by the president and chaired by High Court Judge Chinembiri Bhunu recommended that Gula-Ndebele be dismissed as attorney general; he duly was in May 2008. Gula-Ndebele challenged his dismissal in the courts. Justice Rita Makarau dismissed his case in the High Court on procedural grounds, a decision the former attorney general appealed in the Supreme Court. In November 2011, the court ruled that Justice Makarau should hear his case again, this time with then President Mugabe cited as a defendant. The new case has yet to be heard.[24]

'Hands-off, AG Warns Chihuri', *Financial Gazette*, 14 December 2007, all accessed on 3 October 2012 at www.zimbabwesituation.com/.

[21] Constantine Chimakure and Dumisani Muleya, 'Gula-Ndebele Tangled in Succession War', *Zimbabwe Independent*, 23 November 2007, accessed on 3 October 2012 at www.thestandard.co.zw/2007/11/23/gula-ndebele-tangled-in-succession-war/.

[22] 'Zimbabwe State Prosecutor Refuses to Handle Treason Case after Threats from Security Agents', *Zim Online*, 13 March 2006; Clemence Manyukwe, 'Prosecutor in Chinamasa Case Resigns', *Zimbabwe Independent*, 13 October 2006, both accessed on 3 October 2012 at www.zimbabwesituation.com/. Levison Chikafu previously worked on cases brought against ZANU-PF supporters. He was intimidated by war veterans and CIO operatives when he pushed for the arrest of CIO operative Joseph Mwale on murder charges, and during his prosecution of two ZANU-PF MPs, Enoch Porusingazu and Fred Kanzama, on charges of theft.

[23] Lance Guma, 'Chikafu Case Highlights Intimidation of the Judiciary', *SW Radio Africa*, 25 April 2007, accessed on 9 October 2012 at www.zimbabwesituation.com/apr26_2007.html#Z3.

[24] 'Court Watch 2/2011 [Cases in the Supreme Court]', *Veritas* (November 2011).

During these wrangles Bharat Patel once again became acting attorney general. In December 2008, however, President Mugabe controversially appointed Johannes Tomana to the office.[25] The two factions of the MDC protested against Tomana's appointment. Contrary to the stipulations of the GPA, signed with ZANU-PF after the violent 2008 elections only three months earlier, on 15 September, they had not been consulted. The MDC also noted Tomana's declarations of support for ZANU-PF in his previous positions as deputy attorney general and deputy head of the Anti-Corruption Commission.[26] In a similarly controversial appointment, Tomana went on to replace the director of public prosecutions, Joseph Jagada, with Florence Ziyambi, the former chief law officer under Gula-Ndebele. Transparency International noted that 'Johannes Tomana was desirous of a Director of Public Prosecutions who would go along with his manipulation of cases'.[27]

Although Jagada had a long track record of prosecuting MDC members and civil society activists, prosecutors working within the attorney general's office explained that Ziyambi's connections with Police Commissioner Augustine Chihuri and the security agents probably influenced her appointment. Ziyambi's appointment, the prosecutors argued, was a 'reward' for her support for the security agents and police in the violent abductions of civil society members, such as Jestina Mukoko, in 2008.[28] For his support of the same abductees, human rights lawyer Alec Muchadehama was placed on trial: the trial in which, as shown earlier, state prosecutor Andrew Kumire 'clicked' at the magistrate. Several members of the attorney general's office also

[25] Transparency International, *Johannes Tomana's Reign*, locates Tomana's political partisanship in an unwillingness to prosecute ZANU-PF supporters accused of (political) crimes.

[26] 'Ardent Mugabe Supporter Now AG', *Zimbabwe Times*, 18 December 2008; Tichaona Sibanda, 'MDC Decries Appointment of Johannes Tomana as Attorney-General', *SW Radio Africa*, 18 December 2008, both accessed on 4 October 2012 at www.zimbabwesituation.com/.

[27] Transparency International, *Johannes Tomana's Reign*, p. 60. Jagada himself had succeeded Loice Matanga-Moyo, who had served as director from 2000 to 2006, when she was forcibly removed from her post after ordering the prosecution of ZANU-PF officials. Lebo Nkatazo, 'Zimbabwe's Top Prosecutor Removed from Post', *New Zimbabwe*, 11 December 2009, accessed on 4 October 2012 at www.newzimbabwe.com/pages/judges9.14841.html.

[28] For an account of these experiences, see Jestina Mukoko, *The Abduction and Trial of Jestina Mukoko: The Fight for Human Rights in Zimbabwe* (Sandton, KMM Review Publishing, 2016).

noted that Ziyambi's ability to 'disable those lawyers she deems problematic' probably motivated her appointment. Ziyambi, they continued, 'openly boasts at the office that she can fix judges who humiliate her in court or find against her usually incoherent legal arguments'.[29]

Prosecutors argued that they experienced the most notable decline in professional standards within the attorney general's office once it came under the control of Johannes Tomana and Florence Ziyambi in 2008. Following a series of tensions between the attorney general and ZANU-PF, first over the political independence of the position as with Chigovera, and subsequently over party political wrangles as with Gula-Ndebele, a qualitative change took place with the appointment of Tomana. This change, prosecutors argued, came about as, in the context of the formation of the GNU following the contested 2008 elections, ZANU-PF sought to exert its control more firmly over the actions of the office, specifically its authority to start criminal proceedings and to run trials. In the following sections I demonstrate that these efforts to control the office created a working environment in which prosecutors willing to 'follow instructions' on behalf of ZANU-PF were rewarded, while those who operated independently were threatened.

'Good Boys' and 'Rebels': Enticement and Intimidation among Prosecutors

The most complete description of the working conditions in the attorney general's office emerged from interviews I conducted in Harare in 2010 with two prosecutors, John and David. In our discussion the two men described the appointment processes of their superiors as politically partisan, and focused on how these appointments influenced their working conditions. In the context of a rapidly deteriorating economy the prosecutors argued that their professional office was infiltrated by political demands, facilitated by material corruption within the judiciary as a whole. Their superiors further relied on prosecutors who 'didn't question' their 'instructions' in cases involving members of

---

[29] 'Staff at AG's Office Expose External Intervention', *Zimbabwe Times*, 8 March 2009, accessed on 8 July 2010. Content of the email cited in this news article was confirmed in several of my interviews and discussions. See further, field notes, reflections on discussion with John and David, Harare, 11 September 2010.

ZANU-PF's opposition. These practices split the office into the 'good boys', prosecutors who went along with political instructions, and the 'rebels', who did not.[30]

John and David met in Judicial College before joining the Ministry of Justice in 2002.[31] John started at the Judicial College after he had been expelled from the University of Zimbabwe's law department for participating in a student protest. David had also wanted to study law at the university but had not achieved the necessary grades in his A-levels. He was working as an accounts clerk when he saw an advertisement for the Judicial College and applied. Human rights lawyers regularly noted that, though graduates of the Judicial College had not received the same length and quality of training as those studying at the University of Zimbabwe's law department, they were of a high calibre owing to their personal dedication to the profession.[32]

Asked in 2010 whether they enjoyed their jobs, David stated, 'it's rather problematic. You still have the zeal for your job, but you are demoralised by the remuneration, and the work conditions.' David and John explained that the government might address the question of remuneration if prosecutors were able to strike as a unified group. Prosecutors were not, however, unified. John explained: 'you cannot look at the prosecution job in isolation [from] what is happening, the political climate, the polarisation that is there and how it impacts on your work as a prosecutor'.[33]

In their discussions of the 'political climate' and its implications, John and David began with a description of broader perceptions of corruption in the judiciary and attorney general's office, which they argued enabled the politicisation of prosecutors. As we have seen, Zimbabwe experienced a rapid economic decline after 1998, which

---

[30] Interview, John and David, prosecutors, Harare, 10 September 2010.
[31] Law degrees could be obtained at the University of Zimbabwe as of 1965 and Midlands State University as of 2005. From 1989 on the government closed the University of Zimbabwe multiple times following student protests. The Ministry of Justice, Legal and Parliamentary Affairs established the Judicial College in 1995; in September 1999, the college separated from the Ministry of Justice under the Judicial College Act. Through an eighteen-month taught course the college primarily trained judges, magistrates and prosecutors. In 2008, in the midst of Zimbabwe's economic crisis, the college closed due to a lack of funding.
[32] Interviews David Hofisi, human rights lawyer, Harare, 12 August 2010, and Tafadzwa Mugabe, human rights lawyer, Harare, 18 September 2010.
[33] Interview, John and David, prosecutors, Harare, 10 September 2010.

culminated in extreme economic collapse after 2007. Human rights lawyers argued that this economic collapse in particular facilitated political interference within the judiciary.[34] Lizwe Jamela, a ZLHR lawyer based in Bulawayo, argued:

The judiciary is not spared either, with the political interference, with the economic challenges, whereby the judicial officials are now being forced to resort to unorthodox means as far as trying to earn a living. ... It's almost like a known secret now, that magistrates take bribes.[35]

An often cited example of the form that political patronage took was Reserve Bank Governor Gideon Gono's allocation of plasma TVs and vehicles to High Court judges in August 2008.[36] Alec Muchadehama explained that these gifts had seriously tainted the perception of judicial independence in Zimbabwe: 'The problem is that the perception is that most of the judges are now compromised. ... They [judges] were given trinkets by people who had no authority to give them. ... Chief Justice Gubbay, and other judges in the region, said that that was wrong.'[37] In 2009, Gubbay repeated that 'a payment or perquisite accepted by a judge from any source other than the treasury inevitably raises the taint of undue influence'.[38] This 'taint of undue influence' was evident for instance in the case of notorious magistrate Samuel Zuze.[39] In January 2010, Zuze, a magistrate in Chipinge, convicted four white commercial farmers of failing to vacate their farms, for

---

[34] Interviews with Lizwe Jamela, human rights lawyer, Harare, 6 September 2010; Tafadzwa Mugabe, human rights lawyer, Harare, 18 September 2010; David Hofisi, human rights lawyer, Harare, 11 August 2010; and Alec Muchadehama, human rights lawyer, Harare, 19 August 2010.

[35] Interview, Lizwe Jamela, human rights lawyer, Harare, 6 September 2010.

[36] Frank Kuwana, 'Gono Splashes US$1M in Bribes ahead of Presidential Bid', *ZimDiaspora*, 24 January 2009; Fidelis Munyoro, 'Judges Get Vehicles, Goods', *The Herald*, 1 August 2008, both accessed on 3 October 2012 at http://zimbabwesituation.com; HRW, 'Our Hands Our Tied', pp. 17–18.

[37] Interview, Alec Muchadehama, human rights lawyer, Harare, 19 August 2010.

[38] Anthony Gubbay, 'The Progressive Erosion of the Rule of Law in Independent Zimbabwe', *International Rule of Law Lecture* (unpublished lecture, December 2009), p. 2.

[39] At the time of fieldwork in September 2010, Samuel Zuze was in the news for sentencing a young man to one year in prison for insulting President Mugabe. Allegedly the man had called President Mugabe 'old': 'Chipinge Man Jailed for Insulting Mugabe', *Radio VOP*, 3 September 2010, accessed on 2 October 2012 at www.radiovop.com/index.php/national-news/4442-chipinge-man-jailed-for-insulting-mugabe.html.

which an acquisition order had been issued. Zuze had been offered one of the farms by the minister of lands and resettlement in November 2009.[40] Muchadehama commented:

Judges have been given land that has been seized from white commercial farmers; they have made certain pronouncements upon the same thing. This land, there were a lot of disputes about that, and the disputes were going to the court, where the same people who decided, benefitted. ... It's horrible.[41]

John and David also identified a 'whole system' of corruption which operated within the Magistrates' Courts and which involved prosecutors, magistrates, lawyers and clerks of court. John observed that, 'if you are talking about the total[ity] of the perception of the justice system at the moment, ah, the feeling that ... especially the Magistrates' Court, there is no justice there anymore. It's either you buy yourself out [of prison], or somebody buys yourself in.' David agreed: 'justice is for sale in the Magistrates' Court'. As a result, John continued, 'people have lost confidence in the entire court system. Knowing that the prosecutor can shout and shout, or the lawyer can shout and shout, but as long as there is no money, nothing will happen.'[42]

David explained that such corruption led to much uncertainty, as a person's sentencing was no longer tied to the prosecutor's abilities to convince a judge or magistrate by law. As he stated, 'you will be surprised at, when you think, "ah, I've done a thorough job here" and then the magistrate says "I find you not guilty and you are acquitted", because he has been given some money'. John added that this unpredictability extended to the appeal process. As the majority of the magistrates' records were written by hand the record was 'malleable': the magistrate could 'simply take that record and start writing something that you never said'. In this environment, David held, there was little incentive for prosecutors to prepare their cases: 'The only preparation they can do is the preparation to solicit that money from

---

[40] Sokwanele, 'Compromised Judgement: Magistrate Samuel Zuze's Offer Letter', *ThisisZimbabwe Blog*, 30 January 2010, accessed on 2 October at www .sokwanele.com/thisiszimbabwe/archives/5401; Violet Gonda, 'Magistrate's Conflict of Interest Exposed in Land Case', *SW Radio Africa*, 1 February 2010, accessed on 2 October 2012 at www.zimbabwesituation.com/feb2_2010 .html#Z5.
[41] Interview, Alec Muchadehama, human rights lawyer, Harare, 19 August 2010.
[42] Interview, John and David, prosecutors, Harare, 24 September 2010.

the people'. David lamented that individuals on trial for criminal offences regularly told him, 'your colleagues are very difficult to work with nowadays'.[43]

David and John described these corrupt practices as 'horrible' not simply because this system favoured 'the lawyer with the cash' as opposed to 'the lawyer who knows the law'. In addition, the deteriorating economy and increased bribery had opened up space to establish networks of political patronage that favoured people with the 'right' connections within the attorney general's office. These links were forged not just with prosecutors willing to take bribes, but also with prosecutors who were willing to follow political instructions. Lawyers and prosecutors thus distinguished between two forms of corrupt practice. While certain judicial officials depended on occasional bribes from the accused, their family, their lawyers or the complainant to supplement their minimal income, others accepted material and financial gifts that tied them into a network of ZANU-PF patronage.

As I have shown, such gifts included plasma televisions or land deeds. John and David agreed, however, that there were also subtler indications that certain prosecutors were implicated in the extensive networks of ZANU-PF patronage. The two men had a lengthy exchange about the types of cars prosecutors drove, concluding that those who benefitted most from political corruption drove cars imported from South Africa, while David and John could not 'afford a bicycle'. 'It's horrible', John lamented.[44]

John explained that prosecutors who benefitted from such political patronage were easily identifiable not only on grounds of the type of car they drove, but also by the types of cases they prosecuted. David said that if a prosecutor worked on a case against ZANU-PF's political opponents, 'you can just conclude that this is their man who can easily listen to their instructions, and follow them diligently, doesn't question anything'. These were the 'good boys': prosecutors who did not disagree with their superiors or question their orders and were thus linked into wider patronage networks. 'Good boys' benefitted from the 'whole system' of corruption. In the Magistrates' Courts and through their partisan superiors they received trips abroad, promotions or assignments to particular courtrooms in which one was more likely to extract bribes, such as the remand court.[45]

---

[43] Ibid.   [44] Ibid.
[45] Interview, John and David, prosecutors, Harare, 10 September 2010.

Not all prosecutors could be persuaded to follow ZANU-PF's instructions, however. Grace had worked as a prosecutor for almost twenty years, prosecuting cases in Gweru, Bulawayo and finally joining the attorney general's office in Harare. In 2007, she moved to the Ministry of Lands. She explained that she left the prosecution services because of the working conditions that she encountered in Harare. Specifically, she was unhappy with being pressured to prosecute individuals under POSA for political reasons. Grace declined to take such cases, explaining that she 'didn't really like to have people convicted of those types of offences, because they didn't feel right'. She was only handed one POSA case, involving a group of church leaders who had organised a peaceful prayer meeting. Grace argued against her superiors, saying that the charges were 'ridiculous ... I didn't think that there had been any offence that had been committed'.[46] The file then disappeared off her desk, and 'the same file was given to another different prosecutor, to also get their opinion'. This prosecutor, she continued, could be persuaded to follow political instructions through a combination of intimidation and economic enticement.

Prosecutors such as Grace, who refused to follow political orders from their superiors, were labelled 'rebels'.[47] John explained that, essentially, prosecutors:

Have to make a choice, to say, if I don't comply I face the risk of getting arrested or even charged. If I comply, I have an added advantage of probably managing to win one or two foreign trips, and get one or two advantages ... I can be promoted.[48]

To illustrate the consequences for 'rebel' prosecutors, John referred to an example where he had refused his superiors' orders. The case he had to work on involved Thamsanqa Mahlangu, the former deputy minister of youth for the MDC. Mahlangu was arrested on 28 July 2009 and was accused of stealing notorious war veteran leader Joseph Chinotimba's phone. John recalled:

That case was handled at Harare Magistrates' Court. He [Mahlangu] was acquitted. The instruction was to take up that case on appeal, and it was given to me. I went through that case, the record of proceedings, I formulated an opinion on that, that we could not successfully appeal against the

---

[46] Interview, Grace, former prosecutor, Harare, 16 August 2010.
[47] Interview, John and David, prosecutors, Harare, 10 September 2010.
[48] Ibid.

acquittal. I wrote a memo to that effect and sent it back to my seniors. I was called and I was asked to think again, to think seriously and to think again about it ... So then it becomes a problem.[49]

Shortly afterwards, John:

was called by the director [of public prosecutions, Florence Ziyambi] ... She clearly told me that she didn't like me, she thinks I'm after her, I exposed the office, and a lot of other accusations, for almost an hour ... I even requested a transfer after that meeting. I requested a transfer to Bulawayo, and she again stood in the way of that transfer.[50]

John continued that, after this incident, he had decided not to oppose a bail application as 'the instruction was that that person should not get out, but I was saying, the principles that pertain to bail, the principles that I know, it was clear, this is a good candidate for bail'. John was certain that he had handled the case according to the law. He was, however, arrested and charged with obstructing the course of justice. Although John knew he had not committed an offence, he was concerned that the prosecutor on his trial would 'want to project a picture of a good boy, and in the process manipulate the system'.[51] If this was so, John held, the merit of his case was of no consequence. He attributed these events to 'the leadership', explaining that 'the director [of public prosecutions], she runs the entire prosecution department nationwide, prosecutors report directly to her. ... Unfortunately she, she's political, she's allowed herself to be swayed by political affiliation.'[52]

David explained that he was 'in the same boat', as he was 'accused of inciting other prosecutors to be rebellious to the system'. This was partly due to his friendship with John but also because he worked in a similar manner. As David explained:

If you are given instructions, and you think otherwise, you write them a note, a memo to say that 'I am of the view that this thing should be done this way, and not what you have instructed me', and it's a fact that they'll allocate that matter or that case to someone else who'll be willing to comply with that instruction.[53]

---

[49] Ibid.; 'Chinotimba Sues Minister for US 19 Million for Loss of Business', *The Insider*, 2 December 2011, accessed on 5 October 2012 at www.insiderzim.com/stories/2964-chinotimba-sues-minister-for-us19-million-for-loss-of-business.html.

[50] Interview, John and David, prosecutors, Harare, 10 September 2010.

[51] Ibid.   [52] Ibid.   [53] Ibid.

Human rights lawyers expressed their awareness of, and concern over, these conditions within the attorney general's office. Lizwe Jamela explained that a prosecutor who is 'progressive', 'gets victimised. ... There are prosecutors that have been prosecuted simply because they did not obey orders from above when dealing with certain cases.'[54] Tawanda Zhuwarara similarly commented that, as a judicial official, 'you need to be politically correct to maintain your job'.[55] John and David, however, both agreed that they would rather be labelled 'rebels' than 'good boys'.

When being a 'good boy' had such tangible advantages, and being a 'rebel' had such high costs, their decision needs explanation. To do so, I turn to the alternative understanding of 'good' prosecutors that John and David articulated. I illustrate how they held this understanding within a wider community that shared their commitment to professional and ethical behaviour, thus reinforcing their belief that they were acting in the 'right' or 'proper' manner.

An Alternative Understanding of 'Good' Prosecutors

The very real material benefits accorded to the 'good boys' who were tied into ZANU-PF's system of political power and patronage were counter-balanced for John and David by their moral culpability. In the actions of the 'rebels' there existed an alternative authority that was bound up with a different understanding of what it meant to be 'good'. This authority was tied to the imagination of a prosecution service as a rule-bound and professional state institution, and shared within a larger community which included certain judicial officials, human rights lawyers and Zimbabwean citizens.

In the context of the economic recession, John and David explained that the low salaries for civil servants, together with the threats of unemployment if one did not follow orders, made acting as a 'good boy' increasingly appealing and explicable. At the same time, such 'good boy' behaviour was judged harshly by certain magistrates, civil servants and the imagined public they engaged through their court-room performances. Grace, for example, explained that she 'preferred a straightforward theft or murder ... those kind of things you

---

[54] Interview, Lizwe Jamela, human rights lawyer, Harare, 6 September 2010.
[55] Interview, Tawanda Zhuwarara, human rights lawyer, Harare, 7 September 2010.

prosecute with a clear conscious, you know, but other cases sometimes make it difficult'.[56] As John explained:

So I can say that there are people who sold their souls. I wouldn't say so, maybe it's too harsh, but there are people who have said, 'I have come here to work, what I want is to make sure that I do my work and probably get advancement of the system', so those kind of people would comply. Even if it amounts to showing your stupidity in court, [by complying with an] instruction that is stupid and unprofessional.

Complying with political instructions, John and David argued, might necessitate breaking the law, as 'our superiors want a certain position, ᴡʜɪᴄʜ ᴍɪɢʜᴛ ɴᴏᴛ ʙᴇ ᴄᴏᴍᴘʟɪᴀɴᴛ ᴡɪᴛʜ ᴛʜᴇ ʟᴀᴡ'. Tʜᴇ ᴄᴏɴꜱᴇǫᴜᴇɴᴄᴇꜱ ᴏꜰ ʙᴇɪɴɢ ᴀ 'good boy', they explained, were not just financial benefits and career advancement, but also embarrassment and shame stemming from unprofessional behaviour in an open court. As we have seen, Andrew Kumire's contemptuous behaviour at Rotten Row was punished by the magistrate and condemned by human rights lawyers in their recollections and reporting. Though Kumire showed little remorse, John and David expressed an expectation that 'good boy' prosecutors would experience shame and embarrassment brought on by their behaviour, as they were performing before the larger human rights community as well. They discussed what they saw as the benefits and risks for 'good boys' at length:

DAVID: At times, as you know, people do communicate, and they read the newspapers, and they will notice that ah, for instance, this [guy], he is doing these cases ... prosecuting all MDC activists, MDC MPs and officials, etc. People will be reading the newspapers and then if you pitch up in Masvingo, obviously magistrates will just laugh, 'so they [the accused] are the MDC MP so that prosecutor is around'.

JOHN: Some of them will sympathise with such a person. Even myself, I agree and I mention it in our offices, saying it's pathetic when you are, when you cannot exercise what you think you have learnt and ...

DAVID: when you just do what you're told.

JOHN: I feel pity for them, honestly, and even the judges at the High Court, they feel pity for them for such kind of persons. It happens, it has happened in my presence. Where a person tries to support an argument that cannot be supported at law, completely. This argument is, the judge will say ... 'no, I know, I know that you have instructions but it's unfortunate but, don't you see that you should have made concessions on this one? In any case even if you maintain that position I am going to rule this way, it is not your fault that you have your instructions'.

DAVID: That judge would say that in an open court even, in the presence of many lawyers, and the public, because also the public are present. And he would actually tell you that, and you would feel bad.

JOHN: Yea, and he was struggling there.

DAVID: Because you are under instructions, you were making stupid [*sic*] of yourself because of these instructions.

JOHN: It is embarrassing. It is embarrassing.

DAVID: You are showing the world that you don't know. When you know.

JOHN: You know it.

DAVID: You are degrading the office, you are degrading the office, and everyone will see, [and ask] 'what is it with the officer? What is it with these people? Why can't they do what they have learnt at college?'

JOHN: Yeah, and some judges are not very friendly. They lambast you in court, in their ruling or whatever. If it is a bail ruling, and your instruction is to oppose even if it's very clear that there are no grounds, yeah you struggle trying to say one of those things, but in their ruling they will lambast you to say, 'we don't know which school you were at', and they will say that you are 'advancing something that is out of the ordinary'. ... Remember, some of these things are recorded in the press and everybody knows that.[57]

John referred to the high-profile trial of MDC-T MP Roy Bennett, who was charged with treason in February 2009, shortly after Morgan Tsvangirai appointed him as deputy minister of agriculture in the GNU. Attorney General Tomana led the prosecution over the course of the lengthy trial. John commented: 'even a half-lawyer could tell that case is political. But the attorney general himself had to go and humiliate himself, you see. Because he was trying to pursue a certain political agenda, not a legal agenda.'[58]

---

[57] Ibid.   [58] Ibid.

Following this 'political agenda' marked out the 'good boys'. John, David and Grace, however, all agreed that it was adhering to a 'legal agenda' that identified a genuinely good prosecutor. Their definition centred on professional, fair and impartial conduct. This could only be achieved by applying the law in an independent and informed manner, rather than being driven by political or economic concerns. This view of a 'good' prosecutor was shared among numerous actors within the Magistrates' Courts, contributing to the imagination of a shared ethical community which authorised a rule-bound state governed by professional rather than partisan civil servants.

Sarah had worked as a magistrate for over twenty years before moving to a senior consulting position in a Harare-based legal assistance organisation in 2007. She described a good prosecutor as 'a prosecutor who does his homework, who will get his docket well before the trial, to really look at the case and do whatever research he would want to do before the trial'. She continued:

I remember when I was in Chinhoyi [from 1997 to 2007], I worked with these two brilliant prosecutors, you know, even now I would say the same thing, that those prosecutors were so good, they would write the judgment for you. You know, each time, like the trial was going on ... you would actually have a question ... it's like they were reading your mind, they would ask exactly that question. They were such a pleasure to work with, they would never leave out anything.... And they would do the research. Even that address at the very end, you could actually tell that this person would know what they are actually talking about.[59]

Grace explained that, when she was working as a prosecutor, she was aware that 'magistrates, what they like is for you to lay out the entire case properly, to make it easy for them to either convict or acquit. You know, and when you don't do your job properly, then it also makes it difficult for them.' At times when she was not prepared for a case, Grace feared such magistrates. For the most part, however, she appreciated magistrates who focused on the content of the case, rather than being swayed by political or economic concerns: 'Just working with a good, upright magistrate is always a nice feeling'.[60]

Both Sarah and Grace gave similar reasons for why it was important for prosecutors to be prepared for their cases, binding them to a

---

[59] Interview, Sarah, former magistrate, Harare, 5 August 2010.
[60] Interview, Grace, former prosecutor, Harare, 16 August 2010.

community of like-minded professionals and citizens who were concerned with 'substantive justice'. For Sarah, a prosecutor who was not
prepared to argue a case prevented her from doing her job as a
magistrate, which she described as 'to really try and see whether the
real substantive justice is being done'. In her understanding of 'substantive justice', Sarah echoed E. P. Thompson, locating the authority
of law, and of her legitimacy as a magistrate, in facilitating 'just'
outcomes. She elaborated:

The magistrate is there to listen to both sides and in the end come out with a
well-reasoned judgment. ... And do it in a way that everyone will understand, and no one will go away probably thinking 'so what were they saying,
what were the reasons for them coming up with that decision?' ... You are
supposed to at least make sure that what is being done is being done fairly.[61]

This 'substantive justice', Sarah explained, should be performed before
an audience. For the benefit of the accused, the witnesses and their
families, no interaction in or outside the courtroom should give them
the impression that their case was predetermined, as 'justice must not
only be done, but it must be seen to be done'. Judicial officials had to
give all those involved a sense that a fair trial was a possibility:

Because I always said with the accused person, yes, he may have some rights
kind of curtailed because of [being accused], but that doesn't make him any
less a human being, he is still a human being who deserves to be respected. ...
A trial is not a game, where you are on the look-out, if a person is supposed
to make a certain move, and they are probably not seeing it, and you kind of
keep your fingers crossed that they are not seeing it, and then you punish
them for that. I have always said that a trial is not a game like that, a trial is
something like a process, where you are trying to, to assist the court in
arriving at the truth. ... I have no problems using my prerogative as the
court to try and see where the truth lies ... [because] we are fallible, so each
time I think to myself that 'Lord, I hope I have never sent an innocent person
to prison', because eish, that is something that can really weigh heavily on
your conscience. So I think it's really a question of people appreciating that
[an accused] person is just like me, and the law guarantees nothing, the next
time you might be in the dock and then you'll appreciate how important it is
to be courteous.[62]

---

[61] Interview, Sarah, former magistrate, Harare, 5 August 2010.   [62] Ibid.

Grace similarly explained that, although she liked winning as a prosecutor, she could also:

Feel quite happy, either way, the person gets acquitted, but justice has been done. If you win your case, you also feel quite good. . . . You are dealing with people, and people's lives, and I think to some degree the opportunities as a prosecutor that you aim to actually just get the truth before the court, and let the court decide, you know, if you win or lose.[63]

John shared Grace's ethics. He defined the 'bad' prosecutor as someone who sidelined legal arguments in favour of political considerations. He explained that he would like to see a change both in 'leadership' and in 'attitude'. He hoped that prosecutors would be professional', and that there would be no more 'talk of rebels'. He continued, 'if it can be dealt with, we would be the happiest, and not as rebels, but as people who are prosecutors, because that's our job'.[64] David agreed, explaining that it was precisely this shared perception of the professional prosecutor as a good prosecutor that was important, both to him and to those accused of any sort of offence. Recalling an incident where an accused person he had prosecuted, and who had been found guilty, approached him in Chinhoyi prison, David related, 'it's good to hear an accused person whom you prosecuted, he actually says, in as much as he tried to plead not guilty and explain himself out, I did my job by prosecuting him and he was found guilty'.[65]

John, David, Grace and Sarah positioned themselves within an imagined professional and ethical legal community that, as I showed in Chapter 1, had deep historical roots. Reflecting the long-standing importance of professionalism among civil servants, for instance, all four judicial officials echoed the country's first black judge, Enoch Dumbutshena, who argued in 1989 that 'the process of justice does not begin in the courtroom. It begins in the chambers of the Attorney General.'[66] For John, David, Grace and Sarah, the attorney general's office should be non-partisan, staffed by prosecutors who are able to follow legal procedures correctly and who aim to facilitate a fair trial so as to allow a magistrate to deliver 'justice'. In their view, and in the

[63] Interview, Grace, former prosecutor, Harare, 16 August 2010.
[64] Interview, John and David, prosecutors, Harare, 10 September 2010.
[65] Ibid.
[66] Dumbutshena, 'Address to the Harare Magistrates and Prosecutors Forum', p. 4.

view of a much wider community, ZANU-PF's 'good boys' shamed the attorney general's office and embarrassed themselves not only because they flouted legal procedures in order to comply with political instructions. Through their behaviour, 'good boys' also failed to uphold the authority of the law, and of the state, as they failed to follow the rules to 'arrive at the truth' and to guarantee 'substantive justice' during the legal proceedings, and in their outcomes.[67]

Conclusion

In post-2000 Zimbabwe, ZANU-PF not only undermined the rule of law by strengthening the executive, passing repressive legislation and ignoring court orders. The party also extended its political control over the decisions made by the courts by staffing judicial institutions with political appointees. Prosecutors, lawyers and independent media and human rights reporting found evidence of this politicisation both in the appointments of attorney generals themselves, and the manner in which prosecutors within the office were tasked to follow 'political instructions' in trials of ZANU-PF's opponents. In a context of rapid economic decline, the expansion of corruption, both on a smaller scale as a means of survival and at higher levels in the form of government handouts, facilitated the spread of political patronage. Characterised by partisan appointments and top-down enticement and intimidation, the attorney general's office was brought under increased political control, culminating in a more overt takeover after 2008 with the appointment of Johannes Tomana.

Despite these appointments, ZANU-PF's efforts to extend its political control to the prosecution services did not unsettle the long-standing commitment of legal professionals and civil servants to 'professional' conduct, understood to be key to the delivery of 'substantive justice'.[68] Prosecutors who were willing to set aside their professional conduct to follow 'instructions' – the 'good boys' – worked alongside 'rebel' prosecutors who articulated an imagination of law's legitimacy

[67] Interviews with Sarah, former magistrate, Harare, 5 August 2010; Grace, former prosecutor, Harare, 16 August 2010; Alec Muchadehama, human rights lawyer, Harare, 19 August 2010; John and David, prosecutors, Harare, 10 and 24 September 2010.
[68] Dumbutshena, 'Address to the Harare Magistrates and Prosecutors Forum'; Welshman Ncube, 'Controlling Public Power: The Role of the Constitution and the Legislature', *Legal Forum*, 9, 6, 1997, pp. 12–22.

that was tied to the delivery of 'substantive justice' through ethical, impartial and professional behaviour. 'Rebel' prosecutors like John and David engaged with a wider community that shared their legal consciousness, to argue that 'good boy' prosecutors faced 'embarrassing' themselves, and by extension the ZANU-PF-led government, through their behaviour in court. In Chapter 3 I turn to the wider community that 'rebel' prosecutors engaged with, to examine the ways Zimbabwean citizens invoked the law to hold the state and its institutions to its own rules.

3 | *'Zimbabweans Are Foolishly Litigious'*
Debating Citizenship When Engaging with a Politicised Legal System

Law works in the world not just by the imposition of rules and punishments but also by its capacity to construct authoritative images of social relationships and actions, images which are symbolically powerful.[1]

In a discussion of Zimbabwe's legal system after 2000, the late Professor John Makumbe, then an active supporter of the MDC and outspoken critic of ZANU-PF who taught political science at the University of Zimbabwe, argued that the police force and the judiciary were rife with political interference.[2] Zimbabweans nevertheless continually appealed to the law. He stated, 'Zimbabweans are very litigious … I mean, you call [then President] Mugabe an idiot, somebody takes you to court. If I call my colleague next door a bum, he'll say that is defamation of character and take me to court. Zimbabweans are foolishly litigious.' Professor Makumbe argued that it was irrational to appeal to the law in Zimbabwe as ZANU-PF did not respect the rule of law. Laws were applied in a partisan manner, and citizens could face personal repercussions for articulating legal demands.[3] As I have established, the country's judiciary certainly was politicised. In a context where legal institutions had become spaces in which government officials could commit violence sanctioned by ZANU-PF, citizens' regard for, and reliance upon, judicial institutions to address social or political wrongs may indeed appear 'foolish'. I have also shown, however, that the legitimacy of law, and its relation to the authority of the state, were subject to debate among those who worked within its institutions. In this chapter, I ask how these dynamics shaped Zimbabwean citizens' legal and state consciousness.

[1] Merry, *Getting Justice and Getting Even*, p. 8.
[2] John Makumbe planned to run as an MDC-T MP in the country's 2013 parliamentary elections but he passed away on 27 January 2013; interview, John Makumbe, political analyst, Harare, 11 January 2012.
[3] Interview, John Makumbe, political analyst, Harare, 11 January 2012.

To examine articulations of consciousness I turn specifically to the ways certain Zimbabwean citizens chose to engage with the legal system, and examine their understandings of law to ask whether they were indeed 'foolishly litigious'. I argue that these citizens mobilised a legal consciousness which allowed the law to meaningfully serve both as a marker of their identity in relation to, and as a guide for engaging with, Zimbabwe's state. In their interactions with the law, individuals articulated a robust understanding of their citizenship which, in turn, shaped their state consciousness in a way that allowed them to differentiate their ideas of the state and their belonging to it from the actions of ZANU-PF and its politicised legal institutions.

I first briefly situate this chapter in the literature on law, consciousness, state repression and citizen resistance, and argue to move beyond the binary of repression and resistance to examine the legal engagements of Zimbabwean citizens. In order to tease out the complex ideas of law and citizenship articulated by citizens who turned to the law to challenge political abuse, I then focus on the narratives of two men, Patrick and Father Mkandla, who were not directly involved in political activism but who sought out the police to report cases of political violence. During interviews, both Patrick and Father Mkandla began their narratives by recounting their attempts to report crimes committed by ZANU-PF-aligned war veterans or youth within their community to the police. They had urged the police to take what they saw as the appropriate action, that is, to act according to their own rules and procedures by taking down a formal statement, investigating the crime and apprehending the suspects. The men articulated these expectations in their interactions with the police, but they were frequently disappointed as police officers refused to hear their complaints, or even threatened them with violent repercussions for reporting the crime. They nevertheless persisted. Their commitment to continue to engage in such interactions with the police and the law was sustained for two reasons. First, they occasionally encountered civil servants who, like John and David in Chapter 2, remained committed to behaving 'professionally' by following the law, performing in an ethical and impartial manner and delivering 'justice'. Second, they viewed these interactions as opportunities to perform their understanding of citizenship as an expression of belief in a state that protected their rights, and in the process safeguarded what they saw as their civility, dignity, humanity and morality. This, both men argued, was the kind of state they hoped to belong to as citizens.

Resistance, Repression and the Law

From E. P. Thompson's observations of eighteenth-century British revolutionaries' 'sense of legal wrong' to Sally Engle Merry's discussion of working-class New Englanders' 'legal consciousness', literature on the law as a double-edged sword of repression and resistance indicates that there are a multitude of ways that citizens express their agency when turning to the law.[4] Citizens' decisions to engage with the law are also frequently described as double-edged in their effects. Merry concludes her discussion of the impact of citizens' legal consciousness on their position in society by drawing attention to a paradox. She writes that by 'seek[ing] to use the law to establish a more autonomous life, one regulated by law rather than by violence', those appealing to it 'become more dependent on the law to order their lives', opening themselves up to increased state governance.[5] Nandini Sundar's exploration of the citizenship struggles of India's adivasis similarly highlights that 'even as they try to resist or transform the state, subalterns are bound by state categories'.[6]

In this chapter, I argue that not all citizens' efforts to engage the law in repressive regimes need be about positioning oneself against the state. Citizens may also invoke the law, and engage with legal institutions and practitioners to reaffirm their idea of the state, and to demand that the government recognises and is held accountable to this idea. The law as a repressive mode of governance should not be conflated with the ways law works as a language through which ideas about the state and citizenship can be expressed. With this in mind, I propose to examine 'state consciousness' as a conceptualisation that connects mobilisations of the law and citizens' 'legal consciousness' more explicitly to the ideas of the state that are at stake in their contestations. When examining Father Mkandla's and Patrick's accounts, I show that it was because of the way the ZANU-PF government *denied* their belonging to what they understood as full citizenship – a richly elaborated citizenship through which, for example, they could fit into the category of victims of politically motivated violence – that they engaged with the law.

---

[4] Thompson, *Whigs and Hunters*; Merry, *Getting Justice and Getting Even*.
[5] Merry, *Getting Justice and Getting Even*, p. 182.
[6] Sundar, 'The Rule of Law and Citizenship in Central India', p. 422.

Reporting: Demands that the State Follow Its Rules

In this section, I examine the demands that Patrick and Father Mkandla made when they travelled to the police station to report a crime. As noted above, both men insisted that the police should record an official report, placing the case on record and starting an investigation into the crime. Following the report, they visited the police station to check whether the police were in fact investigating their cases. Ultimately they hoped that the police would apprehend a suspect, who would be judged by the courts.

Both men put themselves at risk when articulating these demands. Following the March 2008 presidential and parliamentary elections, Human Rights Watch observed that violence was a common police response to civil society members or MDC supporters who travelled to a police station to report a case of political violence.[7] For Patrick and Father Mkandla, their interactions with the police often involved members of the ZRP Law and Order division, who were notorious for their violent and partisan behaviour. They explained that their continued visits to the police increased their awareness of the risks they were taking by engaging with a violent and politically partisan police force. At the same time, their exchanges with the police and later the courts increased their knowledge of, and in Father Mkandla's case access to, Zimbabwe's extensive human rights networks. The men's heightened awareness, and to some degree protection, of their rights served to reinforce their commitment to reporting crimes to the police as a mechanism to demand that the state and its officials followed their own rules to safeguard these rights.

The first case focuses on Patrick, who worked as a teacher at a rural high school in Manicaland province, about an hour's drive from Harare, Zimbabwe's capital. Prior to the 2008 elections he had no interest in politics. He described himself as 'just a neutral citizen'.[8] He was the breadwinner for not only his own family of six, but also for two out of his four brothers and their families. Like many others in his hometown, Patrick and his younger brother, who was an MDC member, were victims of ZANU-PF youth violence in the run-up to

[7] Human Rights Watch (HRW), *'Bullets for Each of You': State-Sponsored Violence since Zimbabwe's March 29 Elections* (New York, HRW, June 2008), pp. 56–8.
[8] Interview, Patrick, teacher, Harare, 20 January 2012.

the June 2008 presidential elections. Patrick reported the two incidents of violence involving him or his family to the police.[9]

Patrick first went to the police to report damage to, and the looting of, his property in June 2008. In this turbulent period, Manicaland was one of the provinces where 'ZANU-PF [was] deliberately displacing thousands of people from their homes in the rural areas ... through a campaign of beatings, burning of huts and homesteads, the deliberate slaughter of livestock, and the looting of property'.[10] Teachers like Patrick were targeted due to their positions of influence among the youth, and their often assumed trade unionist and MDC affiliation.[11]

At a time when severe hyperinflation in Zimbabwe had dramatically devalued the incomes of civil servants, Patrick was in a relatively self-sufficient economic position as he had invested in building his homestead and raising cattle. In June 2008, he lost much of his material savings when his homestead was attacked. Combined with Patrick's work as a high school teacher, his brother's political affiliation may have contributed to Patrick's homestead being targeted. Several individuals – whom Patrick recognised from his hometown and identified as ZANU-PF youth – destroyed his granary, slaughtered some of his animals and broke into his home. Patrick filed a police report following the incident in the hope that the police would 'come, apprehend the perpetrators, maybe recover part of the property, get it back to me and maybe make those people pay reparations, or ... what can I say, sort of rebuilding what they destroyed'.[12]

After filing the police report Patrick left town with his wife and children to 'get some shelter'. A week later he received news that his younger brother and sister-in-law had been forced to attend a ZANU-PF meeting, where they were severely beaten. Three days had gone by before one of their neighbours felt safe enough to take the couple to hospital for medical attention. Two days after being admitted to hospital Patrick's brother died. Patrick recounted that, although 'the

[9] Ibid. [10] HRW, *Bullets for Each of You*, p. 46.
[11] Zimbabwe Human Rights NGO Forum, *Teaching Them a Lesson: A Report on the Attack on Zimbabwean Teachers* (Harare, Zimbabwe Human Rights NGO Forum, 2002); Progressive Teachers Union Zimbabwe (PTUZ), *Every School Has a Story to Tell: A Study into Teacher's Experiences with Elections in Zimbabwe* (Harare, PTUZ, 2011); PTUZ and Research and Advocacy Unit (RAU), *Political Violence and Intimidation against Teachers in Zimbabwe* (Harare, PTUZ and RAU, 2012).
[12] Interview, Patrick, teacher, Harare, 20 January 2012.

police would not do anything' following his first report, when he 'heard about the death of my young brother, I went again to the police. ... I was lucky to find the police officer in charge present. I went straight to his office. The officer in charge walked out of the police station.'[13] Patrick explained the police officer's departure as a political act of evasion. He noted that, because his younger brother had been an MDC supporter, the police were unwilling to take the case as 'they play according to the tune of ZANU-PF. Once they hear that you are aligned to the MDC, then they do nothing.' He nonetheless believed it was important to report cases to the police. In part, Patrick sought out the police because he hoped they would facilitate his efforts to negotiate economic compensation for both acts of violence. The economic consequences of the attack on his homestead remained costly for Patrick and his family in the years that followed, especially with the added pressures to care for his deceased brother's family as well.

Patrick was further motivated to report the looting of his house and the murder of his brother to the police, as he was shocked by the extent of the violence he witnessed in his home area, and by the knowledge that his brother was not the only person beaten and killed on that day. It was important, he argued, that the perpetrators be brought to justice in order to set an example that such behaviour would not be tolerated in his community. With this in mind, Patrick persisted in his attempts to have the police take down an official report of the attack on his brother, approaching several police officers and asking them to open a docket although he realised the odds were stacked against him. The unevenness of ZANU-PF's control over legal institutions, shown in the previous chapters, also allowed for certain police officers to follow a professional code. As a result of this, Patrick was eventually able to sit down with a police woman in the charge office, who took notes on the attack on his brother and opened a formal investigation.[14]

In a second case, Father Mkandla, a Catholic priest without any ties to political activism who worked in the provincial capital of Matabeleland North, Lupane, regularly reported cases of political violence in his home area to the police. When making his reports he also demanded that the police follow the rules by investigating cases and apprehending suspects. In 2002, a man died in close proximity to

[13] Ibid.   [14] Ibid.

the mission where Father Mkandla was working and people in his parish suspected that ZANU-PF-aligned war veterans had murdered the man. The man's family asked Father Mkandla to attend the funeral, and at the funeral he spoke broadly about human rights abuses that were prevalent in the region and the innocent victims that they claimed.[15]

Following the funeral, Father Mkandla went to the police to enquire after the progress of the case. Instead of informing him of their progress, the police warned him that he 'was now on the hit list' of the police and the CIO, because he 'was critical of the government'. This conduct angered and upset Father Mkandla, who felt that the police should have been concerned with the case at hand:

> I don't know how the government came in, here was an issue of a person who had been murdered and I went to the police station just a kilometre from there, and they told me they did not apprehend anybody, no suspects. I made a lot of noise in that police station.[16]

For Father Mkandla the police's threat that he was 'on the hit list' was a first indication of the dangers he could face when reporting cases of ZANU-PF political violence. After he had 'made noise' at the police station he was arrested under POSA, an Act primarily aimed at regulating public gatherings and demonstrations. Father Mkandla was, however, arrested for carrying an axe in his trunk, which he used to clear the road to the mission at which he was stationed. After an uncomfortable three nights in police custody he was remanded out of custody for approximately three-and-a-half months before his case was dismissed due to lack of evidence.[17]

Similar to many of the young political activists I interviewed, Father Mkandla's arrest in 2002 did not discourage him from bringing new acts of political violence within his parish to the attention of the police. For example, he recounted that, in November 2007, when he was living in Regina Mundi mission near the town of Lupane, his driver had gone to run an errand in town. There, several war veterans approached him and threatened to murder him. Father Mkandla explained that his driver was also a village head, a position of local leadership that ZANU-PF officials occasionally called upon to mobilise

---

[15] Interview, Father Marko Mkandla, priest, Hwange, 30 November 2011.
[16] Ibid.   [17] Ibid.

support in rural areas. The war veterans were angry as the man had failed to organise a ZANU-PF rally in his village. Father Mkandla met the driver on his return and recalled:

The man was shaking, a 73-year-old man, he was shaking. And I said to him, 'what is it?' and then he said 'ah Father, they said I was going to die.' I then drove straight to the police station in Lupane, I went to the officer in charge, I met him outside his office. Then I said, 'I have come here to report a case of death threats by some political elements here.'

I talked to the detective inspector, and said 'I've come to report a case here of, of political harassment. My driver was threatened by people that he knows, and I know them. It's not a hidden thing. He had been instructed, he's the kraal-head, to organize a meeting.'

Then, instead of responding to that, he said to me . . . 'Actually we have been instructed to investigate you from above.' Then I said 'What investigation? I have come here to report a matter. I think if you have been instructed to investigate me, that is at Regina Mundi, this is not Regina Mundi, I stay at Regina Mundi. Here I have come on a different matter.' They said 'No, no, no, you are making a mistake, we know that you have been so vocal and critical about the government so we have been instructed, we are following you.' Then he began to tell me the types of cars that I was using, and he said, 'We know all the number plates of your cars, and we are following you.' And I said, anyway, I was angry, and I didn't want to stick to that. So I said, 'I am saying I have come to report a matter, what are you talking about, who stopped you from coming to Regina Mundi, don't tell me that here, I am talking about this matter.'[18]

In this exchange with the police Father Mkandla articulated what he thought was the appropriate action for the police to take. He wanted the police to investigate cases of political violence in his parish, and to detain the perpetrators. For Patrick, the appropriate action consisted of investigating his brother's murder, apprehending the murderers and providing his family with some security. For both men, these expressions of legal consciousness were not always performed before an audience that shared their understanding of law. In their efforts to engage with the legal process by reporting crimes to the police, the men were obstructed, threatened, ignored and, in Father Mkandla's case, arrested. Both men nevertheless repeatedly demanded that the police follow what they saw as the appropriate legal procedures.

[18] Ibid.

In the following section, I show that while such efforts to demand rule-following behaviour, and the police responses to these demands, did not necessarily follow standard procedures or yield what were viewed to be 'just' outcomes, both men nonetheless felt they experienced a degree of success when engaging with the law because they were able to engage in a shared set of ideas about professionalism and 'substantive justice' that persisted within these state institutions.

The Occasional 'Success' of Engaging the Law

When Patrick and Father Mkandla felt that police officers or judicial officials engaged with their views on citizenship as tied to rule-bound behaviour and the law, the men described their interactions with the law as rewarding or successful. To achieve such successes both men displayed their legal and state consciousness as they played on the productive tensions that existed between some civil servant's commitment to the law in their professional capacities and the 'instructions' they received from ZANU-PF officials that inhibited them from carrying out their jobs in an independent manner.

Father Mkandla was aware that when he demanded from police officers that they take down an official report of politically motivated violence in his parish, he often engaged with individuals who appeared to be above the law within Zimbabwe's politicised legal system. In these interactions Father Mkandla engaged with police officers such as those who reported to Human Rights Watch that they were working 'under the instructions of senior army and government officials'.[19] These officials instructed them 'not to interfere with "political issues"' or to 'assist victims'. As a result, many police officers felt 'unable to operate independently in dealing with the violence'.[20]

By reminding police officers of the proper legal procedures, however, Father Mkandla noted that he could either threaten them or appeal to the official's own moral compass or professional norms in an effort to encourage them to make the 'right' decision. He drew particular attention to two instances where the government official he had engaged with 'softened up' or became friendlier and more cooperative after he had reminded them of the correct legal procedures to follow.[21]

---

[19] HRW, *Bullets for Each of You*, p. 57.   [20] Ibid.
[21] Interview, Father Marko Mkandla, priest, Hwange, 30 November 2011.

In the first, Father Mkandla highlighted the fact that in response to political intimidation and harassment he frequently alerted the police, ZANU-PF youth and war veterans that he intended to take action against them through the courts. For example, in the run-up to the March 2008 elections, ZANU-PF youths came to his house to intimidate him. He asked who had instructed them, and the youths informed him that it was a war veteran. Father Mkandla, who knew the man, drove to the war veterans' office the following morning. The man initially denied he had sent the youths, but admitted when Father Mkandla told him, 'you cannot deny it because the people you sent are even ready to testify [to] that in the court. So you said it.' The man then 'softened up'.[22]

When reporting the death threats made against his driver in 2007, Father Mkandla again drew on the law to challenge the government officials who, he explained, were acting on political instructions and thus not following the law. As shown above, in Father Mkandla's exchange with the officer in charge, a detective he had met before, the detective did not deal with the violence against the village head but rather took the opportunity to threaten Father Mkandla. The detective warned him that 'what you are doing, what we have heard you are doing, criticising the government almost all the time, you are influencing people badly here, you see this is very dangerous'. In response, Father Mkandla challenged the detective, saying that if there were an appropriate time and place for such threats, this was not it:

I was adamant, and I stuck to 'I have come here to report on this matter, I am not interested in discussing what you are telling me, OK?' Then I said, 'And if you are not taking this matter, say so. But I will testify against you in the court of law, if anything happens to that man, you bet I will.'[23]

Following Father Mkandla's warning that he would take the matter to court, the detective stopped intimidating him and instead created an official record of the threats made against Father Mkandla's driver. In the end, they 'parted on almost kind of soft terms, on kind of [a] friendly basis'.[24]

In this exchange both Father Mkandla and the detective were acting out a script partly focused around ZANU-PF's efforts to politicise the application of the law to exclude those Zimbabwean citizens defined

[22] Ibid.   [23] Ibid.   [24] Ibid.

by the party as constituting an illegitimate political opposition, and partly shaped by certain civil servants' continued commitment to professional, rule-following governance. To challenge his exclusion from the rights-based citizenship he felt entitled to, Father Mkandla attempted to (re)negotiate his relationship with a government official, and to express his view that he would grant authority only to a state that offered him protection. His role included reminding the detective that it was his duty to facilitate the reporting and investigation of a crime. To enact his adherence to ZANU-PF directives, which allowed war veterans relative freedom to undertake violent political intimidation within the area, the detective initially avoided taking this report. However, when reminded of his professional obligations and confronted with further legal action which would involve the creation of a case – and thus a record – against the detective himself, the man conceded. The precise reasons for this remained unclear to Father Mkandla, who explained that in such interactions government officials often refused to explain their decisions. He assumed, however, that the detective's change of heart was linked to his understanding that law and professionalism were valued in Zimbabwean society.

Impressing on both the war veterans and the police detective that he would take them to court, Father Mkandla was not only reminding them of proper legal procedures; he was also invoking the courts as record keepers of their wrongdoings in the present, for justice in the future.[25] In doing so, Father Mkandla resembled the African human rights lawyers in Sally Falk Moore's study, who valued the courts for their ability to expose the shortcomings of governments through their record keeping, and fought for the rule of law despite the politicisation of judiciaries across the continent. She notes that, in part, these lawyers were driven by their 'hope in the future', when 'the injustices of today will be remembered tomorrow, and that culpable people will be called to account'.[26]

Describing an encounter with some war veterans who had caused much damage in his area in the run-up to the 2008 elections, Patrick recalled, in similar vein, that he had threatened to take them to court.

---

[25] Sally Falk Moore, 'Systematic Judicial and Extra-judicial Injustice – Preparations for Future Accountability', in Richard P. Werbner (ed.), *Memory and the Postcolony: African Anthropology and the Critique of Power* (London, Zed Books, 1998), pp. 126–51.

[26] Falk Moore, 'Systematic Judicial and Extra-Judicial Injustice', p. 128.

Upset that 'these murderers are still … roaming the streets', he cornered two of them on the streets of his hometown one morning and told them:

'We are waiting for the time, we are really waiting for the time. The time shall come where you are going to face the courts' benches.' And I am still very sure that these people will be brought to court some time.[27]

Following what he experienced as an unanticipated success in the case of his brother's murder, the courts became more firmly rooted in Patrick's political imagination not only as record keepers, but also as institutions able to acknowledge injustices, and to convict and sentence those who committed them. The police had obstructed his attempts to report and thus record his brother's murder, and so Patrick had lowered his expectations of obtaining a positive outcome when the case came to court. He nevertheless focused much of his time and financial resources on ensuring that the two men accused of murdering his brother went to trial. Supported by his local MDC-T councillor, Patrick repeatedly went to the police station to check on the progress of the case and became acquainted with the prosecutor. His persistence paid off when the prosecutor decided to take the case to trial.

Initially, Patrick described his attendance at the trial as 'a very bad experience'. The presence of CIO agents and war veterans in the courtroom 'frightened' him; he hesitated to put himself 'in the lime-light' for fear of the consequences. He further found it 'painful' to hear the two accused recount the details of his brother's abuse. While this was difficult to witness, Patrick valued the fact that, through the narrative and emotional elements of the court proceedings, the crimes committed against his brother by ZANU-PF supporters were publicly recognised. The courts, he explained, exposed 'the truth of what happened to my brother'. By allowing the repressive atmosphere within the court and the narrative construction of a 'truthful' account of his brother's ordeal to co-occur within the trial, Patrick demonstrated his awareness of various ways law was used within Zimbabwe's courts.

In the demeanour of the magistrate especially, Patrick found evidence for the delivery of 'substantive justice', and it was this use of the law that he granted legitimacy. He was, for example, 'satisfied' when

---

[27] Interview, Patrick, teacher, Harare, 20 January 2012.

listening to the witnesses recount the events leading up to his brother's death, as 'they were fluent, they were very very fluent, they were capable of saying the things as they were, as they happened ... they were telling the facts as they were ... the facts were very convincing, and I was very happy about it'. Patrick was further especially 'touched' when he witnessed that the magistrate too was emotionally affected by the case. Through his response, he recognised the severity of the case. Patrick recalled how his presence in court:

was very painful, and I could not stop myself shedding tears ... I was at times driven off, out of the court, I could not stop that. Until one other time, when the murderer was asked to explain what happened, he started by refusing, and later on he started narrating, he'd throw in bits and pieces, I also could see that even the magistrate was touched, he was touched. Because he kept quiet for some time, he looked at me, he looked at some of the people who were there, he shook his head, he was again quiet for some time, he looked on the floor. He was really touched.[28]

The manner in which the witnesses narrated the ordeal his brother suffered, and the magistrates' empathetic response to these statements, were key in enabling the law to form a shared language that allowed for the construction of a connection between the courts as a state institution and Patrick as a citizen whose legal consciousness could authorise this state.[29]

While the magistrate's empathy, and his subsequent decision to convict the men for the crime, satisfied Patrick, he was not content with the magistrate's initial sentencing of the men to four years in prison. For Patrick this sentence was 'too short, because these people have committed a lot of crimes'. He again had success, however, when the case was reviewed by a High Court judge, who sentenced the accused to an additional twelve years in prison.[30] Patrick explained that he welcomed this decision because the men's behaviour posed a danger to 'peace and stability' in his hometown. In addition, it was

---

[28] Ibid.   [29] Ibid.

[30] From conversations with Heal Zimbabwe Trust officials it would appear that the longer sentence passed by the High Court in the case of Patrick's brother's murder was in keeping with the crime of manslaughter for which two men were convicted, and that the initial sentence was relatively lenient. The original presiding magistrate had been reluctant to pass a tougher judgment given the political nature of the case. (Fieldnotes, discussions with C. M., Harare, 13 January 2012).

important to him that such behaviour be 'punished' in order to 'make an example of them'.[31]

For Father Mkandla, as for Patrick, the selective and changeable application of the law at times opened up spaces for 'success', spaces in which 'truth' was told and 'justice' was delivered by police officers and judicial officials following the 'proper' procedures and reaching the 'right' conclusions. In these spaces the men interacted with people who appeared to be above the law, such as the police officers who refused to take Father Mkandla's case, the war veterans who threatened him or the ZANU-PF youth and war veterans who murdered Patrick's brother. In their exchanges, Patrick and Father Mkandla highlighted the proper application of the law, reminding the people who frequently disregarded it that they might face repercussions for their illegal actions. These exchanges further opened up spaces which offered police officers or judicial officials an opportunity to display their own professional commitment to upholding the law. Patrick and Father Mkandla measured the 'success' of their appeals in the ways that the law allowed them to communicate this aspiration for equality under the law within the Zimbabwean state, in the space the public court-room offered for the accurate and truthful recounting of injustices, in witnessing empathy and in whether or not they 'won' in legal terms through convictions and punishment.

Remaining on 'the Right Side of the Law'

Father Mkandla and Patrick persisted in their demands not only because of the law's potential for perhaps unanticipated successful outcomes that granted their legal consciousness legitimacy. Their efforts to report crimes of political violence, and their demands that the government officials, who they drew into these efforts, follow the rules, were opportunities to perform their understandings of citizenship and to articulate their state consciousness. Citizenship is itself a social and political construction.[32] After 2000, ZANU-PF offered to defend and uphold a narrow construction of it, conditional on expressions of support for the party's agenda. In this context, Father Mkandla's and Patrick's appeals to the police to take their cases, to

---

[31] Interview, Patrick, teacher, Harare, 20 January 2012.
[32] Neveu, 'Discussion: Anthropology and Citizenship'.

uphold legal procedures and to safeguard the rule of law should also be examined as alternative efforts to construct and defend their imaginations of citizenship. Both men held a richly elaborated understanding of citizenship based on notions of civility, morality, dignity and values which, in turn, they expected the police and judicial officials to protect. In this manner their understanding of citizenship was intricately linked to their state consciousness, informing their views that only a law that would safeguard their citizenship could grant the state authority.

As we have seen, ideas of citizenship as connected to law have long been widely and firmly embraced in the Zimbabwean public imagination. Of particular interest here are the values that the 'prisoner government' of nationalists under Rhodesian rule upheld, which alongside education and discipline included 'civility and restraint'.[33] In performing their attachment to 'remaining on the right side of the law' in an effort to critique ZANU-PF's exclusionary citizenship, both Patrick and Father Mkandla embodied values similar to these upheld by Rhodesian-era litigants and political prisoners.

During his arrest and interrogation by the police, for instance, Father Mkandla specifically sought to distinguish his behaviour from the actions, speech and mannerisms of police officers. At the time of our discussion in November 2011, Father Mkandla was on remand for organising a healing service on 14 April 2011 in a village near Lupane. As his trial was in progress at the time of our interview, Father Mkandla was not in a position to elaborate on these proceedings and instead focused on his interactions with the police while he was in detention. In these interactions he described how he challenged the police for failing to follow the 'proper' procedures when arresting and interrogating him.[34]

Father Mkandla described the healing service for which he was on trial as 'a programme meant to empower those victim/survivors' of the *Gukurahundi* massacres of the 1980s. Among citizens in Matabeleland, this violent period and its continued lack of redress contributed much to their experiences of exclusion from the Zimbabwean nation. Following the turbulent elections of 2008, which led to the formation of the GNU, Father Mkandla was not alone in expressing his hopes that the new ZANU-PF and MDC coalition

---

[33] Alexander, 'Nationalism and Self-Government in Rhodesian Detention', p. 552.
[34] Interview, Father Marko Mkandla, priest, Hwange, 30 November 2011.

government would open up spaces to address this violent history, and facilitate the 'healing' of these abuses.[35] In an effort to demonstrate his faith that government was committed to assisting this process, Father Mkandla invited Moses Mzila-Ndlovu, the co-minister of national healing for the MDC under the GNU, to address the meeting. On a visit to the area before the service, however, Father Mkandla was informed that, as had happened in the past, government officials, specifically agents from the CIO, had come to the village to intimidate people.[36]

Nonetheless, several people from the village encouraged Father Mkandla to continue preparing the service, which eventually attracted 250–300 community members. At the start of the service, five CIO agents appeared:

I saw a twin cab coming; it stopped about five hundred metres away from us. And I noticed it earlier, that vehicle was used by the State security agents ... I thought they would come straight to me, I was prepared ... But they didn't, they went behind some school toilets and hid there.[37]

The service finished without any interruption, and Father Mkandla returned home. He was just about to make dinner when 'a very big group of police officers, with baton sticks' came to his gate. He noticed the cars with no licence plates, and also recognised some war veterans. This large group of people at his gate 'frightened' him, but when they informed him he was under arrest, he asked: 'my friend, you were at that service. If I was doing something wrong, why didn't you arrest me there?'[38]

Father Mkandla recounted that throughout the process of his arrest he continually challenged police officers to demonstrate their ability to follow the 'proper' legal procedures. He explained that this was necessary because 'the system is very cruel'. Father Mkandla did not simply seek to challenge his arrest. He challenged the manner in which the illegality of it diminished and dehumanised him:

[35] For a broader discussion on the legacy of the *Gukurahundi* in Bulawayo, see Chapter 7.
[36] Interview, Father Marko Mkandla, priest, Hwange, 30 November 2011. For details on violent government responses to commemoration ceremonies historically, see Alexander et al., *Violence and Memory*; Richard Werbner, 'Smoke from the Barrel of a Gun: Postwars of the Dead, Memory and Reinscription in Zimbabwe', in *Memory and the Postcolony: African Anthropology and the Critique of Power* (London, Zed Books, 1998), pp. 71–102.
[37] Interview, Father Marko Mkandla, priest, Hwange, 30 November 2011.
[38] Ibid.

A violation of my rights as a person, my freedom, I mean, I am not yet charged, I am not a criminal, I have not been charged by the courts, I am still innocent ... I am there [at the healing service] trying to help people come to terms with their pains. Not even making a reference to those who killed them. But this is the way I am treated. The dignity of the person is not something important here.[39]

To challenge this treatment, and to confront the police officers inflicting it, Father Mkandla demanded judicial due process, and performed his urge to stay on the 'right side of the law' from his arrest until his release from detention a few days later. After some deliberation with the men at his gate, Father Mkandla went inside to call his lawyers, his housekeeper and Minister Mzila-Ndlovu. In the process, he was surprised by the police officers and war veterans, who had climbed over the fence. He challenged them on the rough nature of the arrest:

They kicked the door open to the house 'you are wasting our time here', and then straight away they took away my cell phone and checked on it 'you are phoning while we wait', and I said, 'I have to inform people, does getting arrested, does that mean that people shouldn't know where I am?' Then they were very rough, they handcuffed me.[40]

He was subsequently taken to the police station, where 'they played all tricks, to try and intimidate' him. Father Mkandla explained that the manner in which the police continually flouted the 'proper procedures' during his arrest and interrogation made it clear that they were acting on instructions from ZANU-PF. This meant that the police could:

[D]o whatever they want to do to people, you are just there. As an accused in Zimbabwe when the police officers are dealing with you, you are a sub-human. They can say what they want, they can do what they want. Even before you are charged by the courts, they can do whatever they want.[41]

Father Mkandla was aware that ZANU-PF relied on the legal system to harass and intimidate perceived opponents. He 'accepted' his arrest as he was one among 'so many people [who] have gone through the same thing'. His experience in detention had taught him that there was no 'civility' within the arrests, and that the police officers who followed ZANU-PF's order were 'very cruel, very rough. ... These men lack the semblance of humanity, simple.'[42]

---

[39] Ibid.   [40] Ibid.   [41] Ibid.   [42] Ibid.

It was against their 'lack of humanity' that Father Mkandla judged his own performance as an exemplary Zimbabwean citizen under interrogation. By responding to police intimidation in a calm and dignified manner, Father Mkandla felt he maintained the upper hand:

Someone was looking at me, popping their eyes open, 'tell us why you are doing all these things against the government!' It was, I don't know where I got that gravity from. I just looked at them, and I was questioning them, 'where are you taking all these things from?' I was so calm. And they wanted even to speak up in loud voices and I was calm. I said, 'I don't know what you are talking about.'[43]

Father Mkandla further distanced himself from the police officers interrogating him by underlining their ignorance in matters that concerned Matabeleland, specifically those relating to the *Gukurahundi* and the needs within the region to address the consequences of the violence and lingering ethnic tensions. The police informed him he was charged under Section 42(2) of the Criminal Law (Codification and Reform) Act for 'causing offence to persons of a particular race or religion'.[44] Father Mkandla explained to the police that his service had not been about politics or ethnicity, but was concerned with healing the wounds of people in Matabeleland in line with debates around the importance of commemorating the *Gukurahundi* in the region. When the police responded that 'those things are past, it's healed', Father Mkandla replied:

If you are trying to obliterate the memory of the people, then you can say that. If you are saying that people do not have memories anymore, what happened, the people know it. People know what happened to them … *Gukurahundi*, Fifth Brigade, you are working here in Lupane, and you don't know that, then probably you are a misfit.[45]

The 'misfit' police officers Father Mkandla encountered demonstrated a lack of 'civility', 'respect for human rights' and 'the semblance of humanity', degrading him and treating him as if he were already convicted. Instead of simply dismissing his interrogation as a technique of political repression, however, Father Mkandla chose to engage with

---

[43] Ibid.
[44] Government of Zimbabwe, *Criminal Law (Codification and Reform) Act* (Harare, Government Printer, 2005).
[45] Interview, Father Marko Mkandla, priest, Hwange, 30 November 2011.

the police officers. When he had reported cases to the police, this engagement allowed Father Mkandla to 'soften up' detectives, parting with them on friendly terms. During his arrest he could not persuade his interrogators to show 'civility', or to respect his rights. Faced with contradictory and changeable government officials, Father Mkandla explained, all he could do was to remain consistent in his own reliance on dignified and proper conduct under the law. Understanding the case against him as 'all their creation' to intimidate him and stop his engagement with healing in the area, he concluded that this sort of behaviour by government officials only strengthened his reliance on law:

I am seeing through their systems, there are too many loopholes. They only depend on when people are afraid, fear[ful]. That is their strategy, fear. To make people so much afraid that they would not move, they would not do anything. But fear is something that is very temporal. You can frighten me now, as you come in. But when I look at you steadily, then I will say come on, I will gather my courage.[46]

In a similar manner, Patrick explained that his interactions with the police and judicial officials in the court had 'strengthened' him. While the police had disappointed him, the narratives created by the witnesses, and the emotional and empathetic response from the magistrate to the recounting of his brother's murder, provided Patrick with recognition for the injustices that had been committed against his family. This success in the courts, Patrick explained, was a result of his personal commitment and persistence with the case as much as it was a result of the correct application of legal procedure. Patrick therefore stressed that it remained important for him to continue performing his commitment to law as a fundamental component of his citizenship.

Patrick's strong sense of the value of his citizenship inspired his initial trips to the police station to report the looting of his homestead and the murder of his brother, in an effort to seek justice not only in the form of economic compensation but also as a mechanism to deter the culprits and to increase the safety of his community. This was a commitment he sought to uphold and to carry forward as his interactions with the police and the courts had increased his awareness of what constituted a crime, and how the legal system worked. To do so,

[46] Ibid.

Patrick started a programme to train young people on the judicial process. He elaborated:

Though the police are doing nothing, I always try to make sure that such cases [of politically motivated violence] are brought out. And to show that I want these cases to be reported, I have introduced what we call a junior police in school, where our young people are … enlightened on some of the offences which they commit and all those things, there's penalties which you might face. In line with that, we are educating these people so that they don't do that, they don't commit crimes. So if I do that, if I educate kids not to commit crimes, it means I am also educating my fellow people to report cases to the police, so that we stay peacefully.[47]

Although he had no clear indication when, and if, the Zimbabwean state would become rule-bound, it gave Patrick courage to act as if this state could exist. It was only by remaining on 'the right side of the law' that he could be 'fearless' in the face of the physical harassment and intimidation. Patrick accepted that his past behaviour of reporting the looting of his homestead and his brother's murder to the police, and his continued attempts to inform young people of the workings of the legal process, could incur violent repercussions from perpetrators within his hometown. This was, however, also part of the reason why the programme was important for him. It was high time, he explained, for Zimbabweans to demonstrate what state they wanted to be a part of. The manner in which ZANU-PF had ruled the country needed to be changed. 'If we remain under the hands of these people, these unscrupulous people, then it means we continue to see hell. We continue to suffer. And we are fed up, we are really fed up.'[48] Patrick's experience in court, and his belief that, in the future, the Zimbabwean state would function as it was intended to do, and as it had done in the idealised past, allowed him to conclude that, if the ZANU-PF supporters in his area 'could do anything, let them do harm'. In the future they would be tried and sentenced for the harm caused.[49]

In their engagement with the police and the courts, Father Mkandla and Patrick thus tied their actions and demands to understandings of their belief in their rights to a richly elaborated citizenship to the authority of a state that protected social order through legal institutions.

---

[47] Interview, Patrick, teacher, Harare, 20 January 2012.   [48] Ibid.   [49] Ibid.

Conclusion

The articulation of identity or belonging under the law, or the mobilisation of the law for the purposes of marginalisation or repressive rule, need not be primarily shaped by a government's control over legal language and practice. ZANU-PF's selective application of the law extended to endangering the safety of individuals reporting crimes to the police, and increased their uncertainty regarding the behaviour of the police and the courts. Against these conditions, Patrick and Father Mkandla situated themselves as assertive, law-abiding citizens rather than political pawns within Zimbabwe's contested state institutions. Through their demands for rule-bound institutions and their continued treatment of politicised legal institutions as if they were rule-bound, Patrick and Father Mkandla articulated a legal consciousness that was tied to their ideas of what kind of state and which forms of citizenship they considered to be legitimate.

Patrick and Father Mkandla were able to maintain their legal and state consciousness throughout their engagements with politicised judicial institutions because they could acknowledge, and occasionally mobilise, divisions among police officers and judicial officials over which uses of law were legitimate. These division were tied to long-standing debates over professionalism and justice. Patrick and Father Mkandla found that, due to these divisions, experiences of political violence could be recounted, wrongs could be acknowledged and the names of perpetrators could be filed for future reference. As a result of their occasional successes the men also viewed the police and courts as institutions through which to produce and perform a richly elaborated understanding of citizenship which were based on notions of dignity, morality and humanity. When they engaged with the law, Patrick and Father Mkandla were also articulating a state consciousness that connected this imagination of their citizenship and the state's responsibility to protect it by 'following its own rules'.

In Chapter 4, I look at what happens when the state does follow its rules, but against young, urban-based activists who argue they are undeserving of such treatment. Pervasively persecuted by ZANU-PF through violent arrests and inhumane conditions in detention, activists tied their understandings of citizenship to an explicitly political critique of the party's governance. The reactions from their family members, some of whom bought into ZANU-PF's performances of the activists' criminality, highlight the central role legal procedures continue to play in the consciousness of Zimbabwean citizens – at times to the detriment of personal ties and family relations.

4 | 'What Is Abnormal Is Normal'

Performative Politics on the Stages of Arrest and Detention

If you see your neighbours play on very green turf when they exercise their democracy, that is as it should be. But you shouldn't dream of the same here. Here there are potholes. There are stones, there are thistles ... and you know that is the ground you are playing on. It means that when you are supposed to kick off a ball, someone is going to put a stone for a ball. That is their rules. And those are the normal rules here. So we accept it. But that's what I would change.[1]

Henry, a 28-year-old student and political activist who had been arrested four times when we first met in 2010, described his life as an activist as akin to being 'on a leash that [the police and judicial officials] control. They can make it long, or shorten it ... but you are not totally free.' Henry explained that he chose this analogy because he was 'always policed somehow', with police officers 'able to pick you up at any point' to 'force you into admitting to something you didn't do' by threatening, humiliating and torturing him in detention. The pervasive nature of his experiences with arrest and detention made such treatment 'normal'. At the same time, Henry's legal and state consciousness led him to view his experiences at the hands of the law as 'abnormal', inspiring him to publicly critique the 'unprofessional behaviour' of police and the political party they supported, ZANU-PF, who were not building a democratic state but were engaged in 'some sort of terrorism to really try and silence activists. It has got the face of the law, but it really doesn't use anything along the lines of the law.'[2]

After 2000, young, black, urban-based and predominantly male civic activists were the prime targets for arrest and detention by the ZRP. Targeted for their political affiliation with the MDC, or their capacity to mobilise citizens through their position in civil society or student politics, this group was subject to intimidation, harassment,

---

[1] Interview, Wisdom, MDC supporter, Bulawayo, 5 December 2011.
[2] Interview, Henry, student activist, Harare, 16 September 2010.

humiliation and torture at the hands of the police. Their arrest and their treatment in detention were marked by physical violence, mental torment and isolation, and had long-term impacts on activists' health and well-being, on their educational and job prospects and on their social ties with family and friends.

In the previous chapters, I established that both among officials working in the Zimbabwean state's judicial institutions and among its citizens in the country's rural areas the law was understood and engaged with not simply as a system of rules, but as a moral and professional code of conduct. This allowed certain civil servants and citizens to engage with legal institutions in an effort not to position themselves against the state, but to reaffirm their idea of the state and to demand that the government recognises and is held accountable to this idea. In this chapter, I examine how the arrest and detention of young, black, urban-based and predominantly male human rights defenders, student leaders, political activists and MDC supporters fit within the production of this legal and state consciousness. I first show how, through public, often violent arrests and the lengthy and uncertain periods of detention, ZANU-PF performed its strength of control over aspects of, and members within, the police force and prison services. These performances were also aimed at exerting control over the activists' legal and state consciousness, positioning them as needing to experience the full force of the law, as they were 'dangerous criminals' with a Western-led regime change agenda rather than citizens with legitimate grievances against the government for not delivering on their demands for a rule-bound state.

In an effort to claim 'full' citizenship, activists mobilised their experiences of arrest and detention as political narratives, framed around how the ZANU-PF-led government violated the law's shared professional and moral code of conduct throughout the process of arrest, detention and trial. These narratives illuminate how activists, faced with the continuous threat of violence and abuse expressed in histories of multiple arrests over the years, understood their experiences as attempts by ZANU-PF to limit their political participation, citizenship and by extension humanity. This, in turn, informed how activists understood the relationship between the law's legitimacy and the state's authority. Activists explained that while their arrests strengthened their commitment to activism to fight for a particular vision of citizenship that echoed Father Mkandla and Patrick's imaginations, this commitment also posed a real threat specific to the young men, a threat to becoming a 'man', socially and economically. For activists, such threats underlined the importance of 'exposing' the illegitimacy of the government's actions through the law.

Activists' understandings of their arrest and detention as 'illegitimate' were, however, not universally shared. When engaging with elder family members, many activists were confronted with the manner in which they remained 'criminalised', despite the fact that they were arrested and detained due to their political engagement, rather than on 'real' criminal grounds such as petty theft. Exchanges about their arrests with family members in part highlighted parental concerns for the safety of activists when faced with the might of ZANU-PF. It also pointed to an alternative legal consciousness, however, built less on notions of how the law *should* work and more on a recognition of the power of law itself, where ZANU-PF's efforts to portray activists as criminals indeed marked them out as deviant.

Arrest and Detention as Performances of State Power

In this section, I examine the ways ZANU-PF, often through public practices of punishment carried out by certain members of its police force, performed their control over the bodies and minds of activists. When discussing penality, numerous scholars turn to Michel Foucault's claim that the performance of punishment shifted out of the public eye in the nineteenth century, to be replaced with invisible, pervasive discipline.[3] Julie Stone Peters points out, however, that far from disappearing the performative dimensions of punishment have simply taken on new, but still theatrical and spectacular forms over time.[4] Within the African context, a long history of public displays of punishment to support colonial regimes and settlers, and to pathologise certain social groups,[5] influenced postcolonial states' and citizens'

---

[3] Michel Foucault, *Discipline and Punish: The Birth of the Prison* (New York, Vintage Books, 1979).

[4] Julie Stone Peters, 'Penitentiary Performances Spectators, Affecting Scenes, and Terrible Apparitions in the Nineteenth-Century Model Prison', in Austin Sarat, Lawrence Douglas and Martha Merrill Umphrey (eds), *Law and Performance* (Boston, University of Massachusetts Press, 2018), pp. 18–67.

[5] See, for example, David Anderson, 'Punishment, Race and "The Raw Native": Settler Society and Kenya's Flogging Scandals, 1895–1930', *Journal of Southern African Studies*, 37, 3, 2011, pp. 479–98; Jan-Georg Deutsch, 'Celebrating Power

understandings of criminality and penality, evidenced in, for example, vigilantes' appropriation of certain state penal practices.[6]

Recognising how displays of power through punishment are inter-woven into postcolonial rule raises the question of what was being performed through processes of arrest and detention in Zimbabwe after 2000. Here, arrest and detention provided an important stage of political performance, a stage on which ZANU-PF officials aimed to dissuade their critics from political activism. Jocelyn Alexander pointed out in 2010 that 'the experience of prison has become near universal for leaders (and many members) of the civic and political opposition',[7] As a student leader in the Zimbabwe National Students Union (ZINASU), a leading civic movement with a long history of contesting against the government, George was in his early twenties and had been arrested at least six times between his joining student activism in 2006 and our meeting in 2010. When discussing his arrests, he similarly observed that 'we're talking about things that we activists are experiencing every day'.[8]

The frequency and volume of politically motivated arrests after 2000 is in part explained by their performative efficacy. Henry observed that his four public, violent arrests between June 2006 and April 2009 resulted from his political affiliation with the MDC, and from ZANU-PF's desire to 'make an example out of [him]'. His most memorable arrest took place in the volatile days preceding the March 2008 presidential and parliamentary elections. Henry was with three friends at Bikita Shopping Centre in Masvingo province, 350 kilo-metres south of his home in Harare. Sitting in their car, Henry and his friends were listening to an album that included several pro-MDC songs. These songs attracted the attention of other people in the shopping centre, who formed a crowd 'just to get a snippet of the

in Everyday Life: The Administration of the Law and the Public Sphere in Colonial Tanzania, 1890–1914', *Journal of African Cultural Studies*, 15, 2002, pp. 93–103; David Killingray, 'Punishment to Fit the Crime? Penal Policy and Practice in British Colonial Africa', in Florence Bernault (ed.), *A History of Prison and Confinement in Africa* (Portsmouth, Heinemann, 2003), pp. 97–118.

[6] Julia Hornberger, '"My Police – Your Police": The Informal Privatisation of the Police in the Inner City of Johannesburg', *African Studies*, 63, 2, 2004, pp. 213–30; Barbara Oomen, 'Vigilantism or Alternative Citizenship? The Rise of Mapogo a Mathamaga', *African Studies*, 63, 2, 2004, pp. 153–71.

[7] Alexander, 'Political Prisoners in Post-2000 Zimbabwe', p. 484.

[8] Interview, George, student activist, Harare, 18 July 2010.

album'. Two police officers approached the crowd and asked them to disperse. Henry argued with the police officers, asserting that they were 'not doing anything illegal'. He further told the police that, as they were 'the authorities', they should 'try to disperse the crowd'. The two police officers left, only to return with reinforcements. Henry counted about fifteen police officers approaching the car, with 'every unit of the police squad' represented. This included members of the riot police and police officers with dogs. He stayed in the car, but was lifted out by a police officer who hit him 'in the head with a baton stick' and Henry 'got blind for some time. [Next] I had a police dog grabbing my trousers and another guy was beating me.' After he was 'beaten at the shops', Henry was 'bundled into the truck' together with three of his friends, and driven to Bikita Police Station. Staging such a public and violent arrest, Henry explained, was one of the 'mechanisms the police use to instil fear, and to keep people in check, to silence them'.[9]

By returning to Bikita Shopping Centre with additional manpower and dogs, and beating and arresting members of the crowd for listening to pro-MDC music, the police performed their strength and their lack of tolerance for MDC supporters in the run-up to the 2008 elections. Such performances of strength and control over civic and political activists continued in the police detention cells, where they were aimed less at the general public and more directly at the activists themselves.

George recalled how, as a ZINASU leader and student activist, his exchanges with the police were marked by the question of whether he had anything to offer the nation and its citizens when he did not support ZANU-PF. When he was kept in isolation in police detention, for instance, only one police officer would occasionally come by, repeatedly telling him that he should turn on the other activists in custody, saying they were the 'real criminals' as they had recruited him 'on behalf of the party', the MDC, to train him 'to be a terrorist'.[10] George insisted that he was only a student activist who was fighting for improved learning and living conditions at the university. For the remainder of his time in custody, the police then used every opportunity to undermine George's belief that he could work towards a brighter future for Zimbabwe, highlighting that George was but a 'young boy'

---

[9] Interview, Henry, student activist, Harare, 16 September 2010.
[10] Interview, George, student activist, Harare, 20 July 2010.

rather than a 'real man', who was also not a 'real activist', as he knew very little about the MDC.[11]

To further 'humiliate' him, George remembered how his body was used as evidence that he was not a 'real man'. Such tactics were common practice among police officers in their attempts to control and subvert urban young male activists. In his discussion of masculinity among University of Zimbabwe students between 1980 and 2008, for example, Dan Hodgkinson writes of the increased violence, from beatings to practices such as stripping or forced simulations of sexual acts, used by the police after 2000 to humiliate students and to delegitimise their cause.[12] George recalled how female police officers were instructed to 'find out' whether he could prove himself as a 'man' and a 'real activist'. On one occasion, he was told to strip in front of two female police officers because 'they wanted to measure my muscles, and whether I had even some tattoos, as a real activist'. He was 'very shy' because 'they were trying to understand whether I was a person of strong muscle build-up, a strong activist ... I was just a kid, and of course I had not been regularly going for gym, so I did not have very strong muscles.' George recalled how he 'felt ashamed', a feeling that grew when the police asked him 'what kind of service do you think you can offer to the country when you're only 20 and you behave in this manner?'[13]

These practices of humiliation and delegitimisation extended beyond police custody into the public domain. State media reporting on activists' cases often portrayed activists as 'criminals' who threatened the nation through their violent 'imperialist' behaviour. These portrayals played on the narrow notions of citizenship and colonial history that fit into ZANU-PF's political narrative of 'patriotic history', as discussed in Chapter 1, and justified the removal of activists' rights.

One of George's arrests took place in the volatile period around 11 March 2007, when government repression reached a 'new low' with a violent clampdown on civil society members present at the

---

[11] Ibid.

[12] Dan Hodgkinson, 'The "Hardcore" Student Activist: The Zimbabwe National Students Union (ZINASU), State Violence, and Frustrated Masculinity, 2000–2008', *Journal of Southern African Studies*, 39, 4, 2013, p. 874.

[13] Interview, George, student activist, Harare, 20 July 2010.

Save Zimbabwe Campaign prayer meeting in Highfield, Harare.[14] At the time, political tensions intensified as the two MDC factions launched their election campaigns, and their supporters staged more political protests and demonstrations. Human Rights Watch reported the arrest of at least 400 civil society members throughout the country in February alone.[15] On 11 March, before the Save Zimbabwe Campaign meeting could start, activists were beaten on their way to the venue. In the resulting clashes with the police, the police fired teargas and live ammunition into the crowd. Gift Tandare was killed, other activists were severely beaten, and approximately fifty people were arrested.[16]

Following these events, police camps, stores and a passenger train were petrol bombed. ZANU-PF blamed MDC members for the attacks.[17] The ZRP published a report on the MDC's 'trail of violence' between January and March 2007. In this they detailed the petrol bombing of the ZRP Marimba camp by 'suspected MDC sponsored youth', including photographs of damaged property and graphic images of the burnt victims.[18] The report concluded that:

The events and incidents narrated and pictured above are a clear testimony that the opposition forces under the Save Zimbabwe Campaign Project are on a confrontation path. They no longer have respect for law and order. Intelligence at hand indicates that they want to continue targeting the government and members of the security forces ... There is a need for decisive action to be taken against the organisers of these illegal actions. ... Meanwhile the culprits continue to receive massive moral and material support from Western countries and the European Union.[19]

In ZANU-PF's effort to play up their image of 'terrorists' and 'threats to society', activists often recalled how, when the police transported

[14] Human Rights Watch (HRW), *Bashing Dissent: Escalating Violence and State Repression in Zimbabwe* (New York, HRW, May 2007), p. 1.
[15] HRW, *Bashing Dissent*, p. 10.
[16] This included Morgan Tsvangirai, who was arrested at Machipisa Police Station when enquiring about activists who were detained there. The detainees at Machipisa were tortured, denied legal counsel and refused medical attention. See, HRW, *Bashing Dissent*, pp. 12–16.
[17] Zimbabwe Republic Police (ZRP), *Opposition Forces in Zimbabwe: A Trail of Violence* (Harare, ZRP, March 2007). The MDC contradicted these reports, arguing that the attacks were staged by state agents in an attempt to justify the widespread arrests of its supporters (HRW, *Bashing Dissent*).
[18] ZRP, *Opposition Forces in Zimbabwe*.   [19] Ibid., p. 48.

them to the station, remand prison or the courts they were placed under heavy armed guard and 'paraded' in leg irons and handcuffs.[20] During one of George's arrests in 2009, for example, the police performed their force by demanding his presence at a sports day at Harare Polytechnic, after he had been warned by university security forces not to attend. George initially abided by this warning, but at the games the ZRP arrested ten of the students distributing fliers signed by George critiquing the cost of university fees. George received a phone call from the police, informing him no one would be released unless he came to Harare Polytechnic. After some discussion, in which George pointed out that he had been banned from the ground, he made his way there. He was arrested as soon as he arrived and taken to the police truck in leg irons and handcuffs: 'I was in chains. Like an animal. I explained, I was trying to negotiate with the inspector to release me, and I was telling him "no, there is no crime I have committed". But he would press hard here [shows scars on wrists], he treated me like a dangerous criminal.'[21] Malcolm, a political activist, similarly stated: 'The way the police arrest us, they beat us and put us in leg irons [as if] we are murderers or thieves. In fact all we are is activists fighting for democracy.'[22]

Through such treatment, ZANU-PF and members of the ZRP publicly portrayed civic and political activists as 'dangerous' and 'disordering' citizens. ZANU-PF was not the only actor on this stage, however. Playing into the state and legal consciousness expressed by members of the public, such as Patrick and Father Mkandla, and by certain civil servants, such as John and David, activists challenged these performances of police strength, and by extension their criminalisation. In the following section I show how, while Patrick and Father Mkandla framed their decision to report cases to the police in light of their responsibilities as citizens, and John and David emphasised how their behaviour fit with their understandings of their professional position,

---

[20] In interviews with George, student activist, Harare, 20 July 2010; Philip, student activist, Harare, 21 July 2010; Jeremy, political activist, 25 August 2010; Madock Chivasa, student and political activist, 15 September 2010; Henry, student and political activist, 16 September 2010; Victor, civil society member, Bulawayo, 10 November 2011; and Father Marko Mkandla, priest, Hwange, 30 November 2011.

[21] Interview, George, student activist, Harare, 20 July 2010.

[22] Interview, Malcolm, political activist, Harare, 27 September 2010.

activists concentrated on highlighting the political dimensions of their treatment and their responses to it, more specifically.

Locating the 'Criminal' in Performances of Arrest and Detention

Activists argued that they were targets for arrest and detention as a result of their political affiliation, but that the behaviour they were subjected to during their arrest and in detention was evidence of how it was not their own political engagement, but ZANU-PF's governance that was the real threat to Zimbabwe and its citizens. Although they were being arrested and detained, activists argued that ZANU-PF and its supporters were the real 'criminals'. To substantiate this critique, activists framed their experiences around the way that the ZANU-PF government, through the actions of its partisan police officers, violated their own moral and professional code around the law, a code that resonated, as we have seen, both with a wider public and elements within the state.

Recalling the harrowing physical conditions and the humiliations during his arrest and in police detention, for example, Wisdom, a Bulawayo-based MDC activist in his mid-thirties, commented that the way the police 'kicked, slapped and squeezed' him violated the professional norms of their office. While his treatment was 'normal procedure' in that it was expected, as 'everyone knows it happens', he simultaneously grappled with the fact that 'you know in your head that you are not supposed to be treated like this'.[23] Wisdom could not grant these political practices authority, he explained, as they did not reson-ate with the image of a rule-bound, professional state that he held, and aimed to contribute to by being an MDC member.

Next to the physical abuse the biggest challenge Wisdom faced in custody was thus the manner in which the police framed his political affiliation within ZANU-PF's 'patriotic history' narrative, accusing him of supporting an 'imperial, neocolonial party, the MDC'. He struggled with these accusations not only because they were untrue and inappropriate, but because he found them unbefitting of the role police officers should play in society. 'If a police officer really com-ments and says you are an imperial hand, you are a nuisance of the West. A police officer? You don't expect that'.[24] Wisdom's 'surprise' at

---

[23] Interview, Wisdom, MDC member, Bulawayo, 5 December 2011.   [24] Ibid.

how the police painted him as an 'enemy of the state' did not stem from naiveté or a lack of anticipation of this behaviour on his part. Instead it was an expression of his rejection of how the police violated what he saw as a widely shared moral and professional code. He explained:

I don't want the police to support my party, or my political view. I don't want them to support anybody. I want them to be professional. If they aren't professional, let the judicial system be professional. Just do your job without fear or favour. So that people know, we meet at law, no one should be bigger than the law. No political view should be bigger than the law.[25]

Victor, a civil society member in Bulawayo concerned primarily with exposing the ZANU-PF-made atrocities, similarly explained that while he was in detention the police told him that he 'needed to be reoriented on the history of Zimbabwe'.[26] He realised, however, that it was not him, but the police officers harassing him and the members of ZANU-PF instructing these officers to behave in this manner, who needed to be 'reoriented' to see that they, and not he, were the threat to Zimbabwe's future. To express this, Victor lectured the police officers on 'basic human rights and the squalid conditions in detention'. He also took the opportunity to remind the police officers that they had real reasons to fear him, as he was an active Zimbabwean citizen who did not grant the current regime and its practices authority. He continued: ZANU-PF 'knows I am really a threat to their political security ... I can expose that there are deficiencies in governance'. In his interactions, Victor placed the professional adherence to the law at the heart of his claims about what sort of state he would grant authority, and emphasised that he would not support ZANU-PF as they failed to govern in a manner he deemed to be legitimate.[27]

As Henry observed at the start of this chapter, his arrest and detention had 'the face of the law', but did not work 'along the lines of the law'.[28] It was important to take this seriously, he continued, because it was evidence of how members of an unprofessional police force were responsible for detaining activists in 'horrible' and 'inhumane' conditions. It was, in other words, critical to recognise the discrepancy between the existence of legal institutions, institutions to which the activists' political imaginations granted authority, and the practices of

[25] Ibid.
[26] Interview, Victor, civil society member, Bulawayo, 10 November 2011.
[27] Ibid.   [28] Interview, Henry, student activist, Harare, 16 September 2010.

violence that ZANU-PF carried out through these institutions, practices which activists refused to accept as legitimate, 'normal' or admis-
sible within the society they sought to build.

For George, the violence used by the police during his arrest and in
detention demonstrated their failure to follow 'proper procedure'.
More importantly for George, however, these practices masked a lack
of understanding of the law. He explained that the relationship
between students and the police was tense in part because students
exposed that they were 'better educated on matters of law':

When you raise legal questions to the police, they say 'You know you go
around lying amongst yourself that we're not educated and that we don't
know the law, and that is why you are asking us these questions when you
know we don't know them. Ah fine, we don't know it, but we will deal with
you, we will always beat you, whether you know the law or you do not, we
will beat you.'[29]

While, in the eyes of civil and political activists, performances on the
stage of arrest and detention detracted from ZANU-PF's legitimacy,
activists valued their own performances for the political authority the
experience could accord them. Although he knew that it was likely the
police would arrest him when they summoned him to Harare
Polytechnic in 2009, for example, George felt he couldn't leave his
fellow student activists, and he 'did not want to portray myself as a
coward in the face of our national executive council members having
been arrested'.[30] Going to Harare Polytechnic, George argued, was a
display of his commitment to ZINASU and his ability to occupy a
leadership position, a performance both for his fellow students and
the police.

Activists understood their experiences with arrest and detention
through the lens of their political positionality, and were able to shift
the burden of 'criminality' from themselves to the ZANU-PF-led government, which was treating them in an 'uncivilised', 'improper' and
'unprofessional' manner. Unified in highlighting the degeneration of
the Zimbabwean state, and the 'abnormality' of their experiences,
activists turned their gruelling treatment at the hands of the ZRP into
an opportunity to embody and articulate the strength of their

[29] Interview, George, student activist, Harare, 18 July 2010.
[30] Interview, George, student activist, Harare, 20 July 2010.

commitment to a widely shared legal and state consciousness. Despite finding a receptive audience in their fellow activists, in citizens such as Father Mkandla and Patrick, and civil servants such as John and David, their understanding of the meanings of their arrest and detention were not shared by all Zimbabweans. In the following section, I examine activists' experiences of their family's reaction to arrest and detention.

Encountering an Alternative State and Legal Consciousness at Home

Many of the activists I spoke to highlighted how an important part of their experiences with arrest and detention was not linked to how ZANU-PF treated them, or how this impacted their views of the Zimbabwean state. Rather, they focused on the intimate impact of their criminalisation, lamenting how this isolated them socially. Two MDC activists I spoke to in Mbare, Tasimba and Kumbirai, explained how their interaction with the police and the courts had left them 'really struggling' economically and socially.[31] They were arrested on 26 March 2007 and accused of taking part in a petrol bombing. The police moved them around in an effort to hide them from the human rights lawyers, and tried to 'disappear' Tasimba, blindfolding him and taking him into 'the bush' where he was beaten severely. Eventually both men appeared at Harare's Magistrates' Courts, starting a series of remand hearings, and then a trial that lasted for over a year. Both men had lost their jobs as a result of the protracted court case, and although they were acquitted they continued to 'live in fear'. In part they were fearful because they were 'known criminals'.[32] Tasimba explained that as their arrest occurred 'during the same time when Morgan Tsvangirai was being beaten up, and was in court', there had been a lot of press interest during their trial:

The Herald especially would continue taking photos [of us] as we would go up and down to court in leg irons and with swollen feet. We were not allowed to speak to our relatives, so all they saw was how we were paraded

---

[31] Interviews with Tasimba and Kumbirai, MDC activists, Mbare, 20 August 2010.
[32] Ibid.

like criminals, and then the news would show the same. It was a difficult time, really.[33]

Kumbirai observed that the experience had impacted 'on many levels of our lives. Relationships, social, even health.' Most significantly, however, being a 'known criminal' meant that 'friends and relatives see us differently'. On the one hand, several of their relatives avoided Tasimba and Kumbirai because they feared the repercussions of associating with them after their public arrest. Kumbirai explained that his family members stopped speaking to him as 'they know they may be threatened. They may be beaten and asked "why were you talking to these men". So they don't want to talk to us anymore.'[34] On the other hand, some of their family members were in fact ZANU-PF supporters, who believed that associating with the MDC was a criminal offence to begin with. Tasimba's aunt, who worked as a local ZANU-PF chairperson for example, had been the person to report him to the police to begin with. While he was being detained she had also moved into his home, throwing out all his belongings and refusing to return the property to him when he was acquitted. Tasimba tried to negotiate with his aunt, and asked his mother, her sister, for support. His mother, who had initially applauded his activism, refused to help, explaining that when Tasimba had been in detention ZANU-PF youth had come to the house to beat her up, and that she had now 'suffered enough' for his political cause. It was time for him to 'grow up, be a man and not a criminal', she told him.[35]

Henry similarly observed that his multiple arrests isolated him socially, as they resulted in his suspension from college, a loss of contact with classmates and friends who were frightened off by the possibility of being linked to his activism, and challenges in connecting with his family, who were now balancing their worries for his safety, concerns for the potential repercussions for his behaviour on family members more widely, who were being threatened by ZANU-PF youth, and having to come to terms with their perception of Henry as a 'criminal' or deviant after 'seeing me paraded around in handcuffs'. Eventually Henry's parents advised him that his 'only interest should be to your books, go to school, go finish your education and

[33] Interview with Tasimba, MDC activist, Mbare, 20 August 2010.
[34] Interview, Kumbirai, MDC activist, Mbare, 20 August 2010.
[35] Interview with Tasimba, MDC activist, Mbare, 20 August 2010.

then get to a life which is non-political. Because really, things that are political are very high risk.'[36]

George's family too showed unease, troubling George because his 'parents have always been very consistent in blaming me [for being involved in student politics], saying that "you are the first person to do these things. Your father has not been arrested, not even your brothers, why you now?".' Although he thought his parents were 'speaking this out of love rather than hate', it remained difficult for George to accept their view of him. After his first arrest, he found it 'very, very difficult' to reconcile himself with the consequences of his involvement in student politics when noticing that after each of his arrests, 'relatives changed their perception of who you are, and began to question if you are normal. They begin to think you are a hooligan of some sort.'[37]

Activists had to contend not just with notions of criminality, but with expectations of masculinity. Their experiences with arrest and detention impacted on their ability to be 'men', not just before ZANU-PF-instructed police officers but also in the eyes of their families and within society. Student activists in particular noted that while university had previously been a space for self-invention – which often went hand in hand with the exploration of their political understandings of themselves as citizens – this space became increasingly constrained. Henry observed that the fact that his parents were paying his school fees and bills opened him up to their criticism as:

they were saying 'look, now you are really losing direction. You didn't go to college to start activism, it's somewhere where you go to learn life skills and to get a profession. Just try to build on your life.' So it was like maybe I was digressing from what I was really supposed to be doing. It didn't go down well with them, because my father had to sell his cattle at times to pay off fees. He really wasn't happy when he heard the news that I was arrested for activism.[38]

Dan Hodgkinson remarks on how the changing fee structures at the University of Zimbabwe in 2006 'shifted the financial burden to students' parents',[39] which in turn extended parental control into a space which previously served as a site for youth's reinvention and

[36] Ibid.   [37] Interview, George, student activist, Harare, 20 July 2010.
[38] Interview, Henry, student activist, Harare, 22 September 2010.
[39] Hodgkinson, 'The "Hardcore" Student Activist', p. 874.

independence.[40] Henry explained that he, at times, questioned his commitment to fight for 'full' citizenship, especially when he felt deep shame because his arrests disappointed his parents and prevented him from completing his education or finding stable work. Because of ZANU-PF's denial of his imagination of citizenship, Henry explained, he was still not living an 'adult life', an aspiration that he felt might only be achievable if he quit politics.[41] In this way, activists' experiences of arrest and detention made being a 'citizen' incompatible with being a 'man'. The conditions in police detention, and activists' treatment in custody, not only motivated them to continue their political engagement and quest for citizenship. Their interactions with family members also exposed the costs of this demand for citizenship, as they were cast as 'hooligans' and 'criminals' whose transition from 'boys' to 'men' was delayed.

Conclusion

Young, black, urban-based and predominantly male civic activists were the prime targets for arrest and detention by the ZRP. Targeted for their political affiliation with the MDC, or their capacity to mobilise citizens through their position in civil society or student politics, this group was subject to intimidation, harassment, humiliation and torture at the hands of the police. Their arrest and treatment in detention were marked by physical violence, mental torment and isolation, and had long-term impacts on activists' health and well-being, on their educational and job prospects, and on their social ties with family and friends.

ZANU-PF, and the police officers following their instructions, cast MDC supporters like Tasimba, Kumbirai and Wisdom, political activists such as Henry and Victor and student leaders like George as the 'enemies of the state' through public arrests, physical and emotional torture and the squalid conditions in the detention cells. This had consequences that reverberated through their personal and family lives, occasionally threatening their commitment to political and civic

---

[40] Ibid. See also, Teresa Barnes 'Politics of the Mind and Body: Gender and Institutional Culture in African Universities', *Feminist Africa*, 8, 2007, pp. 8–25.
[41] Interview, Henry, student activist, Harare, 22 September 2010.

engagement and highlighting diverging understandings of the extent to which their run-ins with the police 'criminalised' them.

While activists understood their criminalisation within police narratives as evidence that their imagination of citizenship was threatened, and would therefore continue to assert themselves as if they were 'full' citizens, it was more challenging to position themselves in this way when faced with the criticism of their families, and society more broadly. The perceptions articulated by activists' family members also exposed a less tangible, harder to articulate discord between how activists experienced their arrests and detention, and how the legal system was regarded within society more broadly. To varying degrees family members shared, or bought into, ZANU-PF's portrayal of activists as 'criminals'. In this manner the spectacle of penality that was staged during arrest and detention was able to play into a long-standing, public legal consciousness that authorised the police, prison systems and the courts to deal with, and pass judgement over, deviant or disordered members of society. While activists were clearly arrested for their political affiliation, rather than, for example, petty theft, the fact that they were targeted through the legal system still shaped public opinion of them. Despite their efforts to criminalise the police officers responsible for displaying them as such to Zimbabwean society, activists also accorded a level of legitimacy to the legal process when confronted with such public perceptions.

In Chapter 5, I look at how these dynamics entered the courtroom. For many activists, their efforts to bring attention to and 'expose' the horrific experiences of arrest and detention extended into their trials. In an effort to express their commitment to the rule of law, and to cast the offending civil servants as those who really ought to be arrested, detained and tried, activists drew attention to their time in detention when they stood in the dock. I turn to the material and sensory conditions in Harare's Magistrates' Courts at Rotten Row to illustrate how the stages of arrest and detention worked with the more ambient dimensions of the court to strengthen the political performances that activists and their lawyers engaged in to bring ZANU-PF's unacceptable governance to light.

5 | *Material and Sensory Courtrooms*

Observing the 'Decline of Professionalism' in Harare's Magistrates' Courts

Law is not confined to what is semiotically understood as legal, but permeates life in terms of bodies, objects, and spaces.[1]

The courtroom can be conceived as a theatrical space, as well as a highly oppressive space. The courtroom contains and twists bodies into its tiny caverns and grand paneled auditoria, with walls built to ensure the painful silencing of already terrorized bodies.[2]

The previous chapters have established that, within Zimbabwe's judiciary, the law is debated through notions of professionalism, justice, morality, human dignity and normality that expand definitions of law beyond a system of rules to encompass wider claims to citizenship and conceptualisations of state authority. Through performances and performativity, an extensive range of actors – from prosecutors, magistrates, police officers and clerks of court to human rights lawyers, defendants, journalists and audience members in the gallery – engage with these broader debates upon entering the courtroom. As we have seen, legal scholars, anthropologists, sociologists, geographers and architects have all approached the question of how the power and authority of the law and the state are constructed through the actual and symbolic orderings of courtrooms. Through the notion of performance and the metaphor of theatre, these authors highlight how courtroom actors can use their scripts, demeanour and props to assert different state imaginaries and ideas about citizenship. In recent years, scholars have extended the focus on performances within the courtroom to include the study of the architectural and material dimensions of this theatre and its stages. Neither of these bodies of scholarship,

---

[1] Andreas Philippopoulos-Mihalopoulos, 'Flesh of the Law: Material Legal Metaphors', *Journal of Law and Society*, 43, 1, 2016, p. 59.

[2] Victoria Brooks, 'Interrupting the Courtroom Organism: Screaming Bodies, Material Affects and the *Theatre of Cruelty*', *Law, Culture and the Humanities*, 2014, p. 3.

however, elaborate on the sensory dimensions of courtroom performance. During my research, however, the spatial, material and sensory
dimensions of the courtroom, and of the courthouse in which the
courtroom is located, emerged as mutually reinforcing elements which
shaped courtroom experiences. In this chapter, I thus focus on how
state power and authority were established and critiqued through the
material and sensory characteristics that marked the courts at
Rotten Row.

I do so by first discussing several key architectural, material and
sensory features of courts that are foregrounded in a wider literature.
I then turn to my observations and the accounts of human rights
lawyers and their clients, to ask how they experienced and interacted
with the space and materiality of the court. Through a description of
Harare's Magistrates' Courts at Rotten Row, I demonstrate that these
courts were full of the expected spatial trademarks of the law, which
worked to separate the actors present within it in order to put the
defendant in his or her place as the subject of judgement. The defence
lawyers and their clients recognised that the courtroom was a potentially violent space. In addition, they observed that the political and
economic situation in Zimbabwe after 2000 had caused a decline of
the conditions in the Rotten Row courtrooms. As a result, the material
conditions in the courts were read by lawyers and their clients not only
as a mark of the authority of law, but also as symbols of decay, which
highlighted the ZANU-PF-led government's disrespect for the rule of
law. The material evidence of this disrespect served as a basis for
criticising the government.

The declining material conditions impacted lawyers' ability to push
for accountability and to employ the 'proper legal tactics' they relied
upon. The conditions also assaulted the senses of all those present in
court. Confronted with the sight of police officers, badly treated
defendants who 'smelt of decay' and the sounds of rattling chains
and 'booming voices', the lawyers discussed the visual, olfactory and
auditory experiences of the courtroom as evidence that they worked
within a 'collapsed system'.[3] These sensory experiences were intimidating. They reminded the defendants and their lawyers of the manner in
which ZANU-PF coercively asserted its authority over people's bodies

---

[3] Interview, Tawanda Zhuwarara, human rights lawyer, Harare,
   7 September 2010.

and minds prior to their appearance in the courtroom by 'bringing the prison within the space of the court'.[4] Lawyers, and occasionally the defendants, also used the run-down conditions of the courtroom and the defendants' battered bodies as opportunities to contest the state's authority. In the material and sensory dimensions of Harare's Magistrates' Courts, signs of decay, experiences of intimidation and efforts to resist and expose this 'cruelty of the state' converged. These courtroom performances brought into stark relief the contending views of the law, its relationship to state authority and the promise of 'justice'.

Legal Architecture: Expressing Power through the Court's Spaces

Linda Mulcahy argues that 'understanding the factors which determine the internal design of the courtroom are crucial to a broader and more nuanced understanding of state-sanctioned adjudication'.[5] Focusing on the physical structure and layout of English courts, she specifically examines the architecture of Criminal Assizes, and connects the structures of the court to historical socio-political developments and the changing ideas about public space and justice. Mulcahy highlights the longevity of processes of segregation or separation within the court, which she notes work through the creation of rarely overlapping routes of circulation for the various actors present in the courtroom.

Mulcahy's work echoes Julienne Hanson's earlier observations of the architecture of English courts. Hanson writes that 'a courtroom is like a theatre in that the negotiations must take place and be seen to take place in public, but unlike a theatre in that the "stage" is compartmentalised into separate spatial domains, and the actors confront one another across an unbreachable physical divide'.[6] She explains the physical segregation of actors as an effort to 'prevent contamination between the criminal, citizen and those officiating at the ritual process'.[7] Mulcahy also notes that the courthouse was constructed to

---

[4] Ibid.   [5] Mulcahy, *Legal Architecture*, p. 1.
[6] Julienne Hanson, 'The Architecture of Justice: Iconography and Space Configuration in the English Law Court Building', *Architectural Research Quarterly*, 1, 4, 1996, pp. 55–6.
[7] Hanson, 'The Architecture of Justice', p. 58.

facilitate the 'degradation ritual for those subjected to the violence of the law'.[8] Sociologist Harold Garfinkel referred to the 'degradation rituals' as central to practices of exclusion or reintegration of individuals constructed as 'deviant' within societies.[9] Applied to the courthouse, the degradation ritual is embedded within its structure: the courthouse and courtroom are set up to facilitate a view of the trial as a 'rite of passage' during which defendants are temporarily taken out of society before they are either reincorporated once found innocent of breaking societal rules, or recategorised as 'criminal' if found guilty of 'deviant' behaviour. In the latter instance, such a ritual punishes the deviant for defying the norms or rules of society, and in doing so re-establishes the legitimacy of these norms.

This process of segregation extends beyond the courtroom to the entire layout of the courthouse, as '[t]he social programme of the building, put simply, is to engineer separations between these different groups of users, and selectively to reintegrate them under highly controlled conditions'.[10] The location, shape and style of courthouses both set them apart from other buildings and mark them as sites where justice is dispensed.[11] While Hanson and Mulcahy's observations apply specifically to English courthouses, Nigel Eltringham makes a similar observation about the routes visitors are instructed to follow within the ICTR in Arusha, Tanzania, signalling that comparable observations can be made about courtroom architecture across the globe.[12]

In addition to its outer structure, the inner passages of the English courthouses Hanson and Mulcahy described were designed to avoid overlap between citizens and the potentially criminal, with different actors entering the courthouse through separate entrances, or following different routes within it. The courtroom, too, was built up of architectural features aimed at setting various actors apart. The interior design of the courtroom, with its dark wooden panelling, raised platforms, distinct benches or desks and the display of symbols

---

[8] Mulcahy, *Legal Architecture*, p. 9.
[9] Harold Garfinkel, 'Conditions of Successful Degradation Ceremonies', *American Journal of Sociology*, 61, 5, 1956, pp. 420–4. See also, Ervin Goffman, *Asylums: Essays on the Social Situation of Mental Patients and Other Inmates* (Chicago, Aldine Publishers, 1962).
[10] Hanson, 'The Architecture of Justice', p. 55.
[11] Mulcahy, *Legal Architecture*, p. 8.
[12] Eltringham, 'Spectators to the Spectacle of Law'.

of justice, guided the actors to their predetermined positions in a way that avoided contact among actors when navigating the space. Such distinctions were particularly evident in the construction of the dock, which separated the defendant from the court proceedings by placing him or her behind a raised screen or bars.[13]

Building on both Hanson and Mulcahy's descriptions of the vertical organisation of the courtroom, and the separate and segregating circulation routes of 'citizens' and 'criminals' within the courthouse, Victoria Brooks argues that the manner in which one acts within a UK courtroom is constructed and constricted by the space. Movement is constrained because 'the space and the correct articulation of bodies is essential to the process of the court hearing and to disrupt its functioning, is to disrupt the law'.[14] Scholars examining the court as a theatre have pointed to the importance of disruption and interruption as resistance. Brooks also follows this perspective, arguing that 'the howl of anxious bodies enduring the process and space of the law can be materialized through interruptions to the courtroom, such as when bodies stand when they should not and when they speak when they should be silent'.[15]

Scholars have thus analysed how authority is embedded in the court's architecture, and how the courtroom's spatial design perpetuates this authority and impacts on a diverse range of actors. They do not, however, discuss the power of sensory experiences, particularly of smells and sounds, within these spaces. In the remainder of this chapter, I go beyond the focus on spatial elements to ask how the ZANU-PF state, through its invocations of the law, materialised itself in the conditions of the courts and on the bodies of its opponents, and how these bodies, when on display in the courtroom, could disrupt the party's efforts to legitimise its rule in the eyes of a specific subset of its citizens. I first turn to the spatial layout of the Magistrates' Courthouse at Rotten Row as a whole, and to the courtrooms contained within it specifically, to illustrate how, while their architectural design and layout were aimed at facilitating performances of the power and authority of the law, and by extension the state, their material decay undermined this aim.

---

[13] Mulcahy, *Legal Architecture*. See also, Linda Mulcahy, 'Putting the Defendant in Their Place: Why Do We Still Use the Dock in Criminal Proceedings?', *British Journal of Criminology*, 53, 2013, pp. 1139–56.
[14] Brooks, 'Interrupting the Courtroom Organism', p. 5.   [15] Ibid., p. 1.

Figure 5.1 Aerial view of Harare's Magistrates' Courts
Source: Google Earth Map data, Google, 2020, Maxar Technologies

Harare's Magistrates' Courts at Rotten Row

Harare's criminal Magistrates' Courts are located on the south-west outskirts of Harare's busy central business district, just south of ZANU-PF's headquarters. They were opened in 1963 as part of a new 'civic centre' on Rotten Row, designed by modernist architects Peter Oldfield and Nick Montgomerie, and which also included the Harare City Library and the Museum of Human Sciences. Driving further to the south along the Rotten Row road brings you to Mbare, the first and largest of Harare's high-density suburbs. Standing in front of the courts, however, these bustling places felt far removed.[16] The large and impressive circular building, adorned with symbols of justice and the Zimbabwean nation, housed the pretrial detention cells, magistrates' and clerks' offices, and the ordinary and regional courtrooms. When looking at the courts, Linda Mulcahy's observation, that 'when we imagine a courthouse we tend to think of a public building which uses massing, shape and style to convey a sense of importance or foreboding',[17] rang true.

The courts stood on a spacious plot, back from the road, surrounded by parking spaces and trees (see Figure 5.1).

Spread over two floors, twenty courtrooms branched off the hallway that encircled the central courtyard. With the power of the law

[16] Field notes, Harare's Magistrates' Courts, Harare, 21 July 2010.
[17] Mulcahy, *Legal Architecture*, pp. 7–8.

Figure 5.2 Journalist Hopewell Chino'no on entrance ramp to holding cells
Source: Original photograph by Kumbirai Mafunda, 2020

embedded in an outer design that resembles Jeremy Bentham's disciplinary surveillance model, the panopticon, the court's layout further symbolised the power relations between the different actors operating within it.[18] On the top floor sat the courts with the highest sentencing jurisdiction, the regional Magistrates' Courts. Separate staircases for the public, and for clerks of court and magistrates, led up to these courts. On the ground floor were the ordinary magistrates' courtrooms. Separate entrances for the public and the defendants still in custody further facilitated efforts to 'prevent contamination' between the various users of the courts. The defendants who were brought in under police custody from police stations or from remand prison (often from Harare Central Remand Prison) were led in between the courtrooms into the holding cells underneath these courts (see Figure 5.2).

---

[18] The connection between Jeremy Bentham's panopticon prison design and techniques of governmentality and (self-)discipline was made famous by Michel Foucault. See, Foucault, *Discipline and Punish*.

When I was there in 2010 and 2012, police officers prevented groups from gathering on the stairs leading up to the court. As a result, people assembled under the trees in the parking lot to the right of the steps, or climbed up these stairs and passed through the double doors.[19] On either side of the doors a security officer stood before a small white guardhouse, searching visitors' bags and checking identification.[20] Once a visitor passed the guards they crossed the entrance hall, walked up some more stairs and passed through one of three double doors to step into the halls of the circular courthouse, to wait in the halls and eventually sit down in the gallery benches of the courtroom.

As noted in the Introduction, Nigel Eltringham has recounted how both his entry into, and his presence and actions within, the ICTR were highly regulated, and argued that such control was a central element in his transformation from a mere visitor into a member of the 'validating, silent public' that lent legitimacy to the trial.[21] Although the hallways at Harare's Magistrates' Courts were often crowded in the mornings before the trials commenced, the control of the public extended beyond the security checks at the entrance way into these halls. On first glance the open spaces of the waiting areas offered a multitude of actors a chance to mix, to discuss their cases and to observe one another. Prosecutors, police officers, clerks of court, interpreters and court reporters walked between the courtrooms. Defendants and their supporting family members, friends or colleagues waited on benches outside the courtrooms. Lawyers frequently stood chatting with a client, or went in search of the prosecutors or clerks of court to get an update on their cases. The conduct of the public was, however, heavily policed within this space. Police officers walked along the halls, breaking up larger groups of visitors, asking people to find a seat or enquiring which case they were waiting for. If someone was

---

[19] Field notes, observations at Harare's Magistrates' Courts, Harare, 14 July 2010.

[20] In 2010, when I visited the courts three or four times a week over a period of three months, I tended to walk through the door on the right side, where my bag was checked by the same female police officer most times. I thought of this as a simple security check until I returned to the courts in 2012 and this female police officer was still at the door. As she checked my bag, she looked up and said 'ah, you're back again. We've not seen you in a long while now. Welcome back.' While her greeting was warm, being recognised made me feel observed and served as a real reminder of the extent of state surveillance (field notes, observations at Harare's Magistrates' Courts, Harare, 17 January 2012).

[21] Eltringham, 'Spectators to the Spectacle of Law'.

wearing jeans, a skirt above the knee or a low-cut shirt, the officers would further comment that the clothing visitors were wearing was not appropriate in court and bar them from entering.[22]

This control over the manner by which members of the public entered into the courts, and conducted themselves within it, also resonates with Mulcahy's description of how courthouse architecture creates distinct routes in order to separate members of the public from the defendants or the magistrate. She observes that 'the public are first searched, then channelled through space, and finally positioned within tightly controlled zones within the courtroom'.[23] When looking at the architectural design of the courtrooms at Rotten Row, these barriers to the active participation of, or disruption by, the public were evident. Through the use of separate side entrances for the magistrates and for the defendants brought in from police custody, and a main entrance for all other actors such as the spectators, lawyers, prosecutors and the clerks of court, and through the raised platforms and the bars of the dock, the magistrate was elevated above, and the defendant was isolated from, the other courtroom actors. The allocation of different sides of the courtroom for the defence council and the prosecutors maintained the separation of these actors (see Figure 5.3).

Once the doors to the courtroom opened, the defendants on remand, their friends or family members and general audience members filed into the three rows of benches facing the raised platform with the magistrate's desk. In front of the magistrate's desk stood a table, sometimes with a tape-recording machine, and two chairs facing the gallery. The clerk of court sat by the tape recorder; a police officer or security guard filled the other chair. Opposite this table was a desk behind which the defence lawyers and prosecutors sat facing the magistrate. The dock stood to the left of this desk. Behind it was a door leading down to the cells holding the defendants from remand prison and police custody. The witness stand was opposite the dock, on the right-hand side of the courtroom. The defence counsel was

[22] For a thought-provoking reflection on how the choice of courtroom attire can shed light on the history of law and construct the courts' present popular legitimacy, see Lee Cabantingan, 'Fashioning the Legal Subject: Popular Justice and Courtroom Attire in the Caribbean', *Political and Legal Anthropology Review*, 41, 1, 2018, pp. 69–84.
[23] Mulcahy, *Legal Architecture*, p. 10.

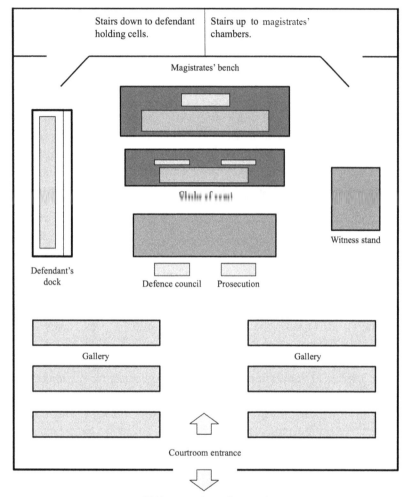

Figure 5.3 Layout of the courtroom at Rotten Row

therefore meant to sit on the left, and the prosecution on the right of the desk.

Speaking of her experience working as a magistrate within various courts across Zimbabwe, Sarah recalled that when she was on the bench she would occasionally remind herself of how the courtroom must look for those entering it as spectators or defendants, in order to better understand their reactions in court. In her view, 'the whole environment can be intimidating', because of the magistrate's dress and elevated position on 'the bench … on this high chair, in the black gown'. The grandeur of the courtroom, she continued, became evident to the public as soon as they walked in, as:

even before you go into the court there is this loud 'stand up' and then the prosecutor goes 'silence in court', and you know, that in itself is actually enough to get a person to say, 'ah, look at this, what kind of place is this?' And then, well, of course they have to stand up when the magistrate walks in, and then you sit down, and then they sit down.[24]

When the defendant or spectators were unfamiliar with the proceedings, these intimidating aspects were further exacerbated. Sarah imagined that the presence of recording equipment, and of different actors all assigned to specific locations in the courtroom, meant that 'for people who do not even know the set-up and what, who is who and what they are supposed to be doing, it's very unfamiliar, and all the more intimidating'.[25]

Indeed, many of the activists I spoke to reflected on how their first experience in court was particularly frightening because they did not understand what was happening, who was fulfilling which roles or where they were meant to go. George, for example, explained that on his first visit to court he had much trouble 'presenting my own self, my own story'.[26] As I show below, however, George's trouble with presenting himself in court was not only the result of his lack of knowledge of the legal system or court proceedings. The material conditions he encountered at the courthouse, and the manner in which the police transported him to the courts, also contributed to George feeling intimidated and disoriented by the space of the courtroom.

In the following section, I examine the material conditions and police presence in the Magistrates' Courts in further detail. In line with their understanding of the law as granting legitimacy to a rule-bound state, human rights lawyers articulated their perceptions of the manner in which ZANU-PF had lost its authority over the law and the state by invoking the dilapidated conditions they encountered at the courts. These material conditions, and the politics that allowed for these conditions to persist, threatened the lawyers' ability to perform their

---

[24] Interview, Sarah, former magistrate, Harare, 5 August 2010.   [25] Ibid.
[26] Interview, George, student activist, Harare, 20 July 2010.

commitment to the law, which further undermined their ability and willingness to grant authority to ZANU-PF's rule. At the same time, I show that the police treatment of activists such as George indicates that ZANU-PF was not attempting to tap into the authority of the law as understood by the defence lawyers. Instead, the party aimed to blur the boundaries between the public, the trial and law enforcement agents to intimidate its political opponents and extend its control over the state's institutions. The lawyers, in turn, understood this, and played on the space these blurred boundaries created in their courtroom performances.

Competing Authorities within a 'Broken' Court

In Harare's Magistrates' Courts, the processes of separation identified by Hanson, Mulcahy and Eltringham in courthouse and courtroom architecture were evident in the security controls encountered upon entering the courts, the policing of visitors' conduct in the hallways and the courtroom design and layout. These processes all contributed to the isolation of the defendant and the separation of judicial officials and lawyers from the general public. The material conditions and politics of the courts, however, undermined these processes of separation.

Unlike the courts in the UK described by Hanson and Mulcahy, or Eltringham's account of the ICTR, the Magistrates' Courts in Harare were severely under-resourced, and extremely dirty. The conditions not only blurred the separation between the public, the defendant and judicial actors within the courtroom. Human rights lawyers also referred to them as one clear sign of ZANU-PF's flawed governance that had resulted in Zimbabwe's dramatic economic downturn and the government's marginalisation of law. The government, they argued, simply did not have the money or the will to invest in the courts anymore. Most critically, the conditions within the courtroom profoundly affected the professionalism of magistrates, prosecutors and human rights lawyers alike.

In many courtrooms, for example, there was only one chair available for the defence and prosecuting councils. As a result, the defence and prosecution needed to share the chair. David Hofisi, a young lawyer working for ZLHR, commented that he did not mind sharing the chair, as most prosecutors were 'cool people' with whom he could share a beer in town after work. He was less comfortable, however, when the prosecutor was one of the attorney general's 'good boys', in part because he noticed that many of his clients were confused or upset by the 'close relationship we seem to have, laughing about the lack of seats. ... They don't understand that we're not really working together to put them away.'[27]

The material dilapidation that spread throughout the Rotten Row court building was shocking to the public and remained a common subject of conversation among those waiting in the hallways. Highlighting their unwillingness to have to separate their view of law as an ideal from its material manifestations, many of the lawyers and members of the public who I spoke to in the court asked whether I had ever seen such a dirty courthouse, drawing my attention to the dust on the benches and the smell of urine in the halls, and expressing their embarrassment that we had to 'wait for justice in a space like this'.[28] In these conversations, many people echoed Daniel Nemukuyu's opinion piece for *The Herald* in March 2009, in which he lamented the disintegration of the courthouse.

His description of the courts remained accurate in subsequent years. He observed that 'the once beautiful fountains and ponds at the centre of the circular building have now been reduced to mosquito-breeding places during the rainy season'.[29] Due to the broken toilet facilities, the hallways often smelt of urine and people had to avoid the 'pools comprising a mixture of leaking water and urine ... while litter floats on top'.[30] Nemukuyu reflected that in these conditions people could only use the toilets if they wore gumboots, and 'it would be strange indeed to see magistrates, prosecutors, lawyers and other court officials trying to find a matching pair of gumboots for their designer suits simply to answer the call of nature'.[31] How, he asked, could these judicial officials be expected to do their jobs professionally in these conditions?

---

[27] Field notes, observations at Harare's Magistrates' Courts, Harare, 17 July 2010 and observations on trial *E. v. State*, Harare, 18 August 2010. See also, interview, David Hofisi, human rights lawyer, Harare, 11 August 2010.

[28] Field notes, observations at Harare's Magistrates' Courts, Harare, July–September 2010; January–February 2012.

[29] Daniel Nemukuyu, 'Zimbabwe: Rotten Row Courts in a Mess', *The Herald*, 26 March 2009, accessed on 5 August 2014 at: http://allafrica.com/stories/200903260048.html.

[30] Nemukuyu, 'Zimbabwe: Rotten Row Courts in a Mess'.   [31] Ibid.

This question was on many visitors' minds. During one of the trials I observed, for example, an activist who had come to show her support was almost refused entrance to the courts because she was wearing jeans. She explained that she had chosen to wear jeans because the courts were so dirty. She was 'surprised' when the police attempted to exert control over her dress and appearance. Like the young, urban-based men in Chapter 4, she expressed 'surprise' as a political claim, in this instance referring to her expectations of the material conditions a court should maintain in order to hold on to its legitimacy, and to transfer authority to the state. Only in these conditions would she 'dress smart' to grant the courts authority. She argued this point with the police officers, insisting that she should be allowed to wear jeans when 'ZANU-PF can't even keep their courts clean'.[32] Turning to me, she further noted how the conditions in the courts led to a loss of professional authority. How, she asked, could a magistrate be tasked with passing judgement on her friend during the trial if she had to work in an environment that did not enable members of the public to 'dress smart'?[33]

Human rights lawyers also pointed to the material conditions in the courts as symbolic of the decline of professionalism and accountability that had spread through the courts. From my first visit in July 2010 to my visits in February 2012, all the clocks at Harare Magistrates' Courts were stuck on 7:10. Lawyers held up these broken clocks specifically. Magistrates were no longer punctual, and the lawyers or the public were no longer able to check on the time. David Hofisi remarked that the government must no longer be able to afford the electricity for the clocks. Running these clocks was likely to be a small expense, but the impact of these broken clocks was proportionally much greater, Hofisi explained, as magistrates were no longer 'accountable to starting their trials on time'.[34] Indeed, in the period I attended hearings at Rotten Row the trials were often delayed. Hofisi acknowledged that the broken clocks did not actually cause delays. The delays were the result of the magistrates' minimal remuneration and the strained economic conditions. Magistrates were paid around US$200 a month, while very basic living costs were easily double this

---

[32] Field notes, observations on trial *E. v. State*, Harare, 18 August 2010.
[33] Ibid.
[34] Interview, David Hofisi, human rights lawyer, Harare, 11 August 2010.

amount.[35] In light of this discrepancy, magistrates not only had less incentive to come to work on time, they were also delayed as they engaged in other businesses next to their legal careers in order to survive. The economic conditions which fostered the corruption and undermined the neutrality of certain judges and magistrates, as discussed in Chapter 2, also weakened magistrates' ability to adhere to a simple demonstration of professionalism: showing up to work on time.

Time itself also had real effects on the lawyers and their clients because most politically motivated prosecutions dragged on for extended periods. This was evidence both of the political tactics deployed by ZANU-PF to discourage activists, as shown in Chapter 4, and the party's decreased interest in claiming the authority that following the rules provided. Eminent human rights lawyer Alec Muchadehama commented that, out of all the different kinds of cases he worked on, those involving civil society members or MDC activists were a 'waste of time and precious resources', as 'the trials will normally not get completed on time. They don't start on time, they don't finish on time, they don't get resolved on time.'[36] For lawyers, the broken clocks thus represented both their real and symbolic inability to hold the magistrates accountable.

Broken tape recorders in the courtrooms were given as further evidence of this 'broken system', which had real effects on judicial actors' ability to do their jobs. Kucaca Phulu, a human rights lawyer based in Bulawayo, explained that, next to confronting political interference in many of his cases, the main challenges of his work emerged because he defended his clients in courts which were not 'properly equipped' and operated in a justice system which was 'not properly resourced'. The broken tape recorders represented the impact of this

---

[35] Ibid. See also, interview, Tawanda Zhuwarara, human rights lawyer, Harare, 7 September 2010.

[36] Interview, Alec Muchadehama, human rights lawyer, Harare, 12 January 2012. These delays were a tactic that had both physical and mental effects on the defendants and put a lot of financial pressure on the defendants as well as their lawyers. Following his arrest at Bikita Shopping Centre in 2008, for example, Henry had to make the 700 km round trip between Harare and Bikita's Magistrates' Courts on a monthly basis for over a year, 'just for a ten to thirty minute court session'. In addition to the financial and physical strain this put on him, he saw the delay as a sign of a collapsing justice system. See, interview, Henry, student activist, Harare, 16 September 2010.

issue most clearly, Phulu continued, because of the way they influenced the lawyers' abilities to perform in court. Indeed, in the majority of the cases I observed magistrates hand-wrote the record of the proceeding as a result of the lack of recorders.[37] Because the magistrates had to 'write everything longhand', courtroom performances could not function 'properly'.[38] Lawyers, the prosecution, witnesses and defendants all had to slow the pace at which they expressed themselves during the trial. David Hofisi explained that he could no longer 'ask questions in rapid succession', because it was 'all about giving the magistrate time to write things down'. This detracted from his ability to make his arguments effectively. In a 'proper' system, Hofisi would expect 'a judicial officer who is taking all of his time to listen and to follow proceedings'.[39]

Kucaca Phulu also noted that the lack of recording technology in court 'distracts the magistrate who is supposed to be listening to the case being presented'.[40] One of Hofisi's colleagues at ZLHR, Jeremiah Bamu, explained that magistrates 'get especially frustrated and irritated when someone is making long submissions ... They get tired of writing the whole day ... so they will restrict what you say.'[41] He stressed that 'it would be better if the recording equipment functioned properly', as the current conditions meant that magistrates were not 'able to exercise their minds as you are making your arguments. That is how they end up missing very critical legal arguments. They are not able to fully concentrate on the argument because all they want to do is to record it.'[42] As a result, Bamu explained, he adapted his own strategies in the courtroom, 'reduc[ing] every argument to writing, and emphasis[ing] the most important aspects orally'. The benefits of this strategy were twofold: it allowed the magistrate to be more focused in court by limiting what they had to write down, and ensured that Bamu could always draw attention to his written statement if he felt that the magistrate had missed a key argument.[43]

---

[37] Field notes, observations at Harare's Magistrates' Courts, Harare, 26 July 2010; 2 August 2010; 6 August 2010; 18 August 2010; 27 August 2010; 10 September 2010; 21 September 2010.

[38] Interview, Jeremiah Bamu, human rights lawyer, Harare, 28 September 2010.

[39] Interview, David Hofisi, human rights lawyer, Harare, 11 August 2010.

[40] Interview, Kucaca Phulu, human rights lawyer, Bulawayo, 29 November 2011.

[41] Interview, Jeremiah Bamu, human rights lawyer, Harare, 28 September 2010.

[42] Ibid.   [43] Ibid.

As magistrates' hand-written records were easily altered, lawyers also expressed the fear that the broken recorders created more opportunities for corruption. Due to their poor remuneration, magistrates, prosecutors and clerks of court were all prone to accepting bribes. If the record of all statements made to the court was 'not extremely accurate' and malleable, this not only opened the case up to individual influence, it also created more space for government-driven politicised changes to the record.[44] Bamu continued that sometimes, during the trial, he would protest against this state of affairs. When he observed that the magistrate stopped writing down his submissions, for instance, he would 'pause a bit from making the submissions and enquire whether they are recording. In some cases, I have requested to be shown the record to see if they are indeed writing.'[45] In this way, he hoped to show that 'the courtroom itself also leaves a lot to be desired'.[46]

Human rights lawyers understood the dilapidated material conditions in Rotten Row's courts within the context of limited financial resources, increased politicisation and declining professionalism in the Zimbabwean judiciary. The failure to start trials on time or to keep accurate records that resulted from the broken clocks and tape recorders, lawyers argued, were not the only expressions of how the authority of the law was undermined through the materiality of the courts.

Human rights lawyers and their clients observed a second, more deliberate shift, in the conditions within the Magistrates' Courts that related specifically to the security measures ZANU-PF took within and around the courthouse. As the material conditions within the courtroom declined, lawyers and activists observed an increased presence of police officers and other state agents such as the CIO officers within and around the courts, particularly during politically motivated trials. I have argued that, for activists, being handcuffed or put in leg irons following their arrest was important as a real and symbolic aspect of their experiences of criminalisation. In this, their journey from the police detention cells to the Magistrates' Courts on Rotten Row also mattered. George described how, following his first arrest in the 2007 petrol-bombing case (discussed in Chapter 4), he was cuffed, loaded

---

[44] In interviews with Jeremiah Bamu, human rights lawyer, Harare, 28 September 2010; and Kucaca Phulu, human rights lawyer, Bulawayo, 29 November 2011.
[45] Interview, Jeremiah Bamu, human rights lawyer, Harare, 28 September 2010.
[46] Ibid.

into an open police truck and taken into court through the secure side entrance (see Figure 5.2, which shows two defendants in leg irons ahead of Hopewell Chin'ono). He was led down 'with prison guards and some members of the police standing by with guns. ... There was very heavy security. It was like I was in a military escort. They tried by all means to create an impression [of me] as a dangerous creature that must always be safely guarded.'[47]

Tafadzwa Mugabe, a human rights lawyer who represented George and the other 'petrol bombers' at the time, recalled that:

every time they would come to court, there would be an armed escort from what is called the Police Support Unit. They would be sixteen. And the guys would come in, escort those guys to the courtroom. And they would establish a perimeter outside the court, inside the court, and at least one of them would always be inside the courtroom with his AK-47. Because they were considered dangerous threats to national security.[48]

The sight of this heavily armed police presence left George feeling 'afraid to come back before court, I thought it was better for me to live in prison. Because it will be very, very terrifying for you to be standing before court, and you also understand that there are armed guards outside the courtroom. ... It's very, very horrible.'[49] Tafadzwa Mugabe expressed that he was also frightened by 'the police, with their guns, and the detective and the intelligence guys'. He continued, however, that 'the court would be packed', as the defence council consisted of five or six lawyers at one time, and the gallery was filled with 'human rights observers'. This, Mugabe explained, created 'an intimidating atmosphere for all concerned'. Even the prosecution and the magistrate were afraid, he explained, because everyone was 'feeling watched'.[50]

This form of intimidation extended onto the benches of the gallery, which were not only filled by defendants, their supporters or members of the public, but also with police officers and CIO agents. Through the inclusion of these state security actors the boundary between the

---

[47] Interview, George, student activist, Harare, 20 July 2010.
[48] Interview, Tafadzwa Mugabe, human rights lawyer, Harare, 18 September 2010.
[49] Interview, George, student activist, Harare, 20 July 2010.
[50] Interview, Tafadzwa Mugabe, human rights lawyer, Harare, 18 September 2010.

'public' and the trial was blurred in a manner that exemplified ZANU-PF's shift away from relying on the authority that upholding the law might accord them in maintaining its control through performances of coercive police power.

Lawyers and activists not only critiqued the material decline of the courtroom but also this shift in state authority when they discussed the sensory conditions they encountered in the courtroom. In particular, lawyers and their clients highlighted the visual, auditory and olfactory dimensions of their courtroom experience. As with its material condition, the sensory experiences of the courtroom created barriers for lawyers to conduct their work in a 'professional', rule-bound manner. In addition, as I show in the following section, the sensory dimensions of the magistrates' courtrooms could be mobilised by ZANU-PF-instructed judicial officials in the government's efforts to intimidate its opposition.

Intimidation in Court: Sensory Reminders of Police Detention and Imprisonment

In human rights lawyers' accounts of their work environment, and in activists' recollections of their trials, both observed the 'normal' intimidating feature of the courtroom, such as the different spatial levels, the separation of its actors and the displays of grandeur. These observations, however, went hand in hand with descriptions of looking into a courtroom filled with the bodies of imposing 'boys in dark glasses' (state intelligence agents), hearing the sounds of police officers yelling and leg irons clanking on concrete, and being affronted by the smell of unwashed bodies. All these sensations reminded lawyers and their clients of police officers' conduct during arrests, the harrowing conditions in the prison and detention cells and the ZANU-PF-led government's ability to expose them to this treatment again at any given time.

On my first visits to the courts in July 2010, the idea of 'feeling watched' quickly came up. Defendants and their supporters frequently talked about how they felt 'the eyes of ZANU-PF' upon them during their trials. Initially I thought they were speaking metaphorically, expressing a sense of being under the constant yet invisible watch of the ruling party. As I spent more time in the courts, however, the notion of surveillance took on more real and recognisable forms. Rather than the imagination of being observed from a remote but ever-watchful centre, as the building's panopticon-like architecture might stir up, the courts' visitors picked up on the consistent and often threatening presence of CIO agents – referred to as the 'boys in dark glasses' – as well as police officers, prison guards, security personnel and plain-clothes police officers among the crowds in the hallways and on the court benches. The presence of these state actors reminded defendants and their lawyers of their previous arrests, their uncomfortable, humiliating and frightening experiences in police detention and remand prison, and the possibility of such experiences being repeated if they failed to behave in a manner the ZANU-PF-led government deemed appropriate.

Such reminders also filtered into the courtroom through the noises coming from just outside it. The police trucks which moved defendants from remand prison into the pretrial detention cells below the courts parked on a ramp between the two courtrooms. Armed police guards led prisoners off the back of the truck into the cells, often in pairs as the prisoners were shackled together around their ankles. The sounds of the prisoners' leg irons hitting the concrete as they walked to the cells, and of the police officers roughly instructing these prisoners, carried into the courtrooms on either side of the gate if the ZRP's trucks arrived while court was in session. Speaking to supporters of defendants in the gallery during political trials, many of them described the noise as a 'harrowing', 'haunting' and 'terrifying' reminder of what they, or their friend or family member, had endured.[51]

For human rights lawyers and their clients, smell was another stark reminder of the 'cruelty' of their treatment in police detention. The impact of the smell prisoners from remand prison gave off was most evident to me on 6 August 2010, when I attended a case that I had followed since early July at the Magistrates' Courts. This was the first time I had sat down on the bench closest to the dock. Just as the trial I had come to observe commenced, a young man was brought in through the door behind the dock. He was in handcuffs and wearing a standard khaki prison outfit of shorts and a shirt. Two guards flanked him. As the man walked in, a strong, unpleasant smell filled the courtroom.

One of the lawyers I had come to court with turned to me, commenting that defendants brought to court from detention or custody

[51] Field notes, observations at Harare's Magistrates' Courts, Harare, 26 July 2010.

often 'smell like they are decaying'. The man, who was accused of robbing a convenience store, had no legal representation. The magistrate nonetheless decided to hear his case first. In my field notes, I described the scene:

The defendant (a man who appeared to be in his early thirties) was asked by magistrate Don Ndirowei why he had been brought to court. He spoke Shona, and explained through the court interpreter that he had been in remand prison for three weeks. He was unclear about the charges against him, but he stated that he would very much like to return home. Magistrate Ndirowei, in turn, stated that he was very busy and could not take the case today. He then remanded the man to another date, two weeks on. The defendant pleaded that the magistrate take the time to hear his case today, but the magistrate firmly reminded him the court was very busy. The guards then urged the man to walk out from the dock to the back of the courtroom. Here, a door led down to the holding cells under the courts, where the man was to wait for the police escort to return him to remand prison. One of the guards forgot to close the door as he came back into the courtroom and took a seat by the dock. In the meantime, magistrate Ndirowei had focused his attention back on the trial he had begun just before the man had come into the court. The prosecutor suddenly interrupted with a loud cough, pulling a face of disgust. The magistrate nodded at him and addressed the police officer seated in front of his bench. He commanded the officer to 'shut the door' behind the dock, and loudly proclaimed to the court that he couldn't 'think with this stench coming into the courtroom'. Once the door was closed, the magistrate returned his attention to the case.[52]

Magistrate Ndirowei appeared able to block out the smell of 'decay' produced by police detention and remand prison simply by shutting a door, and continuing with the case at hand.

Unable to focus on the case, I instead remembered speaking to the former magistrate Sarah just the previous day. Her explanation that, in her work, she often faced the dilemma of sending a defendant to prison because it was 'like punishing a person twice' was suddenly made all too clear.[53] As I showed in Chapter 2, Sarah situated herself as a 'professional' magistrate, working within the rules of the judicial

[52] Field notes, observations trial *E v. State*, Harare's Magistrates' Courts, Harare, 6 August 2010.
[53] Interview, Sarah, former magistrate, Harare, 5 August 2010 and in field notes, observations trial *E v. State*, Harare's Magistrates' Courts, Harare, 6 August 2010.

system to deliver 'substantive justice'. She explained her decisions to
continue to sentence some of the men and women before her to prison
as in line with this duty. She wanted to be sure, however, that she was
making the best possible decision, that is, a 'just' decision. If she had
questions for a defendant during the trial, she did not hesitate to ask
for clarification, especially if the defendant had no legal representation.
She explained:

I have no problems using my prerogative as the court to actually call on that
person and at least try and see where the truth lies. Because we're all fallible,
so each time I think to myself that 'lord, I hope I have never sent an innocent
person to prison', because that is something that i an really weigh heavily on
your conscience.[54]

According to Sarah, some magistrates made mistakes because they
were simply too inexperienced to understand what it meant to remand
defendants into custody. Others, she conceded, had lost interest in
upholding the standard of 'substantive justice' as a result of their
extremely difficult working conditions and poor remuneration.
Human rights lawyers expressed stronger criticism against such behaviour by magistrates. Their working conditions, they argued, should not
be an excuse for magistrates to follow the executive directives pressur-
ing them to return anyone to the horrendous conditions in detention.
The material and sensory conditions in the court, lawyers observed,
were demonstrative not only of limited financial support for the courts,
or of the increased political interference within them. They also
exposed the lengths magistrates and other judicial officials had to go
to in order to 'turn a blind eye' to state excesses of violence and the
cruel conditions of the prisons. In response to this, the lawyers' and
activists' courtroom performances were therefore in part an attempt to
make the magistrates, and the ZANU-PF-led government, 'hear',
'smell' and 'see'.

In the following section I show how, in their interactions with the
defendants in the dock specifically, lawyers worked to turn these
auditory, olfactory and visual reminders of the dilapidated physical
conditions and harrowing abuse in the prison cells and in police
detention to their advantage. Although they were strongly encouraged
not to by the police officers observing them in court, some activists too

[54] Interview, Sarah, former magistrate, Harare, 5 August 2010.

engaged in this strategy when placed in the dock. While police officers and CIO agents were placed within the gallery's benches to 'silently' threaten and intimidate the defendant and their lawyer in politically motivated prosecutions through their presence alone, defence councils often played on their presence to loudly insist on their dissatisfaction with the treatment their clients received in police detention and prison, and during the trial.

Staging Interruptions: Drawing Attention to a 'Broken System'

Of all the architectural trappings within the courtroom, Mulcahy argues that 'the modern dock' in particular 'could be viewed as a brand of incarceration which militates against the presumption of innocence'.[55] The lawyers and activists in the Magistrates' Courts in Harare recognised how the law's violence could be embedded within the courtroom structure, but they used their performances to shift the focus onto the real violence effected by ZANU-PF-instructed state actors. The bodies within the dock, marked by the abuse experienced in police detention, served as 'props' in these performances, which were geared at cultivating a sensory awareness among magistrates, prosecutors and spectators in the gallery of all the signs of the state's abuse of the rule of law.

Such strategies resonate with Victoria Brooks' argument that, by exposing the hidden depths of the court, or by working 'to construct a more sensory courtroom', it is possible to 'interrupt' the potentially violent material and sensory dimensions of the law.[56] For this, she underlines the importance of actor's awareness of 'the potentially sensual affects of space'. In order to cultivate this awareness, 'bodies must be attuned to these affects, that is, these bodies must be able to listen (both to the space and to other bodies)'.[57]

As I have shown, lawyers and their clients were very attuned to the material and sensory conditions in the court. Human rights lawyer Tawanda Zhuwarara's account of being on trial himself demonstrates this most vividly. He not only underlines the powerful and intimidating effect of standing in the dock, but shows how his sensory experiences in that position fuelled his determination to bring the injustices of the

---

[55] Mulcahy, *Legal Architecture*, p. 10.
[56] Brooks, 'Interrupting the Courtroom Organism', p. 11.   [57] Ibid., p. 14.

legal system to light. Alongside other lawyers, and occasionally activists, he sought to raise this awareness among magistrates and prosecutors. He also defied the view of the spectators in the gallery as a 'passive public', portraying them instead as Zimbabwean citizens, charged with communicating to the government, judicial officials and representatives of the state the decay of its judicial system. It was this decay specifically to which the lawyers' performances aimed to attune the public.

Zhuwarara began his career in private practice in 2005 and moved to ZLHR in 2008. He spoke to me about his initial doubts about transferring to work as a human rights lawyer. The long, unpredictable hours he worked, and the constant hostility with which police and prosecutors approached him, raised doubts. Then he was arrested. Zhuwarara was observing a protest organised by the prominent activist group Women of Zimbabwe Arise on 10 February 2009.[58] The police picked him up, and he spent three days in prison before being released on bail. By the time he was brought to court and placed in the dock, he felt 'shell-shocked. Shell-shocked that people live like that [in prison]. Shell-shocked that I am now going through it. Shell-shocked that I am now in court.' Once he was on the other side, he realised the importance of his position at the defence's bench. He recalled:

When you sit down in the accused dock, you can't see anything. It seems silly, but it seems like it's a booming voice from an unknown creature who holds your fate. You can't see anything, it's too high. I nearly asked 'can I be my own defence counsel so I can sit on the bench?' ... It feels like everybody is against you.[59]

Zhuwarara continued that, whereas previously he did not understand why some of his clients hesitated to speak out during their trial, he now understood how much of an 'intimidating space' the courtroom was. 'To tell you the truth, I am a lawyer, and I am one of the feistiest, I would be able to speak till kingdom come, and you know, run rings

---

[58] Interview, Tawanda Zhuwarara, human rights lawyer, Harare, 7 September 2010. He was charged under Section 37 of the Criminal Law (Codification and Reform) Act, for participating in a gathering with the intent to promote public violence. The police further accused Zhuwarara of using his phone to take pictures of the protest.

[59] Interview, Tawanda Zhuwarara, human rights lawyer, Harare, 7 September 2010.

around certain prosecutors. But my spirit was broken by the time that I left the courtroom.'[60]

The three days Zhuwarara spent in detention further affected him in a way that radically heightened his sympathy for his clients, and increased his identification with their plight. It was only by being 'on the wrong side of the bench' that Zhuwarara learned to be fully attuned to the effects of the courtroom. Recalling the 'smell of a human being decaying' that latched on to his clients, for example, he admitted that prior to his own arrest and trial, he kept 'this distance from my clients when I went to visit in person or when I saw them in court'. Then he experienced the shift in physical appearance and smell first hand. 'It was an educating process for me. It gave me a renewed understanding of what it means coming from below the cells. By that time, the suit I was wearing was reeking of human excretion. How that smell latches on to you. I had no idea.' After his own experience, the smell instead served as a reminder to him: 'that was me'. The experience also heightened Zhuwarara's motivation to continue his work. He explained:

I would probably have left this job earlier if I hadn't been arrested. But now I can't, because I need to do something. ... I really need to do something, ... to say the next time when I get arrested, whether it's a driving charge or anything, the conditions must have changed. I should have done something about it.[61]

One way in which Zhuwarara hoped to bring about this change was to ensure that the conditions he endured did not remain invisible. He felt that, given the conditions the prison and police cells were in, it was 'nonsensical ... for the judiciary to apply the normal hard and fast rules without taking into consideration what an individual has gone through ... outside the courts'. Here, the smell defendants brought into the courtroom was not only an unpleasant reminder, it was evidence that 'in Zimbabwe, we operate a collapsed system'. Zhuwarara continued that 'the stench' that attached itself to his clients allowed them to 'carry that part of the prison right into the courtroom'. The smell 'literally means I didn't bathe for the odd three days', but was further symbolic as 'that's very dehumanising, very embarrassing. And for a man, it means, I'm unclean. But it also means that I've been eating in

[60] Ibid.   [61] Ibid.

those conditions, it also means that I've been sleeping in those conditions.'[62]

How, Zhuwarara asked, could a professional and conscionable magistrate just ignore this? A magistrates' silence, he continued, was not only illustrative of the way 'the courts have become numb', but further exemplified that the role of the courts in Zimbabwe was not to uphold justice, but rather to intimidate and restrain ZANU-PF's political opposition. The court process 'endorsed the true injustice happening outside it ... by making it appear that everything is fine'. It was this 'legal fiction' that he, as a human rights lawyer, would have to fight against. One important way to do this, he explained, was by drawing attention to the very ways in which the excess violence of this system materialised itself in the courtroom, and not to remain silent about them.[63]

Alec Muchadehama, a prominent human rights lawyer, took a similar position, arguing that when presenting his case in court he would 'concentrate on the violations, and the evilness of how the state is conducting themselves'.[64] In order to 'expose these violations' and 'put them on record', he would draw attention to his clients' appearance as they were sitting in the dock. His clients, Muchadehama explained, were 'there as the objects for my messaging', as any bruise 'even if it is only a small bruise' represented 'an opportunity which the police have created that they have to regret'. Playing on the presence of police officers and CIO agents, Muchadehama took the opportunity to turn the 'eyes of the state' that meant to intimidate him and his clients back onto its own civil servants. He would:

stand and say 'so and so has assaulted my client, there is my client, look at his eyes, they are hurt'. ... I stand in court, just to make sure it's on the record. Because I know that all the police officers are there, the CIO, they are there. And they are taking notes. They know what I'm saying.[65]

For Muchadehama, performances that called attention to the bruised bodies of his clients in the courtroom served two purposes. First, he aimed 'to deter them [police officers] from violating people's rights. And not to unlawfully arrest people, and not to torture people when they are in their custody. I will not necessarily be doing it for my client,

---

[62] Ibid.   [63] Ibid.
[64] Interview, Alec Muchadehama, human rights lawyer, Harare, 12 January 2012.
[65] Ibid.

but for the future conduct of the police.' Second, he felt that his performances could educate the general Zimbabwean public that the way ZANU-PF used legal processes to 'punish people' and to 'take people through the mud of a trial' was 'totally unacceptable' and 'wrong'.[66]

Tafadzwa Mugabe also argued that he would take any opportunity to be 'the one to make the complaints' about the way his clients appeared in court, constantly drawing the magistrates' and the audience's attention to the 'accused persons, who look clearly battered, hungry, unfed and ill-treated'.[67] Mugabe believed that 'it takes people who work with the system to interrogate those issues and expose them'. Once they were 'standing in the dock', therefore, he would ask his clients to point out the arresting officer and 'say "you arrested me, but in the process you beat me up"', as this allowed him to build 'a public record, a court record that makes a finding of the fact that this was the nature of the arrest'.[68]

His complaints on record were 'grounds for a claim for damages for unlawful assault, unlawful arrest'. These records could therefore be 'very very damning on the police. Because if they have to come and testify, or go through those full-blown trials, some of their tactics are exposed. And it doesn't really bode well for people who are saying that "no, we do everything properly".'[69] Tafadzwa Mugabe emphasised that, as a human rights lawyer, he further felt responsible for using his clients' bodies to draw attention to the facts that were often silenced by the police officers and magistrates. He emphasised that often his clients would be warned by the police not to make a complaint. He also placed responsibility with the magistrate, and was 'very disappointed' that he had 'never come across a case where a magistrate says that "I am taking judicial notice of the fact that you are saying you are not assaulted but your t-shirt is bloodied, therefore I want to find out exactly what happened"'.[70]

Not all magistrates, however, shied away from asking about the bruised bodies of the defendants in their dock. George recalled that, on his first court appearance, it was the magistrate who drew attention to the scars he 'sustained from beatings in police custody'. Once the

---

[66] Ibid.
[67] Interview, Tafadzwa Mugabe, human rights lawyer, Harare, 18 September 2010.
[68] Ibid.   [69] Ibid.   [70] Ibid.

magistrate did this, George felt able to say 'I was beaten by a police officer'. The prosecutor contradicted him, saying 'it had been brought to my attention, my lord, that these scars were sustained by the suspect when he was trying to run away from the scene'. Once again gathering his courage, George spoke to the magistrate: 'No, I was beaten, ask them.' Making use of the presence of the offending police officers in the courtroom, he gestured to them. Just as these police officers had humiliated George for his young age and 'boyish' appearance in detention, a tactic that reminded him that in his efforts to claim 'full' citizenship he would never be a 'man', the prosecutor deployed a similar approach in court. Pointing to his messy, uncombed hair the prosecutor asked George how he could know anything for sure with such an 'unruly', 'youthful' hairstyle. Again, George responded, 'I was arrested two weeks ago. At the time I was arrested, my hair was combed. But now it is no longer combed because of the conditions I have been living in.'

Although the space to speak up from the dock was limited, George explained that this experience strengthened his belief in the importance of taking every opportunity he had in court to call attention to the state's failings through his bodily appearance. The fact that the court appeared able to ignore defendants appearing with 'swollen feet, swollen buttocks, sometimes bruises on their faces, … serious scars, and sometimes with bloodstains on their clothes' not only meant they were not doing their jobs correctly. For George, it also sent a very strong message to the Zimbabwean public that not he, but his government was the 'criminal' in these cases. From the dock, George thus hoped to embody his political narrative to educate his peers, showing them that:

Every member of our nation, every citizen should be knowing and understanding that the struggle that we are engaging in is not a struggle to prove personal oppositions, or to disprove certain personalities, but it is a struggle to entrench a culture of democracy in the country and in the nation. This can only be reliable when the nation, the state, its security apparatus, all citizens are able to understand and recognise the sanctity of human rights and of the rule of law. And we are in an environment where the members of the justice system deliberately do not want to acknowledge that we are not in a democracy. … But we hope that the judges would get to understand that what we are engaged in [we do] because we are trying to fight to inculcate a culture of democracy, not a culture of fighting the government.[71]

---

[71] Interview, George, student activist, Harare, 9 September 2010.

In their performances, human rights lawyers, and at times their clients, played upon the visual, auditory and olfactory senses that reminded the judicial officials and the public observing their performances of the ways the 'collapsed system' of the prisons and police detention cells filtered into the courtroom. Rather than being allowed to 'turn a blind eye', magistrates, prosecutors and the audience in court all had to confront the defendants' 'bruised bodies' and the 'smell of decay' that accompanied them into the dock. Lawyers hoped that those responsible for creating these conditions, from the police officers who beat the defendants' bodies to the members of the ZANU-PF-led government who facilitated the shifting of state authority away from 'professional' rule-bound institutions able to deliver 'justice' to overt displays of coercive power, would face legal repercussions, with their actions captured on the permanent record. More importantly, by selectively attuning those present in the courtroom to the material and sensory dimensions that exposed the state's defects in court, lawyers and activists sought to inculcate the 'culture of democracy' with its commitment to human rights and the rule of law among judicial actors specifically and the Zimbabwean public more generally, and to shift the burden of 'criminality' from the defendants to the state officials instead.

Conclusion

In their architectural design, courthouses and courtrooms awe and impose, communicating the authority of the law and the power of the state. Courts are built to ensure the segregation of the different actors, with distinct 'routes of circulation' separating the potential 'criminals' from the 'citizens', raised platforms marking the magistrates as the arbiters of justice, and sequences of rituals that create a 'validating public'.[72] Yet courts also contain 'hidden spaces', and are filled with material and sensory dimensions that, if actors are attuned to them, reveal such design as a façade, covering up the violence of law.[73] When discussing the material and sensory attributes of the

---

[72] Eltringham, 'Spectators to the Spectacle of Law'; Hanson, 'The Architecture of Justice'; and Mulcahy, *Legal Architecture*.
[73] Brooks, 'Interrupting the Courtroom Organism'.

Magistrates' Courts at Rotten Row, human rights lawyers and activists predominantly drew attention not to typical displays of authority and power in the courtroom, but to how such displays, and the segregation of space they entailed, were inverted and undermined.

In this, the dilapidated material structures of the courts themselves, and the sensory infiltration of the violent, abusive conditions in police detention and prison, served as critical evidence. The broken clocks and tape recorders were read as signs of the ZANU-PF-led government's loss of respect for the rule of law as they threatened the lawyers' ability to hold magistrates accountable, to safeguard the courts from corruption and to perform their crucial speech acts in full force. The visual, olfactory and auditory reminders of the harrowing physical conditions and violent treatment in police detention – aimed at intimidating the lawyers and their clients – were turned against the state with the help of activists' smelly and bruised bodies when they were in the dock. In addition to uncovering the violence of the law, these actors worked to lay bare the 'totally unacceptable'[74] state-perpetrated violence on the bodies and minds of ZANU-PF's political opposition.

To stage these performances, lawyers and activists relied on more than the material and sensory dimensions of the courts, and on their bodies as props within them. In their attempts to attune judicial actors and Zimbabwean citizens to the cruelty of their government, activists and their lawyers also relied on their scripts and demeanour. In Chapter 6, I turn to the scripts of the prosecution and the defence council in more detail to interrogate how human rights lawyers and activists were cast, and challenged their casting, as criminals 'fighting against the government'.[75]

---

[74] Interview, Alec Muchadehama, human rights lawyer, Harare, 12 January 2012.
[75] Interview, George, student activist, Harare, 9 September 2010.

6 | The Trials of the 'Traitor' in Harare's Magistrates' Courts under the Unity Government

The political trial itself reconstructs and rewrites events as they are perceived by the government, and reproduces for the public the image of a just society threatened by people and organisations who seek its violent destruction, thereby serving to justify actions taken by the state against political opponents. ... It was in the political trial most obviously that individual pain was converted into state power on the basis of the multiple rewritings of the state.[1]

On 30 January 2012, I observed the cross-examination of Jonathan Shoko, a policeman and key state witness in what the independent media commonly referred to as 'the Gwisai trial'. The trial took place in courtroom 18 in the Regional Magistrates' Courts in Harare. The courtroom, located on the upper floor of the courthouse, was sun-lit and very dusty. Behind magistrate Kudakwashe Jarabini's bench the wall had been stained by water. Like most clocks in the court, the clock on the opposite wall remained stuck at 7:10. To the left of the magistrate, Munyaradzi Gwisai and five other defendants were seated in the dock as the witness took the stand on the right. While the defendants were barely visible behind the high bars of the dock, Jonathan Shoko towered over the witness stand, cutting an imposing figure in his brown suit.

In front of the bench, facing the gallery, a woman was changing tapes in one of the few working tape recorders in the courtroom. Next to her, a policewoman in uniform was reading a worn novel, waiting for the trial to start. Facing the magistrate, Alec Muchadehama, the main defence lawyer, stood next to state prosecutor Michael Reza,[2]

---

[1] Paul Gready, 'Autobiography and the "Power of Writing": Political Prison Writing in the Apartheid Era', *Journal of Southern African Studies*, 19, 3, 1993, p. 498.

[2] Michael Reza was working together with Edmore Nyazamba, who acted as the main prosecutor on the case during the early stages of the trial. Nyazamba was named Prosecutor of the Year in 2011, while Reza worked on several other

who was occupying the only chair. A female interpreter was perched on a high stool next to the witness stand, and on top of a table behind her sat two female court reporters. During the proceedings, which lasted from 9.30 a.m. to 4.45 p.m., they occasionally passed notes to the prosecutor. Muchadehama explained that while these notes could contain questions about the trial proceedings, it was more likely that they were informal and mocking comments about the trial instead.[3] In the gallery, the three benches were tightly packed, filled mostly with family, friends and co-workers of the six defendants. On the front bench, two men in suits and sunglasses, a trademark of officers from the CIO, joked with the witness and prosecutor before the trial kicked off. A man seated next to me in the gallery pointed the two men out as 'men from the President's Office', the commonly used expression for CIO members.[4]

That morning, Alec Muchadehama asked Jonathan Shoko to explain the reasons for arresting the five men and one woman who were now in the dock. Shoko repeated the state's main line of argument that, while attending a meeting at the Zimbabwe Labour Centre almost a year previously in February 2011, he had signalled for the police via text message to carry out an arrest because he felt the participants at the meeting were threatening to organise 'Egypt-style' anti-government protests. Shoko continued:

I think accused number 5 [Hopewell Gumbo – programme officer at Zimbabwe Coalition on Debt and Development and a former student activist] was the first to mention the Africa Unity Square [a park in central Harare], but I can't remember. I had to send a text message to my superiors because the meeting was getting interesting … Accused number one [Munyaradzi Gwisai] said that the choice was socialism, there was a need to change the current regime of capitalism … This was the move to a socialist state, with equal distribution of wealth. People were to gather at Africa Unity Square on the 1st March secretly, undetected by police forces and from there they would start a revolution. I then texted my superiors that

    high-profile trials in court at this time, such as the Glen View case in which 31 MDC activists stood accused of murdering a police officer in May 2011.

[3] Field notes, informal discussion with Alec Muchadehama on Gwisai trail, Harare, 30 January 2012.

[4] Field notes, trial of Gwisai and five others, courtroom 18 Rotten Row, Harare, 30 January 2012.

it was an opportune time to pounce as a conspiracy to overthrow the constitutionally elected government has been committed.[5]

At this point during the trial, which had started in September 2011 and would run until March 2012, the charge against the six defendants in the dock had been changed twice, first from treason to subverting a constitutional government, and then to conspiracy to incite public violence.[6] In building their case, both the state prosecutors and their key witness focused on a combination of these charges, aiming to prove the intention of the defendants to 'overthrow the constitutionally elected government' through violent protests and demonstrations.

In this chapter, I place this trial in its historical and political context in order to examine the significance both of the methods by which the state presented its case and of the content of the case. I argue that the state's courtroom performances during the Gwisai trial turned the prosecutors' bench and witness stand (rather than the dock) into platforms or pulpits. From the bench and the witness stand, ZANU-PF could articulate the forms of political expression it deemed acceptable under the GNU, the coalition government formed with the two MDC factions following ZANU-PF's parliamentary defeat in the March 2008 elections and the violent presidential re-elections in which then President Robert Mugabe ran unopposed. In Chapter 5, I illustrated that from their position in the dock the defendants and their lawyers drew the attention of the magistrate, prosecution and spectators in court and in the media to the inhumane and degrading treatment they experienced at the hands of the police prior to arriving in the court, to the dilapidated conditions of the courts themselves and to the haphazard and seemingly improvised way in which the state conducted its trials. The techniques the human rights lawyers and their clients relied upon to convey these messages were not only narrative, they also asked their audience to apply all their senses by highlighting the visual and olfactory evidence of their claims. In contrast, as I show below, the state's techniques were highly narrative and relied heavily

---

[5] Field notes, trial of Gwisai and five others, courtroom 18 Rotten Row, Harare, 30 January 2012.

[6] In the Criminal Law (Codification and Reform) Act, treason falls under Section 20, subverting under Section 22 and public violence under Section 36. The first two are crimes against the state, punishable by death or life imprisonment in the case of treason, and a maximum of twenty years in prison for subverting. The last is a crime against public order where the maximum prison sentence is ten years.

on one actor, star witness Jonathan Shoko. These techniques reflect ZANU-PF's shift away from conveying state authority through the material dignity of the courtroom and the law to the party's efforts to legitimise its rule by relying on a select group of actors willing and able to perform a singular historical and political narrative. Through Shoko's narrative, the prosecution focused the trial around the question of whether the defendants sought to overthrow the government, emphasising their alleged intentions to oust President Mugabe. By these means, the activists were cast as a destabilising political force, threatening the safety and security of the Zimbabwean nation and its citizens.

The GNU and the Arab Spring

As Jonathan Shoko recalled, the six defendants in the Gwisai trial were arrested in February 2011, two years after the GNU was formed. Following the contested elections of 2008, and the incorporation of the two MDC factions into the country's government through the formation of the GNU, ZANU-PF was no longer synonymous with 'the government'. The party further felt vulnerable against the backdrop of the Arab Spring uprisings and discussions of the GNU's potential to create spaces for serious political reform. Despite MDC members, non-governmental organisations and political observers' speculations that the newly formed coalition government would unsettle the conflation of ZANU-PF as a political party with the Zimbabwean state, and so open up spaces of accountability, the party continued to use key state institutions to intimidate and coerce the political opposition.

ZANU-PF's sustained efforts to limit space for critical political expression intensified around December of 2010, as uprisings in Tunisia sparked waves of protests across North Africa and the Middle East. These protests, also referred to as the Arab Spring, lasted until February 2012 and were characterised by demonstrations, rallies, strikes and marches, as well as an effective use of social media as a tool of political mobilisation. Following the uprisings, Tunisia, Libya, Egypt and Yemen all installed new governments. ZANU-PF was quick to express its position on these developments. The party threatened MDC-T leader and prime minister, Morgan Tsvangirai, with arrest for expressing support for the uprisings, while taking the opportunity to assert its commitment to protecting the Zimbabwean nation from foreign interference, and publicly expressing its disapproval of any demonstrations and public gatherings that aligned themselves with the 'Western' and 'imperialist' views of the MDC and its supporters.[7]

In January 2011, for instance, the state-owned daily *The Herald* quoted Professor Jonathan Moyo's articulate comparison of the North African demonstrators, not the disputed rulers, to ZANU-PF's leaders. We met Professor Moyo in the Introduction and Chapter 1, who in his capacity as ZANU-PF minister of information and publicity critiqued members of the judiciary and legal profession, such as Justice Michael Gillespie or Sternford Moyo of the Law Society of Zimbabwe, as unpatriotic 'racists'. After 2005, Professor Moyo had run as an independent MP in Tsholotsho district, but by 2011 he was reviving his connections to ZANU-PF. Moyo explained the Arab Spring as a revolt against 'puppet governments', the type of government against which the party sought to protect Zimbabwe. He elaborated:

The leadership in Egypt, Tunisia and Yemen are perceived by its citizens to be American puppets. What is significant about developments in the Middle East is that the protests are essentially anti-American and anti-West and therefore anti-imperialism and anti-neo-colonialism … It is the type of popular anger that we would most certainly have here in Zimbabwe should our country suffer the misfortune of falling into the hands of a puppet MDC-T under massive handholding by the US administration.[8]

Anticipating the parallels that could be drawn between then President Mugabe and the disputed rulers, Professor Moyo suggested that rather than being as a response to ZANU-PF's governance, civil uprisings would result from the MDC's rule.

Later the same month, an independent daily, the *Zimbabwe Independent*, did indeed run an analysis which critiqued President Mugabe by drawing a parallel to Hosni Mubarak. They observed that 'following the oust[ing] of Egyptian leader Hosni Mubarak, many Zimbabweans are of the view that the ejected head of state and his Zimbabwean counterpart, President Robert Mugabe, are mirror

[7] Solidarity Peace Trust (SPT), *The Hard Road to Reform* (Durban, SPT, April 2011).
[8] 'Tsvangirai's Utterances Expose Penchant for Violence', *The Herald*, 31 January 2011, accessed on 3 July 2011 at www.herald.co.zw/tsvangirais-utterances-expose-penchant-for-violence-analysts/.

images of each other'. The article particularly drew attention to the 'uncanny similarities between the two in terms of their policies, time in office and relations with Western countries'.[9] Unlike Professor Moyo, other members of ZANU-PF also picked up on this potential parallel, but framed it as one around which Zimbabwean citizens might (unwisely) be motivated to organise their own demonstrations. Speaking at a military function honouring retiring army officers in Harare in February 2011, then ZANU-PF defence minister, Emmerson Mnangagwa, bluntly warned that 'those who may want to emulate what happened in Egypt and Tunisia will regret'.[10] In March 2011, Mnangagwa further reminded Zimbabweans that 'Mugabe will continue to rule this country. Nobody will stop him, even if the GPA collapses he will continue ruling. Zimbabweans you are actually lucky to have a brave man like him.'[11]

Numerous other media outlets reinforced the message that those who might attempt to oust ZANU-PF would come to 'regret' their actions. In early February 2011, the government-run Zimbabwe Broadcasting Corporation reported that MDC-T supporters were planning violent demonstrations in Harare, but that 'the moves were thwarted by alert law enforcement agents'. The article quoted ZRP's Senior Assistant Commissioner Clement Munoriyarwa in Harare describing the MDC-T's plans as 'wishful thinking. The situation in Egypt will never be tolerated anywhere in Zimbabwe.' He continued: 'people have the right to originate opinion, but as police we are not going to allow that. We want to assure the nation that we are fully prepared for such violent activities and our officers are already on the ground to ensure peace and tranquillity prevails in the country.'[12] As 'Zanu PF began a clampdown on any attempts to organize Egypt style

---

[9] Leonard Makombe, 'Mubarak, Mugabe Regimes: So Many Parallels to Draw', *Zimbabwe Independent*, 25 February 2011, accessed on 25 August 2015 at http://allafrica.com.

[10] 'Demonstrations in Zimbabwe Will Be Crushed: Mnangagwa', *RadioVOP*, 7 February 2011, accessed on 3 July 2011 at www.radiovop.com/index.php/national-news/5463-demostrations-in-zimbabwe-will-be-crushed-mnangagwa .html.

[11] Pindai Dube, 'Mugabe Will Rule Zimbabwe Forever: Mnangagwa', *Daily News*, 25 March 2011, accessed on 26 August 2015 at www.kutabana.net.

[12] 'MDC-T Violence Threats a Fantasy: ZRP', *Zimbabwe Broadcasting Corporation*, 3 February 2011, accessed on 3 July 2011 at www.zbc.co.zw.

demonstrations',[13] the case of Munyaradzi Gwisai and his five co-defendants in particular stood as an example of how the party would respond. The first clear signal came from the police response to the group, which resulted in their dramatic arrest.

On 19 February 2011, forty-five students, civil society members and human rights activists were arrested at the offices of the Zimbabwe Labour Centre (ZLC), in Cross Roads House in downtown Harare. They were arrested for attending a gathering during which a video was shown with recordings of the uprisings in Tunisia and Egypt. The footage, which had also been aired on government-run Zimbabwe Television, was screened to fill the time, and to focus the discussion on the lessons learned from the uprisings. The gathering was also organised to commemorate the death of Navigator Mungoni, an HIV/AIDS activist. The audience at the meeting included many HIV/AIDS activists, who attended 'because they were HIV+ rather than because they were regular members of the International Socialist Organisation', the allegation made against all forty-five attendees when the group first arrived at the courts.[14] Eddson Chakuma, a man in his mid-thirties, was one of the more regular members of the ISO-Z, as he sought to continue his education through the organisation. Chakuma was working at the United Food and Allied Workers' Union when he attended the meeting. He explained that when the police came, he felt 'very very, very frightened', both for his own safety, as he 'had heard of cases [where] people can actually disappear', and for the impact of his possible arrest on his family.[15]

I interviewed Chakuma in Cross Roads House where the arrests were carried out. He described how the police came 'in the middle of that meeting ... and surrounded this building and they parked their cars there, then they actually pounced on us, just like that'.[16] As we walked up the building's main staircase to the Zimbabwe Labour Centre offices, Chakuma recalled that the police operation had been chaotic, pointing to offices on other floors not affiliated with the ZLC

---

[13] SPT, *The Hard Road to Reform*, p. 12.
[14] 'State v Munyaradzi Gwisai and others: Application for Discharge – Court Watch 2/2012', 2 February 2012, *VERITAS*, accessed on 6 April 2012 at http://archive.kubatana.net/html/archive/legisl/120202veritas.asp?sector=legisl&year=2013&range_start=121.
[15] Interview, Eddson Chakuma, labour activist, Harare, 18 January 2012.
[16] Ibid.

and commenting, 'the police just dragged people from these offices as they left with us'.[17] A few months after the arrest, in April 2011, *Question Time*, a programme hosted by a London-based independent media outlet, SW Radio Africa, interviewed Munyaradzi Gwisai, who recalled his arrest as 'a *bamba zonke* [a Shona expression meaning 'grab the lot' or 'take all'] exercise where any and everyone who was in the complex at Cross Roads House was picked up and arrested'.[18]

Munyaradzi Gwisai led the meeting on 19 February, as he was the coordinator of the ISO-Z. In 1999, the ISO-Z had joined forces with the MDC after successfully assisting in the organisation of workers' strikes in the run-up to the party's formation. In 2000, Peter Alexander commented that this connection spoke of the breadth of the MDC's support, describing the ISO-Z as 'a small, but well-rooted, trotskyist pressure group, led by Munyaradzi Gwisai, now an MP'.[19] Indeed, in the 2000 elections Gwisai won a seat as MDC MP for Highfield, Harare. He was expelled from the party in 2002, however, following his criticism of the MDC's lack of a radical position on questions of land reform and the dismantling of class-based hierarchies both in the country and within the MDC's leadership structures, which Gwisai argued were dominated by 'the elite and the rich'.[20]

Although no longer an MDC member at the time of his arrest, Gwisai remained an active and influential figure in civil society, especially in the networks he built up as a student in the 1990s and maintained as a practising lawyer and a labour law lecturer at the University of Zimbabwe. As a university student, Gwisai had been elected general secretary for the ZINASU, at the time when MDC-T minister of finance within the GNU, Tendai Biti, was ZINASU president. As a law lecturer, Gwisai continued to be involved with the

[17] Field notes, reflections on interview Eddson Chakuma, Harare, 18 January 2012.
[18] Lance Guma, 'Munyaradzi Gwisai on Question Time: Part 1', *SW Radio Africa*, 20 April 2011, accessed on 2 July 2012 at http://thezimbabwean.co/2011/04/munyaradzi-gwisai-on-question-time-part-1/.
[19] Peter Alexander, 'Zimbabwean Workers, the MDC and the 2000 Election', *Review of African Political Economy*, 27, 85, 2000, p. 385.
[20] Zvakanyorwa Wilbert Sadomba, *War Veterans in Zimbabwe's Revolution: Challenging Neo-colonialism and Settler and International Capital* (Oxford, James Currey, 2011), p. 168.

ISO-Z, and to 'play a vital role in the formation of student activists'.[21] One of the other defendants in the case, Hopewell Gumbo, became more involved with student activism through his acquaintance with Gwisai. He observed that it was precisely because of Gwisai's and the ISO-Z's political presence that the police responded to their meeting with such force. He explained:

This issue about the uprisings was being discussed everywhere, in pubs and so forth. And this is precisely the reason why the ISO was targeted, the state is also aware of the capacity of the ISO to organise and mobilise. I mean, of all the social forces around in the country, they are ideologically well-placed. [ZANU-PF] are aware of the history of the ISO in the mid-1990's strikes and even in the formation of the MDC, the crucial role it played in terms of mobilisation and so forth. And I think if any intelligence officer is sharp, then they're aware of it and they would want to keep us at bay. They would not even want us to be part of the new and latest issues. ... I'm sure they're aware of the capacity to organise people in that respect ... these are trained activists who conceptualise and actually undertake activities in that respect.[22]

Despite the influential position of the ISO-Z and the potential dangers associated with discussing the Arab Spring uprisings, Gumbo initially thought his arrest was just a straightforward scare tactic on the part of ZANU-PF. As seen in Chapter 4, the ZRP picked up young, black, urban-based pro-democracy activists with such regularity that spending an extremely uncomfortable night in the cells became 'normal' for many. Under the GNU these tactics, aimed at deterring activists from gathering, and thus potentially organising a demonstration, remained unchanged as ZANU-PF kept its hold over members of the riot squad and the Law and Order division within the police forces. In February, the month Gumbo was arrested, the ZLHR was asked to assist with between two to five cases of arrest every day.[23] As the Solidarity Peace Trust (SPT) notes, these arrests were 'often followed by release the same day or within a day or two'.[24]

When the police turned up at Cross Roads House during the meeting, Gumbo thus 'thought it was just another of these routine things

[21] Leo Zeilig, '"Increasing My Value Proposition to the Struggle": Arthur Mutambara and Student Politics in Zimbabwe', *African Sociological Review*, 10, 2, 2006, p. 108.
[22] Interview, Hopewell Gumbo, student activist, Harare, 29 September 2015.
[23] SPT, *The Hard Road to Reform*, p. 28.   [24] Ibid., p. 23.

they do, bundle up activists, take them to the police station, beat them up, and release them without charge or charge them with some flimsy kind of thing'.[25] Gumbo quickly changed his perspective, however, owing to his treatment when he arrived in police detention. The SPT reported that in detention the group was 'denied access both to their lawyers, and to medical care despite clearly having been tortured and showing difficulty walking'.[26] Alec Muchadehama explained that he and his fellow human rights lawyers also rapidly realised that this was a 'special case', a 'politically motivated case', and they acted accordingly. The day after the arrests, for example, Muchadehama had gone 'to take instructions from the clients, and to deal with the police in terms of having them recording statements and so on', together with several other human rights lawyers, 'working as a team … for security reasons, so that none of us is unduly exposed … if one person stands out alone, then they tend to focus on that particular lawyer and try to put pressure on them, including harassing them and arresting them'.[27]

Despite this tactic, the lawyers still 'met with stiff resistance and verbal insults'.[28] Eventually they were able to meet the full group of forty-five defendants for two hours, during which the lawyers were informed that approximately six people had been tortured.[29] As discussed in Chapter 4, activists arrested by ZANU-PF experienced degrading and inhumane treatment at the hands of ZRP. Members of the group arrested with Gwisai were also targets of this treatment. ZLHR consequently reported that some of the accused were 'unlawfully removed from the cells in batches on the first two nights of their detention by people who were not from the CID [Criminal Investigations Department] Law and Order Section for "interrogation" during which they were severely beaten'.[30] Eddson Chakuma

[25] Interview, Hopewell Gumbo, student activist, Harare, 29 September 2015.
[26] SPT, *The Hard Road to Reform*, p. 26.
[27] Interview, Alec Muchadehama, human rights lawyer, Harare, 12 January 2012.
[28] ZLHR, 'Labour Activist Gwisai and 45 Others Languish in Police Custody as Artists Freed on Summons', *ZLHR News*, 21 February 2011, accessed on 7 January 2012 at http://thezimbabwean.co/2011/02/labour-activist-gwisai-and-45-others-languish-in-police-custody-as-artists-freed-on-summons/.
[29] ZLHR, 'Labour Activist Gwisai and 45 Others Languish in Police Custody'.
[30] ZLHR, 'Unidentified People Interrogate Activists as They Remain in Custody', *ZLHR News*, 22 February 2011, accessed on 7 January 2012 at http://archive.kubatana.net/html/archive/hr/110222zlhr.asp?sector=DEMGG&year=2011&range_start=1111.

recalled that the police targeted him and his five co-defendants specifically for these beatings after Jonathan Shoko, the 'policeman who … actually had infiltrated the meeting … pointed at almost six people who had actually addressed the meeting. So that was when we were actually beaten with sticks and brooms [pause] and open fists. And after that we were denied food, sometimes and we were denied medication.'[31]

The six defendants singled out by Shoko first appeared in Harare's Magistrates' Courts on 23 February, alongside the thirty-nine other activists arrested at the meeting. Shortly before the hearing Alec Muchadehama was 'surprised' by the prosecutor, who informed him that his clients would be charged with treason under Section 20 of the Criminal Law (Codification and Reform) Act. Eddson Chakuma explained that the police had struggled to decide on what to charge the group with, recounting that he saw the police 'throwing all sorts of charges around, they didn't know actually what to do'. The decision to charge them with treason, however, still 'shocked' Chakuma, and he understood this to be the first indication that their case would be handled by the 'good boys' of the attorney general's office: 'the prosecutors who act on behalf of the state, who can do what they want to do'.[32] Hopewell Gumbo recalled that this change in the charges was both 'funny', as in his eyes it was a clear indication that 'the state did not have their house in order' to present a well-substantiated and carefully prepared case and therefore decided on an absurd charge to shock and scare them as much as possible, and 'traumatic', as it signalled to him and his co-defendants that 'we should be preparing ourselves for a long haul in prison'.[33]

Following the prosecution's decision to charge the defendants with treason, magistrate Munamato Mutevedzi, who was presiding over the remand hearing, postponed the case for a day to allow the defence to prepare for the new charge. When the case continued, Alec Muchadehama drew attention to the conditions his clients experienced in police detention and asked magistrate Mutevedzi to release his clients from remand. Facilitated by Muchadehama, Munyaradzi Gwisai engaged in a public performance, much like those of his fellow

---

[31] Interview, Eddson Chakuma, labour activist, Harare, 18 January 2012.
[32] Ibid. See also, Chapter 2.
[33] Interview, Hopewell Gumbo, student activist, Harare, 29 September 2015.

The Trials of the 'Traitor'

activists discussed in Chapter 5, which connected his experience in police detention to his physical appearance in the courtroom. From the dock, Gwisai gave vivid evidence of the torture he and his fellow detainees endured. The *Legal Monitor*, ZLHR's weekly newsletter, observed how 'the University of Zimbabwe law lecturer [was] battling to sit and walk because of the torture sessions', and described Gwisai's speech from the dock as a 'tear-rending narration', which 'reminded Zimbabweans of the horrendous experience that many other activists before him went through at the hands of state security agents'.[34] Also reporting on the hearing, the ISO too focused on Gwisai's detailed narrative of his ordeal:

The court was told that they [six of the defendants] were individually taken to the basement where they were beaten by the police officers or those who were working with them. They were beaten under the feet, buttocks and all over the body using broomsticks, metal rods, wood pieces, open hands and other blunt objects.[35]

Positioning himself as one of the 'rebels' within the judiciary, magistrate Mutevedzi, who had a record of critiquing the violent conduct of police officers in detention, and of the prosecutions' inability or unwillingness to comply with legal procedures inside his courtroom,[36] stated that the torture sessions were 'indescribable, sadistic and a tragedy for Zimbabwe'.[37] When the group was brought to the court on 7 March 2011, magistrate Mutevedzi also acknowledged the ramshackle nature of the arrest. He commented that the police had orchestrated a 'dragnet

---

[34] ZLHR, *The Legal Monitor*, edition 82, 28 February 2011, accessed on 3 July 2012 at http://archive.kubatana.net/docs/hr/zlhr_legal_monitor_issue_82_110228.pdf.

[35] ISO(Z), 'Update on Arrests and Detention', *ISO(Z)*, 24 February 2011, accessed on 2 July 2011 at www.kutabana.net.

[36] See, for example, his warning to the police in a case involving two employees of Gays and Lesbians in Zimbabwe (GALZ) that they should not be tortured or mistreated in custody (in interviews with Ellen Chademana, GALZ employee, Harare, 25 July 2010 and David Hofisi, human rights lawyer, Harare, 12 August 2010) or his 'berating' of the prosecutor who attempted to try Alec Muchadehama's contempt of court case in 2009 on a subpoena rather than a summons: in ZLHR, *The Legal Monitor*, edition 13, 21 September 2009.

[37] ZLHR, 'Gwisai Bemoans Torture as Muchadehama Challenges Placement of Activists on Remand', *ZLHR News*, 24 February 2011, accessed on 3 July 2012 at http://archive.kubatana.net/html/archive/hr/110224zlhr.asp?sector=DEMGG&year=2011&range_start=1111; ZLHR, *The Legal Monitor*, edition 82.

arrest', failing to identify or verify on what grounds they were carrying out the arrest of each individual defendant.[38] Following this line of argument, he released thirty-nine people on the grounds that there was no reasonable suspicion they had committed the alleged offence of treason. Alec Muchadehama commented that magistrate Mutevedzi's decision was convenient as the lawyers 'were only left with about six people to deal with in terms of the actual trial'. It was also 'quite brave', because it was evident to him that ZANU-PF was interfering in the case, and by criticising the police and the state's conduct the magistrate risked becoming a target of such harassment and intimidation himself. The Gwisai trial, Muchadehama observed, was 'not dealt with in a normal way … in terms of the law and the procedures with which those cases are supposed to be dealt with, but they are given some form of special treatment [with the state putting] the presiding magistrates under some form of pressure'.[39]

Under this pressure, magistrate Mutevedzi's 'rebellious' behaviour was restricted to his 'brave' decision to release the majority of the defendants, because he ruled that the six remaining individuals should return to police custody. Among those further detained were Munyaradzi Gwisai, Hopewell Gumbo and Eddson Chakuma. Magistrate Mutevedzi also ruled that Tatenda Mombeyarara, advocacy officer at the ZLC, and Welcome Zimuto, a former ZINASU leader, had a case to answer. In addition to these five men, social and women's rights activist Antonater Choto was the sixth and only female defendant in the case. Magistrate Mutevedzi reasoned that there was 'reasonable suspicion' that the six had committed a crime. He argued that Gwisai, Choto and Mombeyarara were responsible for the programme of the meeting. Gumbo, Zimuto and Chakuma, in turn, 'allegedly … incite[d] participants to revolt against the government'.[40] It would be up to the state to prove that the viewing of the footage of the Arab Spring, which in and of itself could not be seen as criminal,

---

[38] ZLHR, 'Hard Labour and Solitary Confinement for Treason Suspects', *ZLHR News*, 7 March 2011, accessed on 2 July 2012 at http://archive.kubatana.net/html/archive/hr/110307zlhr2.asp?sector=CACT&year=2011&range_start=571.

[39] Interview, Alec Muchadehama, human rights lawyer, Harare, 12 January 2012.

[40] ZLHR, 'Hard Labour and Solitary Confinement for Treason Suspects'.

was intended to urge people to revolt against the government, something that was 'certainly criminal' and treasonous.[41]

This ruling, Alec Muchadehama observed, was just the first step in a long process aimed at taking 'people through the motions of a trial, which is not there'. The attorney general's office and the police, Muchadehama continued, 'clearly know there is no evidence, but they take people through the mud of a trial, as well for punishing people and also to send a, some political messages to people who they regard as, you know, anti ZANU-PF'.[42] Examining the case presented by the state prosecutor and their key witness as the trial progressed, the remainder of this chapter asks how ZANU-PF used the prosecutors' bench to send a political message, what message it aimed to send and what effects this message had.

The State's Case

In his closing remarks on 12 March 2012, prosecutor Michael Reza recommended that the magistrate convict Gwisai and his five co-defendants by outlining the central arguments of the state's case. In his narrative, he reminded the court that on 19 February the six defendants had met and conspired to commit public violence in the form of an uprising to unseat the constitutionally elected government. This uprising 'had gone beyond the planning stage. The date had been set (March 1, 2011), the place set (Africa Unity Square), communication method agreed on (e-mail, texting). All what remained was the arrival of the appointed date. The crime had been complete at that stage.'[43] Reza continued that he was therefore convinced that the state had proved the defendants 'guilty as charged', and that they 'should be punished heavily'. Their punishment should reflect that they 'planned to import a strange way of changing Governments from Egypt to Zimbabwe', which would be an 'anathema to Zimbabweans'. The court should further take into account that the six defendants planned such a revolt despite the fact that President Mugabe denounced the protests in North Africa and that Prime Minister Tsvangirai spoke out

[41] Ibid.

[42] Interview, Alec Muchadehama, human rights lawyer, Harare, 12 January 2012.

[43] Tahir Sema, 'Zim Activists in Danger of Unlawful Prison Sentences: Release Them Now!' *SAMWU Press Statement*, 14 March 2012, accessed on 2 July 2012 at www.zimbabwesituation.com/old/mar20_2012.html#Z22.

against violence. Jonathan Shoko, Reza pointed out, had told the court how the defendants agreed that the president had been in power too long, while the prime minister was a stooge of the West. 'Both national leaders have vowed to stamp out violence and yet we have six accused persons Nichodemously [secretly, or with one's own interests in mind] planning violence to assume power ostensibly for themselves ... Were it not for the police, who scuttled the plan, Harare would have burnt on March 1, 2011.'[44]

Michael Reza's closing remarks capture three key elements of the state's narrative performance during the trial, which I explore further in this section. First, they highlight the central arguments that guided the state's construction of the events, namely that the six defendants were planning to oust President Mugabe through an Egypt-style uprising. This was complicated by the fact that the MDC was part of Zimbabwe's government, and so the state included an element in its narrative that expanded the uprising as a threat not only against ZANU-PF, but against Morgan Tsvangirai. To do so, the state constructed an account in which the defendants allegedly marked Tsvangirai out as a Western stooge, language which echoes that of ZANU-PF. Second, Reza's closing narrative indicates that the prosecution was not the only actor needed to perform this story. They relied heavily on the manner in which their second witness, Jonathan Shoko, recounted his evidence. Finally, the state's construction of the events aimed to emphasise the severity of the allegations against the defendants as a violent threat to the stability of Zimbabwe by arguing that this threat, which would have led to the capital city being 'burnt', could not be ignored and the defendants should thus be gravely punished.

The consistent reminder of the danger the six defendants posed to Zimbabwe's constitutionally elected government, and by extension to the safety and security of the country and the nation, was at the heart of the state's narrative from the very start of the trial. When the state first brought the group of forty-five men and women for a bail hearing on 23 February 2011, state prosecutor Edmore Nyazamba charged them with treason and stressed that the meeting's purpose was 'to organise, strategise and implement the removal of the Government of Zimbabwe by unconstitutional means'. He told the court, and members of the public in the gallery, that those present at the meeting

---

[44] Sema, 'Zim Activists in Danger of Unlawful Prison Sentences'.

'actively participated in the proposed plan and supported implementation of a revolt against the constitutional Government of Zimbabwe'. To stress the danger, Nyazamba further stated that the defendants 'expressed their agreement with the plan … for implementation of the illegal revolt'. At a subsequent bail hearing on 6 March 2011, Nyazamba argued that 'clearly the case before this court is not an ordinary case, it is a very sensitive case of extreme national importance and … with extreme repercussions on issues of national security'.[45]

At another bail hearing on 16 March 2011, the prosecution built up its narrative of the threat posed by the six remaining defendants to the country's security by stressing that they were well connected and might 'continue with their plan of removing the government' should they be released.[46] At this point in the case, Munyaradzi Gwisai and his five co-defendants had been redetained in police detention and remand prison following magistrate Mutevedzi's ruling that their case should proceed to trial and had their bail hearings referred to the High Court, as the Magistrates' Courts could not preside over cases involving offences which could result in the death penalty. Despite the prosecution's narrative of the danger the defendants posed, High Court Judge Samuel Kudya granted all six bail. The strict conditions under which he released them, however, did play into the state's story, singling them out as potential risks. In addition to a bail of US$2,000 per person, the six defendants had to report to the notoriously violent CID Law and Order division of the ZRP three times a week, surrender their passports, remain at a specified address and not interfere with state witnesses.[47]

Alongside these strict conditions, however, Justice Kudya also issued a warning to the state that its narrative recounting of the ISO-Z meeting did not match the charges against the defendants:

[45] Tendai Rupapa, 'State Says Gwisai Has Case to Answer'. *The Herald*, 6 March 2011, accessed on 3 July 2011 at www.herald.co.zw/state-says-gwisai-has-case-to-answer/.

[46] ISO(Z), 'Bail Hearing: Gwisai and 5 Others Granted Bail', *ISO(Z)*, 17 March 2011, accessed on 2 July 2011 at: www.kubatanablogs.net/kubatana/gwisai-5-granted-bail-%e2%80%93-but-urgently-fundraise-for-bail-fees/.

[47] ISO(Z), 'Bail Hearing'. On 30 May 2011, Justice Kudya relaxed the reporting conditions to one Friday a month; see ZLHR, 'Relief for the Alleged Treason Activists as State Dilutes Treason Charge and Relaxes Reporting Conditions', *ZLHR News*, 31 May 2011, accessed on 3 July 2012 at www.zlhr.org.zw.

The suggestion of endangering peace and security is again bald and unsubstantiated ... The trial court would have to determine the credibility of the witnesses for the state and those for the applicants. One lesson that we learn from the (Morgan) Tsvangirai treason trial is that treason is often a difficult crime to prove beyond reasonable doubt.[48]

In the run-up to the 2002 presidential elections, Tsvangirai was charged with treason and stood accused of plotting to oust and kill President Mugabe. In this trial too, much of the evidence in the case was based on audio and video recordings of a meeting between Tsvangirai and Canadian-based consultant Ari Ben-Menashe, who was the prosecution's star witness. In 2004, Justice Paddington Garwe acquitted Tsvangirai. In a lengthy, 107-page judgement that detailed the particulars of witness' and accused's statements, the state's charges and the ways in which the state had failed to prove its case, Garwe concluded that 'it cannot be said that the state has proved beyond a reasonable doubt that high treason was committed in this case'.[49]

In the Gwisai treason trial, the state heeded Justice Kudya's warning that 'treason is often a difficult crime to prove'. When the trial date was set in Harare's Regional Magistrates' Courts for 18 July 2011, the case was delayed as the state announced new charges against the defendants. As ZLHR reported, the state prosecutor informed the six defendants and their lawyer Alec Muchadehama that they were now charged under Section 36 of the Criminal Law (Codification and Reform) Act with 'conspiring to commit public violence', which carries a maximum prison sentence of ten years.[50] They also faced three alternative charges under the Act, namely of contravening Section 187, read with Section 36 for inciting public violence; and Sections 37(1)(a) and 37(1)(c) for participating in a gathering with the intent to promote public violence, breaches of peace or bigotry, which carry a sentence of no more than five years imprisonment.[51]

---

[48] 'Free at Last', *NewsDay*, 16 March 2011, accessed on 5 September 2015 at www.newsday.co.zw/2011/03/16/2011–03–16-free-at-last/.

[49] From Judgment HH 169-2004, p. 41 (issued on 15 October 2004 by Justice Garwe in *State v. Tsvangirai*).

[50] ZLHR, 'Charge Shopping State Water down Treason Charges against Gwisai and Five Others', *ZLHR News*, 18 July 2011, accessed on 3 July 2012 at www .zlhr.org.zw.

[51] ISO(Z), 'Update on Zimbabwean Socialists' Treason Trial', *ISO(Z)*, 18 July 2011, accessed on 1 September 2011 at http://isozim.blogspot.fr/2011_07_01_

ZLHR described the state's new charges as 'a dramatic twist' in the case, while one of the defendants, Hopewell Gumbo, commented that this was 'a hilarious window shopping spree'. He continued that he 'hope[d] they have found the dress that fits'.[52] Although the state's seemingly unexpected decision to apply lesser charges appeared 'dramatic' and 'hilarious' to the defendants and their lawyer, the decision appears rational if we understand the aim of the trial to be tied to the creation of a narrative that illustrated what awaited Zimbabweans who planned to protest against the party or the government. In order to bolster this narrative, the state may have opted to favour the charge with a higher chance of resulting in a conviction, an outcome that would affirm the validity of their allegations that the defendants were 'dangerous' and 'threats' to the sovereignty of the Zimbabwean nation. To tell this story the state relied heavily on the testimony of its key witness, Jonathan Shoko. The following section focuses on his evidence as exemplary of the narrative ZANU-PF constructed in court.

The Case of Jonathan Shoko

Although his initial reaction to the change of the charges was contemptuous of the state's ability to prepare their case, Hopewell Gumbo later observed that this chaotic and disorganised appearance was misleading. He recalled that 'as the trial went on, the state was really on us. They wanted to prove a point and just scare everybody.' This view, he explained, was supported by the fact that while the 'ordinary people just on the streets' had dismissed the Arab Spring, the state refused to 'ignore this case and leave it aside'. Instead, 'they really pursued it, vigorously'.[53]

The state pursued the case in order to publicly tell Zimbabweans of the forms of political engagement it accepted and authorised. Discussions of the Arab Spring uprisings were not deemed acceptable, evidenced in the state's efforts to stress the danger the defendants posed

archive.html; and ZLHR, 'Charge Shopping State Water down Treason Charges against Gwisai and Five Others'.

[52] Hopewell Gumbo, 'I Wish to Thank You All for the Overwhelming Solidarity during Our Trial', 7 March 2012, accessed on 2 July 2012 at http://archive .kubatana.net/html/archive/opin/120307hg.asp?sector=PRISON&year=2012& range_start=1.

[53] Interview, Hopewell Gumbo, student activist, Harare, 29 September 2015.

to the nationalist ideals the country was built on. In large part, the state constructed this story through the testimony of Jonathan Shoko. Shoko gave his evidence before magistrate Kudakwashe Jarabini when the state began presenting its case on 14 September 2011. Although it was originally meant to start in July that year, the case had met further delays as four magistrates recused themselves, citing their connections with Munyaradzi Gwisai, who might have taught them during their law degrees at the University of Zimbabwe. Magistrate Jarabini obtained his Bachelor of Law degree from Fort Hare University in South Africa, and was thus less likely to be familiar with Gwisai. He was also one of ZANU-PF's 'good boys'. Having risen through the ranks of the Magistrates' Courts in Harare quite quickly from the start of his career in 2006, magistrate Jarabini was promoted again following the Gwisai trial. In September 2012, he was transferred from Harare to Chitungwiza Magistrates' Courts to take up the position of resident magistrate, a position he held until his death following typhoid on 19 March 2014.

With a magistrate appointed, the state first called Rinos Chari to testify. Chari had been arrested alongside the initial group of forty-five activists, but was released before the group appeared before magistrate Mutevedzi. Under cross-examination by Alec Muchadehama, Chari claimed that he had been arrested and tortured by the police and knew nothing of the allegations against the six defendants.[54] Chari's behaviour on the witness stand was far from unique. Many human rights lawyers discussed their experiences of cross-examining state witnesses whose testimony was 'fabricated' and who recanted when pushed for details.[55] Such behaviour fits into a long history of witness' refusal to perform, going back to the liberation war. Munyaradzi Munochiveyi, for example, referred to the trial against Miriam Nare Nyathi, who stood accused of 'terrorist recruitment' by the Rhodesian Front government in July 1978.[56] Against the backdrop of the country's war for independence, Nyathi was one among many Africans who were

---

[54] 'Court Quashes Gwisai's Application', *The Herald*, 15 September 2011, accessed on 4 July 2015, at http://allafrica.com/stories/201109150395.html.

[55] In interviews with human rights lawyers Tafadzwa Mugabe, Harare, 21 July 2010 and 18 September 2010; Tawanda Zhuwarara, Harare, 7 September 2010; Alec Muchadehama, Harare, 19 August 2010 and 12 January 2012; and Jeremiah Bamu, Harare, 28 September 2010.

[56] Munochiveyi, *Prisoners of Rhodesia*, pp. 112–20.

arbitrarily arrested by the Rhodesian Front, which as we have seen also used the law as a repressive tool to dissuade support for the liberation movements. Munochiveyi demonstrated how, in Nyathi's trial, all witnesses recanted as part of a collective tactic whereby they 'colluded with each other in misleading the courts through giving conflicting and negating evidence', ultimately placing 'prosecutors' cases into disarray'.[57]

In the trial against Gwisai and his five co-defendants, however, Shoko, a member of the security division of the state, proved a formidable witness. He could be led to perform the state's narrative by prosecutors Edmore Nyazamba and Michael Reza. Shoko's court hearings took place sporadically until January 2012 as a result of continued interruptions and delays. In stark contrast to Chari, Shoko supplied a detailed account of the meeting, which he had attended as an undercover police officer. The narrative Shoko presented in court seemed heavily rehearsed and coached by the prosecution, as he recalled in great detail who, out of the six defendants, spoke at what times, the content of their statements, the content of the videos watched and how the defendants reacted to, and engaged with, these videos, as well as the responses of the wider audience to their speeches.

He recounted, for example, how he interacted with 'accused number 6', Welcome Zimuto, before the meeting started. In an effort to gain Zimuto's trust in order to stay at the meeting, Shoko, who 'could tell from his tone that he was anti-President Mugabe', joined Zimuto so they could 'castigate the president together and belittle him'. Shoko went on to claim that, in his recollection of the events of the meeting, Zimuto had stood up to explain that:

He was speaking on behalf of ZINASU and then gave deliberations [that] students in institutions of higher learning were languishing. They were not eating properly, do not have money for necessary things like books, photocopying and so forth. This was blamed on President Mugabe, who they said is living lavishly while students suffer. Apart from suffering in universities due to the lack of government funding, such as grants and loans for students, these students after graduating would find it difficult to secure employment because Mugabe and ZANU-PF had run down the economy. He then stated the affairs before Mugabe running down the economy, that these were good environments. He then bemoaned the situation and said there was a need for

[57] Ibid., p. 112.

unity of purpose and courage on the part of the students because, as can be learnt from the Egypt revolution, once people are united for a common cause the common cause can come to pass. He explained the need to fight the present regime and have a reversal of the situation and that this needed unity. He then sat down. This is what I remember.[58]

In response, Shoko continued, the members of the audience clapped and nodded their heads. In cross-examination, Alec Muchadehama attempted to cast doubt on the conclusions Shoko drew when narrating his detailed memories about the danger the defendants posed by asking him whether the responses he observed by the audience were evidence that they were incited to commit public violence. Shoko, in turn, performed his commitment to the narrative, maintaining that 'to be incited is a matter of the heart'. The defendants, he continued, showed videos of the Arab Spring uprisings to draw out lessons that were 'meant to incite similar occurrences'.[59]

The court viewed the videos as well. In a dramatic decision that played into the prosecution's allegations of how dangerous it was to view this material, magistrate Jarabini ordered the footage to be shown in a closed court session. Although available in the public domain, the magistrate's decision to show the video footage in a closed court session utilised the court's ability to restrict the audience's access to its performances to convey a message. In this case, the court portrayed the six defendants' actions as a threat to Zimbabwe's security that supported their efforts to overthrow a constitutionally elected government. Under cross-examination by one of Zimbabwe's most formidable human rights lawyers, Alec Muchadehama, Shoko upheld the state's line of argument that protest against the government would not be tolerated. In his cross-examination on 1 November 2011, Muchadehama argued that Shoko was in fact a CIO agent, Rodwell Chitiyo, and the national ID and police identity card the court had seen were fake. Muchadehama asked how a reasonable court could admit, and trust, the evidence of someone who was lying about his name and identity. Legally speaking, Shoko was perjuring himself. To strengthen this point, Muchadehama traced the history of the witness, producing

[58] Jonathan Shoko, as quoted by Alec Muchadehama in personal correspondence with author, 25 March 2012.
[59] Field notes, trial of Gwisai and five others, courtroom 18 Rotten Row, Harare, 30 January 2012.

several of his old teachers, one of whom revealed that his nickname in school had been Pinocchio because of the lies he told. In the independent media, these defence tactics were heralded as 'mount[ing] a formidable attack on [the witness'] credibility'.[60] In the courtroom, however, the effect was predominately comic, as Eddson Chakuma recalled that 'it was very funny. Even [Shoko] himself, he was laughing because he knew that nickname Pinocchio.'[61]

This comic moment aside, Shoko side-stepped Muchadehama's attempts to question his identity by continually returning to the main thrust of his narrative: the threat he alleged the six defendants posed to peace and security in the country. Seated in the dock, this was also evident to Hopewell Gumbo, who recalled that Shoko 'had his own drama he wanted to play. And I'm sure he did play that drama. . . . His theory was that an Egypt was about to happen in Zimbabwe and that the ISO was organising it and therefore the government should be careful.' This theory, Gumbo concluded, was meant to 'send a message. They clearly wanted to send a message. This is what they told us even when we were in police custody, that "you will be the examples, you're not going to see your children again, you're not going to see your relatives again, you are the examples of what we can do to you if you try and do an Egypt here".'[62]

When Muchadehama challenged Shoko that 'Zimbabwe is not Egypt' as there were not enough similarities between the two countries to generate the conditions for a revolution, Shoko stated, 'I don't care about those differences', and continued to outline the similarities he had observed instead. He recounted how the defendants:

> were planning to take certain elements, saying that if they were united, they would not be scared. They would gather at AU square and use cyberspace to call people to gather there in large numbers. The plan was hatched. Civil society organisations were told to go back and use cyberspace and they gave reasons of why they would have to remove President Mugabe and Tsvangirai.[63]

---

[60] VERITAS, 'State v Munyaradzi Gwisai and Others'.
[61] Interview, Eddson Chakuma, labour activist, Harare, 18 January 2012.
[62] Interview, Hopewell Gumbo, student activist, Harare, 29 September 2015.
[63] Field notes, trial of Gwisai and five others, courtroom 18 Rotten Row, Harare, 30 January 2012.

Shoko concluded his narrative by drawing attention to the fact that, in his view, the protest he believed the defendants planned was not only illegal, but threatened the survival of the government under the GNU:

everything culminated in accused number one [Gwisai] calling for the removal of Morgan Tsvangirai and President Mugabe ... Tsvangirai was also a capitalist and stooge of the West. ... This was the move to a socialist state, with equal distribution of wealth. People were to gather at AU square on the 1st March secretly, undetected by police forces and from there they would start a revolution. ... The accused wanted the removal of the unity government [and] it is illegal to demonstrate to overthrow a constitutionally elected government.

At the end of his cross-examination, Alec Muchadehama challenged Shoko's interpretation of the illegality of the protest, asking whether it was 'an offence to ask the government to go by peaceful means'. Although the court was reminded by Muchadehama that peaceful protest was not an offence in Zimbabwe, Shoko again took this as an opportunity, this time to challenge the renowned human rights lawyer's authority to make these claims. Protected by his position as a state witness supporting ZANU-PF, Shoko boldly stated: 'We cannot rely on your submission, give me a section [of the constitution that allows for protest] and I will Google it ... without this section I will not be convinced, you may be misleading the courts.' Following Shoko's statement, magistrate Jarabini adjourned the case until the following day, when the defence finalised its cross-examination and applied for the discharge of the defendants on grounds of a lack of evidence against them. I now briefly turn to the final stages of the trial to illustrate how Shoko's evidence was picked up by the magistrate and prosecutors to conclude the trial with a conviction of the six accused.

The Conviction

Although he only had the evidence of one witness before him, it was compelling enough for magistrate Jarabini to dismiss the defence application for discharge on 15 February 2012, arguing that the state had presented sufficient prima facie evidence. In contrast to the long, drawn-out state case, the defence presented its case over three days in February and March. On 18 March, magistrate Jarabini ruled that all six were guilty of conspiracy to commit public violence as defined in

Section 188, read with Section 36 of the Criminal Law (Codification and Reform) Act. In his judgement, magistrate Jarabini reflected two key points of Shoko's narrative: that the videos were aimed at inciting the audience, as 'although watching the video was not a crime, the motive was meant to arouse feelings of hostility among the participants towards the government'; and that this would pose a huge threat to the safety and security of Zimbabweans as 'the meeting was meant to encourage a revolt'.[64]

In response to the magistrate's decision to convict, both the state and the defence teams submitted their proposals for the punishment or sentencing of the defendants. Building on the case that Jonathan Shoko had so successfully presented for the prosecution as of September, namely that the defendants posed a threat to national security by conspiring to protest against the country's government, prosecutor Edmore Nyazamba declared that the six defendants should be imprisoned. Invoking the authority of a regime that had rightfully come to power through armed struggle against foreign occupation, and was now tasked with protecting its independence, Nyazamba argued that any alternative sentence would 'be sending a wrong message to the world that in Zimbabwe you can revolt against the ruling Government and get away with it'.[65] Referring to the Bible, Nyazamba implied that the Zimbabwean government was appointed by God, and reminded the court that 'before civilisation, people accused of committing such an offence would be stoned to death even without trial'.[66] Quoting the book of Romans, Nyazamba concluded that 'everyone must obey the State authorities because no authority exists without God's permission'.[67]

For the defence, Alec Muchadehama's proposal was less dramatically formulated, and appealed not to the authority of a state supported by divine intervention, but to a state that followed its own rules in its

[64] Crisis in Zimbabwe Coalition, 'Court Finds Gwisai, 5 Others Guilty', *CRISIS*, 20 March 2012, accessed on 19 September 2012 at from http://archive.kubatana.net/html/archive/demgg/120320ciz1.asp?sector=HR&year=2012&range_start=661.
[65] 'Gwisai Sentencing Set for Today', *The Herald*, 20 March 2012, accessed on 23 August 2015, at www.herald.co.zw/gwisai-sentencing-set-for-today/.
[66] ZLHR, *The Legal Monitor*, edition 136, 26 March 2012, p. 2, accessed on 3 July 2012 at http://archive.kubatana.net/docs/hr/zlhr_legal_monitor_136_120326.pdf.
[67] 'Gwisai Sentencing Set for Today', *The Herald*.

treatment of detainees. He referred back to Munyaradzi Gwisai's performance from the dock to draw attention to the horrific conditions the defendants faced in police detention, urging the court to keep in mind that 'the six accused persons were brutally assaulted by the police and that is punishment on its own'.[68]

Magistrate Jarabini delivered his sentence on 21 March 2012. His decision captured both the arguments and the authorities of the law that the defence invoked on the one hand, and the power of ZANU-PFs rule that the prosecution played upon on the other. In terms of the degree to which the defendants should be punished, he followed Muchadehama's recommendations, and fined all six defendants US$500 each. In addition, he sentenced them to two years imprisonment, of which twelve months were suspended on the grounds that they each carry out 420 hours of community service and the other twelve months suspended for good future behaviour, that is, that they do not commit a similar offence in the next five years. Magistrate Jarabini justified his decision to fine the defendants by explaining he had taken 'a compassionate approach'. Shoko's narrative from the witness stand was, however, not forgotten by the magistrate. Arguing that he wanted to 'send a message to would-be offenders', magistrate Jarabini continued that the defendants were threatening the 'peace and tranquillity' of the GNU by viewing the video clips at a time when 'it was easy to start a riot'. By finding the defendants guilty, magistrate Jarabini was protecting the nation. By sentencing the six to a fine and community service, magistrate Jarabini felt he was upholding 'the duty of the courts to safeguard the Constitution of the country'.[69]

Magistrate Jarabini's decision failed to satisfy either the prosecution or the defence. The defence appealed against the conviction and the sentencing. In outlining his reasons to appeal, Alec Muchadehama returned to the role the magistrate played in the case. He argued that the magistrate had facilitated ZANU-PF's political persecution of the defendants, and reflected on the role legal performances played in enabling the party to construct its political narrative by taking the six defendants through the motions of a trial. He specifically challenged the magistrate's interpretation of the video footage of the Arab Spring

[68] Ibid.
[69] Tendai Rupapa, 'Community Service for Gwisai', *The Herald*, 21 March 2012, accessed on 23 August 2015, at www.herald.co.zw/community-service-for-gwisai/.

shown at the meeting as having potential to 'arouse feelings of hostility'. This interpretation, he concluded, was an illustration of how 'the magistrate removed the judicial cloak, jumped into the arena and started behaving like the 2nd witness [Jonathan Shoko] who would interpret the video and impute his subjective view to the Appellants'.[70] Embedded in this critique of magistrate Jarabini's actions in court was the authority that the magistrate granted Shoko's politicised narrative.

Read in this manner, securing a conviction in this trial was a victory not only for the prosecution, but also for the narrative it performed in court more broadly. As such, the conviction demonstrated how ZANU-PF's continued control relied upon the judiciary to maintain its political authority under the GNU. As the magistrate's lenient sentencing shows, however, this control was far from complete. In protest, prosecutor Nyazamba appealed the magistrate's decision to pass a non-custodial sentence. Demonstrative of both the continued efforts of judicial officials to exercise their independence, and of the changing political conditions in the run-up to the national elections in 2013, the outcome of which was speculated upon, Justice Charles Hungwe threw out the state's appeal in the High Court on 16 January 2013, noting that he was of the opinion that 'the Attorney-General's appeal does not enjoy any prospect of success'.[71]

Conclusion

In early 2011, as protests spread across North Africa, ZANU-PF responded to the potential threats the Arab Spring uprisings posed to its authority by dramatically arresting forty-five people at a commemoration ceremony and convicting six of those arrested after a drawn-out trial. During this trial, Michael Reza, Edmore Nyazamba and Jonathan Shoko worked to construct a narrative that the six defendants were dangerous, credible threats to the nation's peace and security. Watching a video on the Arab Spring, discussing the possible lessons learned about the power of political protest, and gathering forty-five people for such an event, were portrayed as activities or

---

[70] ZLHR, *The Legal Monitor*, edition 136.
[71] From Decision on State Appeal in *Stave v. Gwisai and Others*, 13-HH-020, p. 6 (issued on 16 January 2013 by Justice Hungwe).

forms of political expression that the government, and particularly ZANU-PF, would not tolerate under the GNU.

ZANU-PF used the trial as a platform from which to articulate the limits to the party's tolerance for protest, and the consequences faced by those testing these limits. The party marked these forms of political engagement out as threats to the party's commitment to maintaining peace and security. Certain judicial officials were reluctant to enable the state to stage a high-profile treason trial. Magistrate Mutongi, for example, released thirty-nine of the forty-five activists arrested, while Justice Kudya warned the state that treason charges were rarely successful. Despite such divisions within the judiciary, the case eventually came before magistrate Jarabini, who was willing to let the drama unfold.

In this drama the state's witness played the starring role. Undeterred by the changing charges and limited evidence against Gwisai and his five co-defendants, themselves characteristic of trials against those accused of crimes against the state, Shoko put forward a cohesive and carefully practised and performed narrative that combined elements from the charges of treason, subverting a constitutional government and conspiracy to incite public violence. In a context where human rights lawyers such as Muchadehama had become very adept at navigating this politically influenced judiciary in their attempts to 'put the State on trial', as illustrated in Chapter 5, Shoko's ability to maintain a consistent, detailed and dramatic story throughout the trial was striking. Alec Muchadehama sought to shame the court for allowing a witness to perjure himself through his challenges on Shoko's identity, and to shame Shoko for his incomplete and seemingly false evidence by pointing out the inconsistencies between the witness' initial evidence and the responses to his questions during cross-examination. These tactics, however, provided Shoko with the opportunity to continually reassert the state's case, and the political narrative that underlay it, as well as his conviction that he had made the right call to stop the meeting. When asked whether he was looking for an offence when none had been committed, for instance, Shoko stayed true to his carefully constructed narrative, responding with the words prosecutor Michael Reza echoed in his closing remarks: 'I was simply doing my job as a security agent, a police officer. I had to be cautious and alert my superiors. As we speak, buildings in Harare could have burnt down.'[72]

Able to maintain this narrative when faced with Alec Muchadehama's efforts to cast doubt on the quality of his evidence, Shoko's theatrical performance sent a very clear 'message to would-be offenders' that did not remain confined to the courtroom. Reported on in both the independent media and the state-owned press, the prosecution in the Gwisai trial constructed a compelling narrative. This narrative was demonstrative of how ZANU-PF continued to position itself as the party responsible for upholding the safety and security of the nation against local manifestations of foreign imperialist influences. Despite the fact that the court's material and sensory conditions undermined it as the representative of the authority of the state and the guarantor of justice, as discussed in Chapter 5, ZANU-PF could still express the forms of political engagement that it authorised through the narrative it presented within the courtroom.

In Chapters 7 and 8, I turn to a different regional and historical context to explore how historical narratives, specifically the narrative around the *Gukurahundi* violence of the 1980s shaped the dynamics of law, state authority and citizenship in Matabeleland.

[72] Field notes, trial of Gwisai and five others, courtroom 18 Rotten Row, Harare, 30 January 2012.

7 | History, Consciousness and Citizenship in Matabeleland
The Impact of the MLF Case

People who live in Matabeleland and parts of the Midlands know only too well what happened to them during the 1980s. Their lives were affected in serious ways by both government troops and also by dissidents and Youth Brigades at this time. However, most people from other parts of Zimbabwe still have no idea what it was like for those who were suffering. They have no idea how people still suffer as a result of the violence that took place.[1]

On 28 December 2010, the MLF was launched as a new political party in Bulawayo.[2] The MLF was part of a growing trend in the formation of political parties and civic movements that focused on Matabeleland's role in Zimbabwean politics, and specifically its history of post-independence violence. With its call for the secession of the region in order to create the 'Mthwakazi Republic', a nation based on the precolonial Ndebele state, however, the MLF found limited support. At its launch, for example, the MLF drew a crowd of only 300 to Stanley Square, where rallies of the MDC-T, MDC-N or ZANU-PF could draw over 800 people. Despite its limited popular appeal, the government violently persecuted the MLF, accusing leading figures within the party of high treason in March 2011. As I have shown, after 2000 ZANU-PF maintained a complex relationship with the law, invoking legal language and practice to authorise its governance, relying on its institutions to exercise coercive power, reminding Zimbabweans of the law's illegitimate roots in colonial domination and using the courtroom to publicise its narratives regarding what it considered permissible politics. Much as in the Gwisai trial discussed in Chapter 6, the state used the trial of the MLF to delineate and display which kind of politics it deemed acceptable and legitimate.

---

[1] CCJP and LRF, *Breaking the Silence*, p. 1.
[2] 'New Zimbabwe Opposition Party Launched', *RadioVOP*, 29 December 2010, accessed on 18 September 2013 at www.radiovop.com/index.php/national-news/5151-new-zimbabwe-opposition-party-launched.html.

This trial was, however, also shaped by a political history specific to Bulawayo and Matabeleland. The *Gukurahundi* violence of the 1980s, which had targeted the region in political and ethnic terms, and the politics of the 1990s and 2000s that resulted from this turbulent period had maintained Bulawayo as an opposition stronghold, first for ZAPU and later for the MDC. This history raises unique questions around the significance and use of the law, mobilisations of ethnicity and constructions of citizenship, that I explore in this chapter and Chapter 8. In this chapter, I focus on the trial of the MLF members to examine how history shapes the understandings of law and its relation to state authority, held by human rights lawyers and members of civil society in Matabeleland. As I have shown, these actors were important in challenging the ZANU-PF government's use of law, playing to the 'rebels' in divided state institutions, and performing and mobilising civil servants' and citizens' legal and state consciousness. This did not mean, however, that human rights lawyers were homogenous in their uses and understandings of law. Although the MLF's arrest and prosecution was politically motivated, and bore many resemblances to the Gwisai case discussed in Chapter 6, Harare-based lawyers affiliated with the largest human rights law network, ZLHR, refused to take the case.

ZLHR's Bulawayo-based colleagues read the Harare-based lawyers' refusal as an indication that they did not understand, or appreciate, the importance of the specific history of violence in the region, and the established role of legal action in addressing this history. In response, five Bulawayo-based lawyers – Lucas Nkomo, Sindiso Mazibisa, Matshobana Ncube, Kucaca Phulu and Robert Ndlovu – withdrew their ZLHR membership on 16 March 2011.[3] They formed a new human rights network in the region, the Abammeli Bamalungelo Abantu-Network of Human Rights Lawyers (Abammeli). 'Abammeli' refers to 'representative' or 'advocate', and 'Bamalungelo' to 'lawyer' or 'rights', which combined gave the organisation 'a name that communicates very clearly our nature as representatives of the members of

[3] Abammeli Human Rights Lawyers Network, 'Statement by Abammeli', *Abammeli*, 16 March 2011, accessed on 5 November 2011 at http://zimdiaspora .com/index.php?option=com_content&view=category&layout=blog&id=38& Itemid=293&limitstart=5205. See also, 'Mthwakazi Trio's Case Splits Lawyers', *New Zimbabwe*, 16 March 2011, accessed on 4 July 2013 at www .newzimbabwe.com/news-4692-Mthwakazi%20trios%20case%20splits% 20lawyers/news.aspx.

community … to fully enjoy their human rights and to lead dignified lives'.[4] I argue that Abammeli's formation expressed a deeply rooted and historically specific experience of political, economic and cultural exclusion from the Zimbabwean nation among Matabeleland's residents, which created region-specific legal strategies. Abammeli's actions created a public performance that cast not only ZANU-PF but also the MDC-supported human rights community in Harare as responsible for curtailing the right-based citizenship of Matabeleland's residents.

To make sense of Abammeli's formation, I first discuss the history and politics of Matabeleland, and illustrate how the MLF included this history in its imagination of the Mthwakazi Republic. I then outline the circumstances of the arrest and detention of three MLF leaders, which prompted the formation of Abammeli. Through explaining Abammeli's mission, and their courtroom performance during the MLF trial, I examine the connection between history, legal and state consciousness, and citizenship in Matabeleland.

History and Politics in Matabeleland

At Zimbabwean independence, much of Matabeleland's population supported ZAPU. In the first elections in February 1980, ZAPU ran as the Patriotic Front (PF-ZAPU) party led by Joshua Nkomo. The party gained 24 per cent of the national vote, whereas Robert Mugabe's ZANU-PF won the elections with 63 per cent of the vote. In Matabeleland North and South, however, PF-ZAPU won with 79 per cent and 86 per cent respectively, an outcome that reflected strategies of recruitment among the two parties during the liberation struggle, and historical regional ethnic divisions. In the majority-Shona provinces, particularly Manicaland and Mashonaland, ZANU-PF won convincingly, whereas in the majority-Ndebele provinces, such as Matabeleland, PF-ZAPU gained more votes. Joshua Nkomo himself stood in the Midlands province, home to an ethnically mixed population. Here, ZANU-PF won 60 per cent of the vote, while PF-ZAPU got 27 per cent.[5]

---

[4] From Abammeli's website, 'Who We Are?' and 'Mission', accessed on 20 December 2016 at www.abammelilawyers.com.
[5] Martyn Gregory, *From Rhodesia to Zimbabwe: An Analysis of the 1980 Elections and an Assessment of the Prospects* (Johannesburg, The South African Institute of International Affairs, 1980).

ZANU-PF initially responded to ZAPU's overwhelming victory in the Matabeleland provinces by incorporating members of the party into government. Joshua Nkomo was appointed minister of home affairs. Shortly afterwards the coalition between ZAPU and ZANU-PF collapsed amid clashes between former ZIPRA and ZANLA guerrillas at, for example, Entumbane, a Bulawayo suburb, between November 1980 and February 1981. Political relations were further strained in February 1982, when the government sacked Joshua Nkomo and other ZAPU ministers after 'discovering' arms caches at a ZIPRA-run company, Nitram, and around ZIPRA Assembly Points. ZANU-PF accused ZAPU of attempting to claim state power through violent means, with senior ZANU-PF government officials increasingly placing the blame for 'disturbances' in Matabeleland and the Midlands squarely on ZIPRA 'dissidents', and on ZAPU's leadership.[6]

Jocelyn Alexander, Joann McGregor and Terence Ranger argue that 'a semantic change occurred in the post-election period: armed men on the loose in Matabeleland came to be called "dissidents", and the problem they represented was increasingly cast in political terms'.[7] ZANU-PF played up regional ethnic differences to portray ZAPU 'as a treasonous, Ndebele party' threatening the security of the newly established nation.[8] Dissidents were 'described as anti-social, criminal malcontents'.[9] In its official propaganda, the government thus framed their response as being in line with the law for the protection of the newly established nation, stating: 'The acts committed are acts against humanity not against a political enemy. The perpetrators are not political weapons – nor even soldiers. They are criminals committing criminal acts in a law-abiding and constitutionally legitimate country.'[10]

The ZIPRA guerrillas' 'return to the bush' reflected in large part a growing distrust and dissatisfaction following their violent persecution within the newly formed Zimbabwe National Army.[11] Far from the dramatic threat the government portrayed them as, however, these

---

[6] Alexander et al., *Violence and Memory*; Werbner, 'Smoke from the Barrel of a Gun'.

[7] Alexander et al., *Violence and Memory*, p. 185.

[8] Alexander and McGregor, 'Elections, Land and the Politics of Opposition in Matabeleland'.

[9] Weitzer, *Transforming Settler States*, p. 169.

[10] Ministry of Information, Posts, and Telecommunications, *A Chronicle of Dissidency in Zimbabwe* (Harare, Government Printer, August 1984), p. 39.

[11] Alexander et al., *Violence and Memory*; Alexander, 'Dissident Perspectives'.

'dissidents' were 'a small, organised group of men on the run, who tried to stay loyal to ZIPRA ideals, even though they were ultimately leaderless'.[12] As discussed in Chapter 1, the government responded with excessive violence against the citizens of Matabeleland and the Midlands, most notoriously by the North Korean-trained Fifth Brigade under the command of Colonel Perence Shiri. The Fifth Brigade was deployed first in Matabeleland North, and subsequently in Matabeleland South between January 1983 and late 1984.[13] The CCJP and LRF assert that 'it is indisputable that thousands of unarmed civilians died, were beaten, or suffered loss of property during the 1980s, some at the hands of dissidents and most as a result of the actions of Government agencies'.[14]

Civilians in Matabeleland made sense of the *Gukurahundi* in ethnic and political terms. The campaign was viewed as a government-led assault targeted against the Ndebele, and against ZAPU supporters. Indeed, much of the violence (especially in the early phase of the Fifth Brigade deployment) was characterised by replications and exaggerations of ZANU and ZANLA's liberation war strategies. Civilians were forced to attend *pungwes*, night-time rallies of ZANU political songs, sung in Shona, and the Fifth Brigade justified 'its violence as revenge for 19th century Ndebele raiding'.[15] Language and ethnic divisions were deepened as many of the members of the Fifth Brigade did not speak Ndebele. As Alexander, McGregor and Ranger argue, 'the Fifth Brigade's greatest "success" may have been in hardening ethnic prejudice, and in bolstering a strong identification between ethnicity and political affiliation'.[16] Writing in 1998, Richard Werbner argues that ZANU-PF's strategies had 'far reaching implications for certain newly-emergent yet basic political realities for nation-building, for state-made ethnic polarisation, for the concentration of power within the state and indeed for the very critique of what state power could or should be'.[17]

---

[12] CCJP and LRF, *Breaking the Silence*, p. 13.
[13] *Breaking the Silence* details the violence of the Fifth Brigade and unpacks the different strategies the government, and the Brigade, used in Matabeleland North and Matabeleland South in this period.
[14] CCJP and LRF, *Breaking the Silence*, p. 15.
[15] Musiwaro Ndakaripa, 'Ethnicity, Narrative, and the 1980s Violence in the Matabeleland and Midlands Provinces of Zimbabwe', *Oral History Forum d'Histoire Orale*, 34, 2014, p. 34.
[16] Alexander et al., *Violence and Memory*, p. 224.
[17] Werbner, 'Smoke from the Barrel of a Gun', p. 79.

Despite the government's violent attempts to crush support for ZAPU, the majority of Matabeleland's citizens remained loyal to the party. In the 1985 parliamentary elections, PF-ZAPU candidates won all nine seats in Matabeleland North and all six seats in Matabeleland South with wide margins. The 1987 Unity Accord brought an end to the violence, but also ended ZAPU's opposition to ZANU-PF in such elections as the party was absorbed into ZANU-PF. Symbolic of one party's continued dominance, the united political forces maintained the name ZANU-PF. Despite this, the period shortly after the Unity Accord was marked by optimism among Matabeleland's citizens – soon to be disappointed – that the region would experience economic development.[18]

As we have seen, the complaints voiced against ZANU-PF's rule grew stronger across Zimbabwe in the 1990s. The MDC rallied around central issues of the declining economy, price inflation, increased unemployment and political corruption scandals. In Matabeleland, citizens voiced additional, specific concerns relating to their experiences of limited development after the Unity Accord, and the lack of an apology and compensation by the government for the violence of *Gukurahundi*. New pressure groups and political parties were formed with such regional, and often ethnic, concerns at the heart of their agendas.

In the 1990s, for example, pressure groups such as *Imbovane Yamahlabezulu* and *Vhukani Mahlabezulu* were formed. They called for 'political autonomy and sovereignty' of the Ndebele population, in an effort to address political and economic inequalities in the country. Several new political parties played on ZAPU's history in the region without being directly connected to the original party, adopting evocative names such as 'ZAPU 2000' or the 'ZAPU-Federal Party'.[19] In 2008, Dumiso Dabengwa 'revived' what he conceived of as the original ZAPU, an act he portrayed as a withdrawal from the Unity Accord. In their various forms, the parties placed Matabeleland's and the Ndebele's neglect by the ZANU-PF-led government at the centre of

---

[18] Terence Ranger 'Matabeleland since the Amnesty', *African Affairs*, 88, 351, 1989, pp. 161–73; Alexander and McGregor, 'Elections, Land and the Politics of Opposition'.

[19] Julian Dube, 'Nkomo's Ghost Rises to Fight Land Grab', *IOL*, 6 May 2000, accessed on 23 September 2013 at www.iol.co.za/news/africa/nkomos-ghost-rises-to-fight-land-grab-36749.

their agendas, drawing attention to uneven development and a lack of redress of the 1980s violence. As I show below, some groups, including the MLF, explicitly advocated for the formation of a state that was built on a shared Ndebele identity and history. None of these parties, however, were able to mobilise widespread support in the region. As Adrienne LeBas argues, such 'new parties … were launched by small groups of [political] elites without any prior constituency-building or broader consultation'.[20] After 2000, it was the MDC-T and ZANU that contended for power in the elections.

The Launch and Agenda of the MLF

The MLF grew out of initiatives within the diaspora community in South Africa.[21] In South Africa, the group was led by Fidelis Ncube, a former ZIPRA commander also known as General Nandinandi. In Bulawayo, Max Mkandla, another ZIPRA veteran, was appointed as the party's national organising secretary. Mkandla had a history of oppositional politics in the region. In 2000, he co-founded the Zimbabwe Liberators' Platform (ZLP), an initiative for war veterans critical of the manner in which ZANU-PF played up its liberation war legacy for political gain while betraying central values of the struggle. In the late 1990s ZANU-PF met the demands for financial compensation of members of the national veteran's organisation, the ZNLWVA, which had formed in 1989 to press the government for compensation and benefits for former guerrillas. In part, the government met their demands because war veterans made up a useful constituency.[22] For ZANU-PF, war veterans were important for the party as symbolic capital within their liberation war narrative. The

---

[20] Adrienne LeBas, *From Protest to Parties: Party-Building and Democratization in Africa* (Oxford, Oxford University Press, 2013), p. 121.

[21] 'New Zimbabwe Opposition Party Launched', *RadioVOP*; Khanyile Mlotshwa, 'New Radical Matabeleland Political Party on the Cards', *Zimbabwe Mail*, 26 December 2010, accessed on 5 June 2013 at www.zimbabwesituation.com/december_2010_archive.html; Kholwani Nyathi, 'New Radical Movements Expose Tribal Fault Lines', *The Standard*, 15 January 2011, accessed on 5 June 2013 at www.thestandard.co.zw/2011/01/15/new-radical-movements-expose-tribal-fault-lines/; Mthwakazi Liberation Front (MLF), 'Open Letter to His Excellency President Robert Gabriel Mugabe', *MLF*, 24 February 2011.

[22] Alexander and McGregor, 'Elections, Land and the Politics of Opposition in Matabeleland'; Erin McCandless, *Polarization and Transformation in Zimbabwe*; Dorman, *Understanding Zimbabwe,* pp. 81–3.

party could not, however, claim the allegiance of *all* war veterans. In Matabeleland, a region generally omitted from 'patriotic history',[23] the relationship between veterans and ZANU-PF was obstructed 'in large part [by] a legacy of the 1980s' conflict, which itself built on older tensions between the two nationalist parties and their respective guerrilla armies during the liberation struggle'.[24] The ZLP was formed to critique the veterans' narrowly partisan use by ZANU-PF.[25] Indicative of the centrality of Matabeleland's history in these political initiatives, however, Mkandla himself split from ZLP to form the Zimbabwe Liberators Peace Initiative in 2001. He explained that, as the ZLP had come under increased control by war veterans from ZANU's armed wing, ZANLA, the movement faced even more difficulties in their efforts to address the *Gukurahundi*.[26]

The MLF itself took on multiple forms within diaspora politics, before its launch as a separatist party within Bulawayo. To legitimise their claims to the separate Mthwakazi 'state' (which would encompass Zimbabwe's Matabele North, Matabele South and Midlands regions) parties such as the MLF relied on a specific narrative construction of Matabeleland's history. In the MLF narrative, King Mzilikazi established 'Mthwakazi' as a multi-ethnic state when he broke away from the Zulu kingdom in the early 1820s and migrated north to present-day Matabeleland.[27] In 1898, following almost a decade of claims to, and struggle over, the territory, the Mthwakazi state and territory to the east of it were integrated into the newly formed colony of Rhodesia. In contrast to ZANU-PF's recounting of 'patriotic history', the MLF's narrative of post-independence history posited that under ZANU-PF's rule the region and its 'Matabele' residents continued to be 'colonised' by a Shona-dominated government.

In 2014, the MLF published a book, *Free Mthwakazi*, in which it argued that 'the nation of Mthwakazi [had] been under inhuman slavery conditions for a total of 121 years: 87 years under European

---

[23] Ranger, 'Nationalist Historiography, Patriotic History and the History of the Nation'.

[24] Alexander and McGregor, 'Elections, Land and the Politics of Opposition', p. 515.

[25] Ibid.

[26] McCandless, *Polarization and Transformation in Zimbabwe*, pp. 91–2.

[27] Various groups feature versions of this history on their websites. For the example closest to the history the MLF wrote in 2011, see the Matabeleland Liberation Organisation website: www.matabeleliberation.org/p/about-us.html.

colonial rule and 34 years under the Shona colonialists'.[28] It argued that:

For thirty four years, the people of Mthwakazi nation in present day Zimbabwe, have resisted extinction, endured major genocide, suffered economic marginalisation and absorbed immeasurable insult and injury from the genocidal regime of Zimbabwe. Mthwakazi nation has lost hundreds of thousands of its people to genocide, massacre and ethnic cleansing. Millions have scattered to exile in neighbouring countries and elsewhere throughout the world, while many thousands are languishing in prisons and hundreds of thousands more continue to silently suffer punishment and torture from a regime that has trampled on human rights and justice with alarming impunity and arrogance.[29]

Unlike the political and civic activists of previous chapters, the MLF's post-independence historical narrative reflected an understanding of citizenship that was tied to ethnicity. By framing 'Mthwakazi' secession as the optimal outcome in a long struggle against 'Shona domination', they articulated a sense of citizenship and state legitimacy tied to a 'nation' separated from the central government in Harare's rule. This historical narrative and political imagination of Mthwakazi as a separate nation was reinforced through the production of symbols of Mthwakazi's 'stateness', such as a map,[30] a calendar with official holidays,[31] a shield and a flag.[32] As I discuss below, Mthwakazi also expected to establish its own constitution, and to abide by the rule of law in a manner that the Zimbabwean government had failed to do since independence.

In December 2010, around the time of the MLF's launch, the Arab Spring uprisings were fuelling anxiety among ZANU-PF leaders. As I discussed in Chapter 6, this created the political circumstances in

---

[28] Mthwakazi Liberation Front (MLF), *Free Mthwakazi: Why Should Mthwakazi Secede from Zimbabwe?* (Bulawayo, MLF, 2014), p. 6.

[29] MLF, *Free Mthwakazi*, p. 9.

[30] 'A Must Read for All People in the Land Currently Known As Zimbabwe!', accessed on 14 October 2016 at http://ikhonaindaba.blogspot.co.uk/2016_06_01_archive.html.

[31] Solidarity Peace Trust (SPT), *Hard Times in Matabeleland: Urban Deindustrialisation and Rural Hunger* (Durban, SPT, November 2011), p. 18.

[32] Don Sikhosana, 'Republic of Matabeleland Flag', *Ezakomthwakazi Blog*, 20 January 2014, accessed on 15 March 2015 at http://ezakomthwakazi.blogspot.co.uk/2014/01/republic-of-matabeleland-flag.html.

which members of the ISO-Z, including Munyaradzi Gwisai, were tried in order for the party to demonstrate what sort of political engagement it would, or would not, tolerate. In the case of the MLF, ZANU-PF members within the government was similarly quick to respond following its launch in Bulawayo in December 2010. In January 2011, Police Commissioner Augustine Chihuri was reported to have ordered police officers to 'monitor and arrest political activists ... calling for a breakaway state of Mthwakazi'.[33] Max Mkandla was detained at Bulawayo Central Police Station on 16 February. The police searched his home and confiscated MLF calendars portraying the 'Mthwakazi Republic'.[34]

The MLF nevertheless persisted, outlining its key demands in an open letter addressed to President Mugabe.[35] The letter, dated 24 February 2011, framed the 'Mthwakazi' people's wish for self-determination in historical, political and legal terms. It proposed that the region's marginalisation and continued tribalism was cause for Mthwakazi independence, which was to be achieved through a constitutional, political process. It stressed that while Zimbabwe as a whole had longed for, and fought for, independence during the colonial era, the independent nation of Zimbabwe had then let the region of Mthwakazi down in the decades following 1980. The *Gukurahundi*, and the president's dismissal of these events as a 'moment of madness', had contributed to promoting 'tribal and ethnic animosity between the Shona and the Ndebele'.[36]

Their call for secession, the MLF argued, had a legal basis in numerous international agreements, and could be viewed in comparison to the successful South Sudanese referendum of January 2011. Attention was also drawn to the Arab Spring uprisings to illustrate that 'power originates in, belongs in, and ends in the people'. The MLF concluded that it sought to remind the government of Zimbabwe that a disagreeable government could be replaced. The party asked the government to

[33] 'Police Ordered to Crackdown on Matland Secessionists', *Radio VOP*, 26 January 2011, accessed on 6 July 2013 at http://67.199.57.196/printableversion.asp?id=24917; Mxolisi Ncube, 'Chihuri Crushes New Party', *The Zimbabwean*, 15 March 2011, accessed on 5 July 2013 at www.zimbabwesituation.com/march_2011_archive.html.

[34] 'Bulawayo's New Party Organising Secretary Arrested', *Radio VOP*, 17 February 2011, accessed on 4 July 2013 at www.radiovop.com/index.php/national-news/5576-bulawayo-s-new-party-organising-secretary-arrested.html.

[35] MLF, 'Open Letter'.   [36] Ibid.

be open for discussions about the process of secession, and to consider that 'change always presents an opportunity not risk, opportunity deserving of an attentive ear, not a threat inviting a dismissive boot in the groin'.[37] The president's spokesperson, George Charamba, refused to comment on whether the government had received the MLF's open letter.[38] The government subsequently, and rather predictably, responded with a 'dismissive boot in the groin'.[39]

The MLF's Arrest and Detention

On 3 and 4 March 2011, five MLF members were arrested at various locations in Bulawayo. Much like the case against Gwisai and his five co-defendants, members of the MLF were threatened, detained for extensive periods and taken through the motions of a drawn-out trial. Surprisingly, these arrests did not include Max Mkandla.[40] Instead, Ntombizodwa Moyo, the deputy information and publicity officer, and Nonsikelelo Ncube, the deputy chairperson, were picked up only to be released on 5 March, while three other MLF members were detained first at Bulawayo Central Police Station and then held on remand at Khami Maximum Security Remand prison. These members, Paul Siwela, John Gazi and Charles Gumbo Thomas were probably targeted as they were key members of the party and occupied leadership positions. At the time of his arrest, Siwela worked as the MLF's secretary general. He had long been active within Bulawayo's political scene but had yet to appeal to a significant constituency. In the 2002 presidential elections he ran as an independent candidate affiliated with ZAPU 2000. He received only 0.38 per cent of the vote, and when ZAPU 2000 refused to contest the elections Siwela broke away

---

[37] Ibid.
[38] 'Secessionists Pile Pressure on Mugabe', *The Standard*, 26 February 2011, accessed on 6 July 2013 at www.thestandard.co.zw/2011/02/26/secessionists-pile-pressure-on-mugabe/.
[39] MLF, 'Open Letter'.
[40] In part because he was not targeted, Max Mkandla was later accused of being an undercover CIO agent. He denied these claims. A more common explanation I was given for Mkandla's exclusion from arrest was that it was both an example of the lack of the police's and the state's preparation in, and understanding of, the case, and a tactic to instil fear as it signalled the unpredictability of who would be targeted. See field notes, reflections on discussions on MLF case, Bulawayo, November–December 2011.

to form the ZAPU-Federal Party. Unable to mobilise significant support for this party, Siwela became involved with the MLF. Before the MLF trial was resolved, however, he again split from the MLF amid accusations over his continued ties to ZAPU-FP, and obliquely cited 'policy reasons' to explain his formation of the Matabeleland Liberation Organisation in 2013.[41] John Gazi's alliance to the MLF was also in dispute during the trial. Then the deputy secretary for security for the MLF, Gazi was a former ZIPRA special weapons expert. In the independent media, rumours circulated that he maintained close ties to the CIO. Amid the reporting on Siwela and Gazi, Charles Gumbo Thomas faded into the background of the trial as the MLF's national economic advisor.[42]

Following their arrest on 3 and 4 March 2011, Siwela, Gazi and Thomas were initially charged under Section 22 of the Criminal Law (Codification and Reform) Act for subverting a constitutional government. In court on 7 March the charge was changed to the more serious charge of treason under Section 20 of the Criminal Law Act. Before the courts, the prosecution argued that the men had met on 1 March 2011 for an 'executive meeting ... during [which] they connived and agreed on ways to influencing [sic] people to rise and demonstrate against the government which would result in creation of a separate state of Republic of Mthwakazi'.[43]

To underline the severity of the charges against Siwela, Gazi and Thomas, and to cast them as dangerous political agitators, the men were kept in solitary confinement at Khami Maximum Security Remand prison, a prison that had already become notorious under Rhodesian rule for its harsh conditions.[44] Their applications for bail before Regional Magistrate John Masimba were repeatedly refused, as

---

[41] Interview with Lance Guma, 'Nehanda Radio Speaks to Paul Siwela', *Nehanda Radio*, 6 January 2014, accessed on 7 January 2014 at http://nehandaradio.com/2014/01/06/nehanda-radio-speaks-to-paul-siwela/.

[42] 'MLF Leaders Still in Police Custody', *Radio VOP*, 5 March 2011 and Khanyile Mlotshwa, 'Government Cracks Whip on Secessionists', *The Standard*, 7 March 2011, both accessed on 4 July 2013 at www.zimbabwesituation.com/march_2011_archive.html.

[43] From Judgment HB 53/11, p. 2 (issued on 24 March 2011 by Justice Ndou in *Thomas, Gazi and Siwela v. State*).

[44] Munochiveyi, *Prisoners of Rhodesia*, pp. 167–8. Munochiveyi provides a detailed account of the conditions in Khami prison, drawing attention to the bare cells, strict routine, forced hard labour, sparse meals and beatings among other evidence of its harsh conditions.

he argued that the defendants had a case to answer because they were 'senior members of the MLF and were found in possession of pamphlets carrying messages which incite members of the public to rise against the government'.[45] As the case dragged on, ZANU-PF extended its intimidation to other members of the MLF. During a bail hearing on 11 March, for example, four more members of the MLF – Nonsikelelo Ncube, Makhiwa Ndebele, Ntombizodwa Moyo and Makhosi Khumalo – were dramatically arrested inside the courtroom and taken to Bulawayo Central Police Station. They were released later that day.[46]

Eventually the matter was referred to the Bulawayo High Court. On 24 March the three men were granted bail at US$2,000, with strict conditions.[47] The prosecution, led by Whisper Madbaudi and Martha Cheda, invoked Section 121(1) of the Criminal Procedure and Evidence Act (Chapter 9:07).[48] In many political trials the prosecution did not act on its use of Section 121, failing to file an appeal to the initial bail outcome. They would nevertheless use the section with the aim of delaying the accused's release from remand prison for seven days. In this instance, in line with its heavy-handed response to the MLF, the state did file an appeal. The prosecution claimed that the High Court had been misdirected to come to a decision that the three men would not commit a similar offence when released on bail.[49]

---

[45] 'Mthwakazi Leaders Have a Case to Answer – Magistrate', *Radio VOP*, 11 March 2011, accessed on 4 July 2013 at www.zimbabwesituation.com/ march_2011_archive.html.

[46] 'MLF Members in Hiding, Four More Arrested', *Radio VOP*, 12 March 2011 and Mxolisi Ncube, 'Chihuri crushes new party', *The Zimbabwean*, 15 March 2011, both accessed on 4 July 2013 at www.zimbabwesituation.com/march_ 2011_archive.html.

[47] From Judgment HB 53/11, pp. 7–8 (issued on 24 March 2011 by Justice Ndou in *Thomas, Gazi and Siwela v. State*). Conditions included that the three defendants would remain at their registered addresses, surrender their passports and were not to go beyond a 40 km radius of Bulawayo's main post office. The men were further banned from attending political gatherings and had to report to Bulawayo Central Police station at the CID Law and Order division's office three days a week.

[48] 'State Blocks Mthwakazi Leaders' Release', *Radio VOP*, 24 March 2011, accessed on 5 July 2013 at www.zimbabwesituation.com/march_2011_archive .html; Veritas, 'Court Watch 8/2012 [Prosecutors' Record of Abuse of Power to Delay Bail]', *Veritas*, 25 April 2012, accessed on 4 July 2013 at http://archive .kubatana.net/html/archive/legisl/120425veritas.asp?sector=POLACT&year= 0&range_start=1.

[49] From Appeal Judgment HB 59/11, p. 2 (issued on 31 March 2011 by Justice Ndou in *Thomas, Gazi and Siwela v. Attorney General*).

Justice Nicholas Ndou heard the state's appeal at Bulawayo's High
Court on 31 March. He upheld Justice Maphios Cheda's decision to
release John Gazi and Charles Thomas, stating that it was likely that
the Supreme Court would come to the same decision. Justice Ndou
rejected Paul Siwela's bail application, however, arguing that Siwela
still had a pending case dating from 2004 when he had been charged
with contravening Section 19 of POSA.[50] This, he argued, could allow
the Supreme Court to consider his case differently.[51] In May the
Supreme Court's Chief Justice Godfrey Chidyausiku indeed requested
that Siwela file an affidavit in which he assured the court he would not
commit similar offences while out on bail.[52] Reporting on the case, SW
Radio Africa interpreted the court's request as 'deliberate
bureaucracy ... to delay the case'.[53]

Following his initial arrest in March 2011, it took almost three
months before Siwela was released from Khami prison on 4 June.[54]
Siwela suffered a range of indignities and threats during his extended
stay at Khami. He was criticised by other members of the MLF for his

[50] In 2004, Section 19 of POSA fell under Part III of the Act, crimes against public
order, and related to 'gathering conducting to riot, disorder or intolerance'. In
2007, Part III of POSA was repealed by the Criminal Law (Codification and
Reform) Act. Corresponding offences were moved to Chapter IV of the Criminal
Law Act. At the time of Siwela's arrest, 'similar offences' would have related to
Section 37 the Act: 'participating in gathering with intent to promote public
violence, breaches of the peace or bigotry'.
[51] From Appeal Judgment HB 59/11, p. 2 (issued on 31 March 2011 by Justice
Ndou in *Thomas, Gazi and Siwela v. Attorney General*); Lance Guma, 'High
Court Orders Release of Mthwakazi Duo, Siwela Still Held', *SW Radio Africa*,
31 March 2011, accessed on 5 July 2013 at http://allafrica.com/stories/
201104010050.html; 'MLF Pair Released on Bail', *NewsDay*, 7 April 2011,
accessed on 6 July 2013 at www.newsday.co.zw/2011/04/07/2011–04–07-mlf-
pair-released-on-bail/.
[52] 'Siwela Suffers New Bail Blow', *New Zimbabwe*, 10 May 2011, accessed on
6 July 2014 at www.newzimbabwe.com/news-5088-Siwela%20suffers%20new
%20bail%20blow/news.aspx; Irene Madongo, 'Mangoma, Paul Siwela Trials
Drag On', 17 May 2011, *SW Radio Africa*, accessed on 6 July 2013 at http://
allafrica.com/stories/201105171044.html.
[53] Madongo, 'Mangoma, Paul Siwela Trials Drag On'.
[54] Tererai Karimakwenda, 'Siwela Awaits Release after Granting of Bail', *SW
Radio Africa*, 1 June 2011; Tererai Karimakwenda, 'Siwela Release Not
Confirmed', *SW Radio Africa*, 1 June 2011; Thabo Kunene, 'Released
Secessionist Leader Siwela Fears for His Life', *RNW*, 8 June 2011, all accessed
on 7 July 2013 at www.zimbabwesituation.com/old/june_2011_archive.html.

affiliations with ZAPU-FP and suffered from high blood pressure.[55] His wife was arrested and questioned by members of the CID Law and Order division.[56] On 15 August 2011, Siwela himself was again interrogated by the CID Law and Order division at Bulawayo Central, where he was held for three hours.[57] Such harassment through detention continued on 20 January 2012, when Siwela, Gazi and Thomas were again remanded into custody by magistrate Tawanda Muchemwa. They were to be held at Khami prison until the start of their trial.[58]

Asked to describe his experiences in prison by Lance Guma on *Question Time*, Siwela commented that 'people have to appreciate that staying in prison is not a good place'.[59] As with the young, urban-based activists whose experiences in detention are discussed in Chapter 4, the prison conditions were central to the narratives of many of the political activists and civil society members I interviewed in Bulawayo. For example, Mkhokheli, a founding member of *Imbovane Yamahlabezulu* who had worked alongside Siwela to revive ZAPU before he decided to join the MDC-T, had been arrested with Siwela twice.[60] He discussed their 'terrible, very humiliating, and dehumanising' experiences in Khami prison and recalled that:

prisoners were being served with yellow maize porridge which was terrible, smelly and, ugh, unappetising … most of the time you were not consuming that food because it was terrible. … And I remember there was a time when it was raining, and rain was coming through the window because the window is just an opening without any windowpane. So the rain was coming

[55] 'Siwela's Condition Worsens in Prison', *Radio VOP*, 25 May 2011; Patience Nyangove, 'Siwela Critically Ill', *The Standard*, 29 May 2011; Brian Chitemba, 'Jailed Siwela Left in Dilemma', *Zimbabwe Independent*, 27 May 2011, all accessed on 7 July 2013 at www.zimbabwesituation.com.

[56] Irene Madongo, 'Paul Siwela Wife Hunted Down by Secret Police', *SW Radio Africa*, 21 March 2011, accessed on 6 July 2013 at www.zimbabwesituation.com.

[57] 'Zim Police Investigates Fliers to Topple Mugabe', *Radio VOP*, 15 August 2011, accessed on 7 July 2013 at www.zimbabwesituation.com.

[58] 'Mthwakazi Liberation Leaders Re-arrested', *Radio VOP*, 20 January 2012, accessed on 5 July 2013 at www.zimbabwesituation.com.

[59] Quoted in 'Paul Siwela on Question Time', transcript of interview with Lance Guma, 30 November 2011 on *SW Radio Africa*, accessed on 5 June 2013 at http://allafrica.com/stories/201112060190.html.

[60] Interview, Mkhokheli, political activist and MDC-T member, Bulawayo, 13 December 2011.

in through the window and our cell, you know, got wet. Even water accu-
mulated inside and we had to spend the rest of the night, you know squatting
because you could not stand all night, and you could not sleep. Then the
blankets were also wet. So those were some of the conditions that we had to
contend with.[61]

As the similarities in prison experiences underline, the MLF members'
harassment through repeated detentions and the threat of a treason
trial had all the hallmarks of politically motivated persecution through
prosecution. Despite this, human rights lawyers based in Harare
refused to represent the three defendants. Following ZLHR's decision,
Bulawayo-based lawyers broke away to form an alternative human
rights network. This organisation explicitly recognised and incorporated the continuing impact of the *Gukurahundi* legacy on the region in
its approach to the law, combining their legal and state consciousness
with a historical awareness that, they argued, was essential to the
practice of law. In this manner, they worked to protect the citizens of
Matabeleland, whose understandings of their belonging within the
Zimbabwean state, and the claims they could make to its institutions,
were fundamentally shaped by history. As Mkhokheli explained, for
example, his experience of the horrible physical conditions in Khami
prison was fundamentally attached to his recognition of historical
injustice in the region. He argued that his incarceration was 'especially
dehumanising' because he was 'mixed with common criminals' despite
having 'raised an issue which is very legitimate ... the issue of the
Gukurahundi'.[62]

The Formation of the Abammeli Human Rights Lawyers Network

Since 2000, human rights lawyers have been concentrated in Harare,
where they were financially and morally supported by the donor
community and its 'good governance' agenda. In the narratives of
Bulawayo-based lawyers, these Harare-based lawyers never had knowledge of, or had lost sight of, Matabeleland's violent past, and the
repercussions of this past in the present day. The *Gukurahundi*,
Bulawayo-based lawyers argued, did not shape the legal and state

[61] Ibid.   [62] Ibid.

consciousness that the lawyers in Harare represented and enacted. With the formation of Abammeli, Harare-based lawyers stood accused of wrongly perpetuating a wider discourse evident in human rights reporting: that Zimbabwe's key human rights challenges emerged with the formation of the MDC and the land reform programme of the early 2000s. In contrast, Bulawayo-based lawyers asserted that the recognition that the struggle for rights and belonging in Zimbabwe started not in 2000, but in 1980, was essential for the mobilisation of law to protect the rights and human dignity of Matabeleland's citizens.

Kucaca Phulu, one of Abammeli's founding members, explained:

We had noticed over a long period of time that this approach where everything is centred in Harare, there is a Harare-centric mentality, tends to overlook a number of critical matters in trying to handle human rights matters in our region. And therefore we thought there was a space that Abammeli Human Rights network could fill and play a critical role.[63]

Phulu continued that Bulawayo would benefit from a human rights organisation that focused specifically on the region of Matabeleland because 'Matabeleland issues are unique and they need people, you know, human rights lawyers who are going to understand the unique nature of those matters, and the sensitivities around those matters of *Gukurahundi*'.[64] For Phulu, this view was vindicated by the debates he had with ZLHR members based in Harare over whether they should represent the MLF leaders.

In early March 2011, Phulu was in Geneva, Switzerland with Irene Petras, ZLHR's executive director, when he was contacted by Matshobana Ncube, his partner at his law firm Phulu & Ncube. Ncube informed Phulu of the arrest of Siwela, Gazi and Thomas, and explained that he had approached Lizwe Jamela in ZLHR's Bulawayo offices to request that ZLHR represent the three men. Ncube recalled that Jamela had explained that ZLHR could not represent the MLF because of 'what they stand for, one of the things they are said to stand for is, they want to chase all the Shonas away from Bulawayo and the second thing is that they want to use violent means in order to divide

---

[63] Interview, Kucaca Phulu, human rights lawyer, Bulawayo, 29 November 2011; also in an interview with Sibusiso, human rights lawyer, Bulawayo, 22 November, 2011.

[64] Interview, Kucaca Phulu, human rights lawyer, Bulawayo, 29 November 2011.

the country'.[65] Ncube explained that ZLHR 'essentially said the guys were tribalists and biased against Shona people. We said we could not vouch for such [ideas] but that the issue was that these guys were facing treason charges and needed to be defended.'[66]

In an interview with Lance Guma on SW Radio Africa, Phulu explained that he had updated Petras on the matter in Geneva. He told her that the MLF stated that they would not use violence, and reminded her that, as human rights lawyers, their professional capacity dictated that 'we must not pre-judge the matter. At least people must be given the right to be heard before we as human rights lawyers begin to condemn them,'[67] Although Phulu communicated with people at different levels of ZLHR, he was not able to convince them to represent the MLF leaders. Phulu remarked that ZLHR 'sat as judge and jury to convict MLF even ahead of the courts'.[68] As ZLHR 'indicated that they were not prepared to deal with the matter', Phulu explained, 'lawyers in Bulawayo proceeded to act on their behalf because we could not wait for the resolution of the matter before they could get representation'.[69] Ncube recalled that following ZLHR's decision, Bulawayo-based lawyers 'were so disappointed in that kind of conduct and decided that if ZLHR was unwilling to assist human rights defenders we [must] step in. So we formed Abammeli [to] provide legal assistance to the communities on the margins'.[70]

Following Phulu's interview with SW Radio Africa, Irene Petras released a statement criticising the Bulawayo-based lawyers who had formed Abammeli. The statement sidelined Phulu's key claim, that ZLHR lacked an understanding of the way the violence of the 1980s continued to impact the residents of Matabeleland, and that by refusing to represent the MLF leaders on the grounds of 'what they stood for' they perpetuated rather than challenged the government's

---

[65] Quoted in 'Kucaca Phulu: Behind the Headlines', transcript of interview with Lance Guma, 24 March 2011 on *SW Radio Africa*, accessed on 7 July 2013 at http://swradioafrica.com/Documents/Kucaca%20Phulu%20Behind%20the%20Headlines.pdf.

[66] Matshobana Ncube, in personal correspondence with author, 19 December 2016.

[67] 'Kucaca Phulu – Behind the Headlines'.

[68] Abammeli Human Rights Lawyers Network, 'Statement by Abammeli'.

[69] Ibid.

[70] Matshobana Ncube, in personal correspondence with author, 19 December 2016.

criminalisation of the concerns raised within such political groupings. Petras stated that the question of whether ZLHR would have represented the three MLF leaders should be considered a 'moot point'. ZLHR's work, she argued, 'speaks for itself'.[71] The statement then proceeded to criticise the Abammeli lawyers in ways reminiscent of ZLHR's frequent allegations against the prosecution in politically motivated trials. That is, ZLHR argued that the correct procedures for requesting legal representation had not been followed:

As a professional law-based organisation with limited funding for litigation, ZLHR has strict standardised procedures for the take-up of cases by lawyers on its behalf. The organisation does not cover cases in which lawyers deploy themselves and then ask, or expect, ZLHR to cover their legal fees after the fact.[72]

The statement continued that, had the Abammeli lawyers been 'genuine and dedicated ZLHR members', they would have known to follow the proper procedures. ZLHR concluded that the Bulawayo lawyers' 'malicious and unfounded' claims resulted from their faulty perception of what human rights work was all about: 'We believe that the unsubstantiated complaints and allegations against ZLHR are being raised by some people who have an unfortunate and regrettable misconception that human rights lawyering is an industry and not a passion.'[73] In their decision to extend legal representation to the three MLF leaders, certain Bulawayo-based lawyers suddenly stood accused of not being 'proper' human rights lawyers, but greedy, rule-breaking entrepreneurs.

Phulu and his colleagues responded to this patronising, disparaging response from Harare's leading human rights lawyers by distancing themselves from ZLHR's network and forming their own. Abammeli members noted that their Harare-based colleagues were guilty of a 'continued and structural failure to adequately represent Human Rights defenders from Matabeleland'.[74] In their rhetoric and through their actions, Harare's human rights community had contributed to the

---

[71] Irene Petras, 'Statement by ZLHR on Formation of Abammeli Human Rights Lawyers', in 'Behind the Headlines', *SW Radio Africa*, 24 March 2011, accessed on 7 July 2013 at www.zimbabwesituation.com/old/mar25_2011.html.
[72] Petras, 'Statement by ZLHR'.   [73] Ibid.
[74] Abammeli Human Rights Lawyers Network, 'Statement by Abammeli'.

misunderstandings and preconceptions of Matabeleland as a violent region, as a result of which ZLHR had failed to recognise that:

[T]hese people [Siwela, Gazi and Thomas] have been arrested for holding an opinion, for advocating for a certain cause. And they have been charged with treason when they have done nothing treasonous. The meeting in question, all they discussed was basic issues that you would find discussed as an organisation. There was certainly nothing treasonous. And human rights lawyers refused to represent them. They refused to represent them because they said 'look, we don't believe in what you believe in', which is not a human rights lawyers job, to decide that I agree with you or I don't agree with you and therefore I'll work with you on that basis.[75]

In the eyes of the Abammeli lawyers, ZLHR had made illegitimate claims to authority by portraying itself as the organisation with the 'right' legal knowledge that followed 'proper procedure'. ZLHR's decision was more than 'bad' human rights lawyering, Phulu argued. It was an indication that the legal consciousness of his colleagues outside of Matabeleland was shaped by a history of repression that did not include the *Gukurahundi*. As a result, these lawyers 'don't understand the dynamics and the things that are happening in Matabeleland', and so could not share in understanding the implications of this history for Abammeli lawyers' choice to practice law in a manner that was based not on fighting for a shared political ideal – the safeguarding of justice and the rule of law – but on acknowledging a shared human experience: the possibility that law could be turned against you.

This also meant that Phulu and his regional colleagues would never belong to the human rights network in Harare, as the Bulawayo-based lawyers' legal and state consciousness could not accommodate a version of history that refused to acknowledge that the law had been used as a mechanism for state-sanctioned violent coercion since independence. Phulu continued:

They don't understand that the person that is advocating for secession, I may not agree with him, but he is still my neighbour. He is still my brother. We are still one person. We suffered through a lot together. There is no way I am going to allow him to be tortured, you know, arrested unjustly and sent to jail and the keys thrown away.[76]

ZLHR's decision not to represent the MLF leaders brought to light what, among the Abammeli lawyers, was a much more deep-rooted

---

[75] Interview, Kucaca Phulu, human rights lawyer, 29 November 2011.   [76] Ibid.

concern, namely that their colleagues in, or with strong ties to, Harare could not, and never would, fully understand what it meant to be a citizen of, and human rights activist in, Matabeleland. Just as Father Mkandla described the ZANU-PF-supporting, Shona-speaking police officer as a 'misfit' for working at a police station in Matabeleland and having no knowledge of *Gukurahundi*, certain ZLHR-affiliated lawyers in Harare appeared unable to fully understand how the violence of the 1980s shaped views on law within the region. Without this understanding, ZLHR failed to engage with the law in a manner that not only protected the MLF leaders, but safeguarded the humanity, dignity and civility of residents in the region. At the root of their critiques of ZLHR's refusal to represent the MLF, then, was the Abammeli lawyers' framing of themselves as residents in, and citizens of, Matabeleland. Rather than focusing on the MLF's ethnic concerns, however, they echoed the young activists in Harare who engaged with the law to express a 'rich' understanding of citizenship. This allowed the Abammeli lawyers to engage popular understandings of citizenship to argue for the importance of incorporating law's history in mobilisations of legal consciousness, as this in turn had effects on state consciousness.

History, Law and Citizenship

Abammeli's lawyers argued that, as a result of their limited understanding of Matabeleland's politics, ZLHR drew the wrong conclusion about the government's motivations in arresting, detaining and prosecuting the MLF leaders. Throughout the trial, which lasted until late October 2012, the defence team found further evidence for this in the way that the state framed the three men as 'dangerous criminals', but presented a procedurally flawed case and eventually acquitted the men. These aspects of the trial all underlined that ZLHR should not have 'sat as judge and jury to convict the MLF even ahead of the courts'.[77]

On 19 March 2012, Siwela, Gazi and Thomas' trial began before Justice Nicholas Ndou at Bulawayo's High Court.[78] The prosecution charged the men with treason, using language reminiscent of the accusations laid against both the 'dissidents' of the *Gukurahundi*

---

[77] MLF, *Free Mthwakazi*, p. 32.
[78] Tichaona Sibanda, 'Bail Hearing for 29 MDC-t Activists Postponed for 7th Time', *SW Radio Africa*, 19 March 2012, accessed on 4 July 2013 at www.zimbabwesituation.com/old/mar20_2012.html.

period, and after 2000 in cases like the trial against Munyaradzi
Gwisai and many young activists, to portray the MLF as 'dangerous
criminals'. During a bail hearing, for example, state prosecutor Martha
Cheda argued that 'the three applicants can't be granted bail as they
are a bunch of unrepentant criminals'.[79] The prosecution continued
that the MLF leaders had designed and distributed fliers with
'insulting, inflammatory' language, aimed at:

inciting members of the army to defect from the army, refuse to carry out
orders from their superiors, to take their weapons and join the army in
Mthwakazi Republic. The messages also incite members of the public, civil
service to rise against the government like the revolt of Tunisia and Egypt.
The messages also incite members of the non-governmental organizations,
political parties, labour unions, churches to join Mthwakazi Liberation
Front in order to liberate the people of Mthwakazi from 30 years of dicta-
torship, 30 years of one-man rule and 30 years of fake independence. It is
submitted that the messages in the fliers are treasonous.[80]

Defence lawyers Lucas Nkomo, who was representing Siwela and
Thomas, and Sindiso Sibanda, who represented Gazi, consistently
drew attention to the discrepancies in the state's case. These discrepancies, they argued, were a clear indication that 'the case against their
clients was a hatchet job meant to silence them from the political scene
in Bulawayo'.[81] Much to the amusement of the public in the gallery,
the defence lawyers' tactics resulted in witnesses admitting they had
altered their evidence, that they had presented a different account
during the bail hearings, or that they were unable to explain why the
calendars and pamphlets were 'treasonous'.[82] To 'the laughter of the

[79] MLF, *Free Mthwakazi*, p. 32.
[80] From Judgment HB 53/11, p. 3 (issued on 24 March 2011 by Justice Ndou in
Thomas, Gazi and Siwela v. State).
[81] Tichaona Sibanda, 'Prosecution Case against MLF Leaders "Shaky"', *SW Radio
Africa*, 23 March 2012, accessed on 5 July 2013 at www.swradioafrica.com/
News_archives/files/2012/March/Frid%2023%20March/ts-mfl-leaders.html.
[82] 'MLF Leaders' Trial Opens, Key Witness Rebuffs Police Claims', *Radio VOP*,
20 March 2012, accessed on 6 July at www.zimbabwesituation.com/old/mar21_
2012.html; 'Police Recant Testimony in Siwela Trial', *New Zimbabwe*,
20 March 2012, accessed on 6 July at www.zimbabwesituation.com/old/mar22_
2012.html; Tichaona Sibanda, 'Treason Trial against MLF Leaders Resumes in
Bulawayo', *SW Radio Africa*, 23 April 2012, accessed on 6 July at http://
allafrica.com/stories/201204241169.html.

packed court gallery', for example, Detective Sergeant George Ngwenya, who was not permitted to testify at the bail hearing in March, had to admit to having very limited knowledge of the details of the case, in spite of being an arresting officer and having searched the MLF's offices.[83] Such performances were not only an effort to convince the courts of the men's innocence. By exposing the flaws in the state's case they also aimed to highlight how the MLF's trial was politically motivated, thus drawing attention to Abammeli's perspective that the Harare-based lawyers had misjudged the situation because they failed to engage with the longer historical trajectory of the law's use as a mechanism of political coercion.

In October 2012, the defence lawyers applied for the release of all three defendants.[84] Justice Nicholas Ndou, however, chose to reserve judgement indefinitely, dragging out the defendants' uncertainty over their futures.[85] These uncertainties were compounded when Justice Ndou resigned as High Court judge effective from 31 December 2012. As ZANU-PF was restored as the single party in government in the July 2013 elections, however, Justice Ndou returned to the bench to finalise the case on several occasions. In December 2013, Gazi was acquitted due to lack of evidence, and in October 2014, Thomas was acquitted as well. Siwela had fled to South Africa in self-imposed exile in August 2013, and as a result the case against him was still pending in March 2021.[86]

Matshobana Ncube commented that once the court acquitted Gazi and Thomas he felt all the more 'disappointed' in ZLHR's response to the case: 'ZLHR's conduct was quite unfortunate because at the same

[83] 'Cop in MLF Trial Admits Some Exhibits Not in Court', *The Chronicle*, 26 April 2012, www.chronicle.co.zw/cop-in-mlf-trial-admits-some-exhibits-not-in-court/.

[84] 'Mthwakazi Treason Trio Seek Discharge', *New Zimbabwe*, 1 November 2012, accessed on 4 July 2013 at www.newzimbabwe.com/news-9445-Mthwakazi%20treason%20trio%20seek%20discharge/news.aspx.

[85] Tichaona Sibanda, 'Prosecution Case against MLF Leaders "Shaky"'. Veritas, 'Court Watch 2/2013 [Supreme Court and High Court Judges and Labour and Administrative Court Presidents]', *Veritas*, 25 January 2013, accessed on 14 August 2014 at http://archive.kubatana.net/html/archive/legisl/130122veritas.asp?sector=LEGAL&year=2013&range_start=61.

[86] Silas Nkala, 'Bereaved Siwela Sneaks Back', *The Standard*, 1 December 2019, accessed on 7 January 2020 at www.thestandard.co.zw/2019/12/01/bereaved-siwela-sneaks-back/; see also Tendai Chinembiri, 'Paul Siwela Poses a National Security Threat', *Bulawayo24*, 25 April 2016, accessed on 17 December 2016 at http://bulawayo24.com/index-id-opinion-sc-columnist-byo-87010.html.

time they were defending Gwisai and others in Harare who were eventually convicted on violence related charges. On the other hand, two of the accused persons with Siwela were acquitted on the treason charges.'[87] By drawing a parallel with the Gwisai case the lawyers were also drawing attention to the way that ZLHR's refusal to take the MLF's case in effect authorised ZANU-PF's framing of the MLF as a serious political threat. This, Kucaca Phulu explained, indicated that the Harare-based human rights lawyers had fundamentally misunderstood the dynamics between law, state coercion and history in Zimbabwe, and as a result had failed to protect Matabeleland's citizens in their challenges to ZANU-PF's repression. The *Gukurahundi*, Phulu explained, allowed Matabeleland's human rights community to comprehend what it really meant to hold a legal consciousness in which the fight for a rule-bound and 'just' state was 'inextricably linked' to the future of the Zimbabwean state. It entailed fighting for a state in which there was no longer 'any way [that] you can stand up and say "your right is better than mine"'.[88]

Conclusion

This chapter examined how Matabeleland's violent history has shaped understandings and uses of law among the region's citizens, and within the country's human rights community. Invoking a specific, ethnic history as justification for their calls for Matabeleland's secession into the 'Mthwakazi Republic', the MLF occupied a marginal position in the region's wider politics. Through their arrest, detention and trial, however, ZANU-PF issued a public warning against expressions of secessionist politics. The Harare-based lawyer's collective ZLHR refused to represent the MLF leaders, thereby siding with ZANU-PF's portrayal of the MLF as a 'dangerous', 'criminal' party and failing to engage with Matabeleland's long experience with law's coercive potential. In response the Bulawayo-based lawyers formed Abammeli. In part, Abammeli was formed to take on the task of defending the legitimacy of the MLF leaders in court, casting them as fellow citizens and human beings deserving of equal and dignified

---

[87] Matshobana Ncube, in personal correspondence with author, 19 December 2016
[88] Interview, Kucaca Phulu, human rights lawyer, 29 November 2011.

treatment and entitled to express their political visions. In addition, the formation of Abammeli was itself a decision by the lawyers to challenge the Harare-based lawyers' lack of understanding regarding, and a respect for, the ways that the historical place of law in Matabeleland continued to shape legal and state consciousness in the region. Ironically, as we see in Chapter 8, the state did have a strong sense of the historical place of law in Matabeleland.

8 | Historical Narrative and Political Strategy in Bulawayo's Magistrates' Courts

The Case of Owen Maseko

So I went Demonstrating
Demonstrating in my bedroom,
Under oppressive blankets of sad, failed
And shattered dreams
Demonstrating in my sitting room
With no room for my hopes to
Sit and maybe blossom
Demonstrating in my toilet
Too stinking a nation gone
Down the blocked drains drained
By the black president
Demonstrating in my kitchen with
Empty dishes, pots and pans
Milling with red berets, club and shield welding,
Black cockroaches
Food burning, fainting in teargas smoke
So I get out, out to free myself
From this black dark Smokey house
In a black dark Smokey country,
Only to find myself in a Jail Cell![1]

On 25 March 2010, visual artist Owen Maseko's exhibition of paintings, installations and graffiti focused on the *Gukurahundi* period opened in Bulawayo's National Art Gallery. Its title, *Sibathontisele*, an Ndebele expression for 'we drip on them', referred to a common torture technique of dripping melting plastic on victims used by government forces in the 1980s and after 2000.[2] The exhibition consisted

---

[1] Owen Maseko, 'So I Went ... ', *The 1980 Alliance*, no date, accessed on 15 November 2016 at http://the1980.org/index.php/so-i-went/.

[2] Owen Maseko, *Trials and Tribulations of an Artist*, 17 July 2011, accessed on 2 February 2012 at www.osisa.org/openspace/zimbabwe/censorship-trials-and-tribulations-artist.

of a series of twelve paintings, three installations and graffiti painted directly onto the gallery walls. Similar in style to his painting on the cover of this book, Maseko primarily used white, red and black paint to demonstrate the bloodshed of the 1980s and the dark and difficult times that followed. The works, Maseko explained, were inspired by his memories, documentation on the *Gukurahundi*, particularly the well-known report on the atrocities by the CCJP and LRF, *Breaking the Silence*, and many conversations with its author, Shari Eppel.[3] A day after the exhibition's opening, Maseko was arrested and the exhibition shut down. It remained shut for the next five years. In April 2015, Maseko was ordered to take down his exhibition and banned from showing it elsewhere in the country by the courts.[4]

In the media and within academic and human rights communities, Maseko's arrest, his trial and the banning of his exhibition were interpreted as a prime example of ZANU-PF's continued closure of democratic spaces for expression and its reluctance to take responsibility for, or to discuss, the *Gukurahundi* period.[5] In Chapter 7, I demonstrated how ZANU-PF made a heavy-handed effort to repress a minor political opposition party, the MLF, which placed perceptions of Matabeleland and the 'Matabele' people's marginalisation at the centre of its agenda. I argued that the case against the MLF exposed regional differences between human rights lawyers that were tied to diverging understandings of how violent history shaped the authority of law and the post-independence state, and how this influenced the protection of citizens within it.

In this chapter, I examine Maseko's trial to demonstrate how the violence of the 1980s shaped the way law was used by various actors in the court to create and contest a historical narrative. For Maseko and his defence team, law worked as a claim to citizenship and as an

---

[3] Interview, Owen Maseko, visual artist, Bulawayo, 8 January 2012.

[4] 'Gukurahundi Exhibition Pulled Down', *New Zimbabwe*, 9 April 2015, accessed on 3 March 2016 at www.newzimbabwe.com/showbiz-21763-Gukurahundi +exhibition+pulled+down/showbiz.aspx.

[5] See, for example, Mbonisi Zikhali, 'Gagged: Owen Maseko's Art in Zimbabwe', 23 May 2010, accessed on 5 June 2011 at www.dispatchesinternational.org/?p= 161; John Eppel, *Owen Maseko and the Gukurahundi*, 5 April 2010, accessed on 4 February 2012, at www.kubatana.net/html/archive/opin/100405je.asp?sector= opin&year=2010&range_start=151; Amnesty International, *Zimbabwe: Continued Clamp Down on Dissent* (New York, Amnesty International, March 2011).

expression of a legal and state consciousness which granted authority to a rule-bound state. Echoing the understanding of courts as record keepers, held by Zimbabwean citizens and human rights lawyers more widely, Maseko saw his trial as an opportunity to continue to 'break the silence' by placing the atrocities of the ZANU-PF regime in the 1980s on legal record. ZANU-PF, in turn, tried Maseko not with the aim of 'silencing' references to *Gukurahundi* history, but with the aim of presenting a historical narrative on the public stage of the courts. In court, the prosecution invoked the 1980s history as a narrative and political strategy to remind Zimbabweans of ZANU-PF's capacity to orchestrate widespread violence.

Owen Maseko's Exhibition and Arrest

Owen Maseko is a visual artist based in Bulawayo. He described himself as someone who 'just did art on canvas', without a 'history of political activism', though he did raise social concerns in his work. In 2005, Maseko organised *Khululeka*, an exhibition of graffiti in public toilets that suggested these toilets were the only remaining spaces for free expression in Zimbabwe. Through this graffiti, Maseko questioned whether ZANU-PF's narrow retelling of the liberation struggle – its 'patriotic history' – was justified given its failure to ensure that the goals of the struggle were met.[6] Maseko's subsequent exhibition, *Sibathontisele*, explicitly broke the ongoing political silence surrounding recognition and discussions of violent history and legacies of *Gukurahundi*.

Maseko organised the exhibition against the backdrop of the GPA and the GNU, the unity government of ZANU-PF and the two MDC factions, and the formation of the Organ of National Healing. He noted that, despite these political changes, the government continued to display a 'lack of commitment to resolve sensitive issues that will create space for peace and democracy', particularly the consequences of violent repression of the 1980s.[7] By placing his art in the public domain, specifically within Bulawayo's National Gallery, a state-funded institution, Maseko hoped he would stimulate debate on the *Gukurahundi*. He explained that he:

---

[6] Taurai Maduna, *Toilet Democracy*, 12 July 2005, accessed on 14 March 2012 at http://swradioafrica.com/Documents/Toilet%20Democracy.pdf.
[7] Owen Maseko, *Trials and Tribulations*.

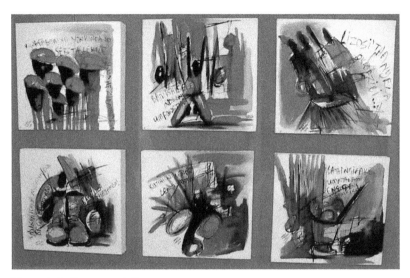

Figure 8.1 *Ongowane'zibomvu*
Source: Photograph of Sibathontisele Exhibition paintings by Owen Maseko. Copyright © 2020 Owen Maseko

did the exhibition in a government institution, I did the exhibition in Zimbabwe, not outside the country ... I think that kind of made everyone feel that this [recognition of the *Gukurahundi*] is a case they should be pushing. I think it gave everyone a lot of energy to talk about this.[8]

Maseko was aware that his art could be interpreted in 'millions of ways' by anyone coming into the gallery, but many of the images he used were central in the memories of the *Gukurahundi* as they persisted in the public imagination in 2010.[9] Describing his painting *Ongowane'zibomvu* (see Figure 8.1) – Ndebele for 'red berets', the cap worn by the notorious members of the Fifth Brigade – at the Oslo Freedom Forum in May 2013, for instance, Maseko noted that the men in red berets made up 'one of those memories that us as Ndebele people, people from Matabeleland remember so well'.[10]

Another of Maseko's paintings, *Babylon Songs*, depicted a *pungwe*, a political education rally, led by the Fifth Brigade soldiers. In the 1980s the Fifth Brigade replicated strategies of political mobilisation

---

[8] Interview, Owen Maseko, visual artist, Bulawayo, 8 January 2012.   [9] Ibid.
[10] Owen Maseko, *Presentation at the Oslo Freedom Forum*, 15 May 2013, accessed on 5 August 2013 at www.youtube.com/watch?v=cMP5iVv0huc.

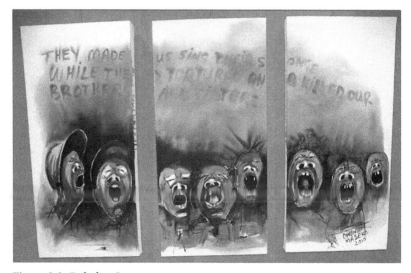

Figure 8.2 *Babylon Songs*
Source: Photograph of Sibathontisele Exhibition paintings by Owen Maseko. Copyright © 2020 Owen Maseko

that ZANU-PF had relied upon during the liberation war, organising *pungwes* at which people were made to denounce ZAPU, and 'forced [to take part in] singing, dancing and sloganeering, often accompanied by grotesque forms of violence, as well as lesser humiliations'.[11] In this context, *pungwes* were a political and cultural strategy to mobilise, discipline and punish civilians.[12] In the painting, Maseko referenced the violence of this strategy with the quote 'they made us sing their songs while they killed our brothers and sisters' (see Figure 8.2).

The exhibition also included an installation of the signing of the 1987 Unity Accord, through which ZAPU was subsumed in ZANU-PF. In the installation Joshua Nkomo is shown bleeding from his back,

---

[11] Alexander et al., *Violence and Memory*, p. 222.
[12] Ibid.; Richard P. Werbner, 'In Memory: A Heritage of War in Southwestern Zimbabwe', in Ngwabi Bhebe and Terence Ranger, *Society in Zimbabwe's Liberation War* (James Currey, Oxford, 1996), pp. 192–205; and CCJP and LRF, *Breaking the Silence*, pp. 50–1. For use of pungwes as a form of political discipline in other contexts, see Gerald Chikozko Mazarire, 'Discipline and Punishment in ZANLA: 1964–1979', *Journal of Southern African Studies*, 37, 3, 2011, pp. 571–91; and Sabelo J. Ndlovu-Gatsheni, 'Rethinking *Chimurenga* and *Gukurahundi* in Zimbabwe: A Critique of Partisan National History', *African Studies Review*, 55, 3, 2012, pp. 1–26.

Figure 8.3 *Unity Accord*
Source: Photograph of Sibathontisele Exhibition paintings by Owen Maseko. Copyright © 2020 Owen Maseko

surrounded by the infamous 'men in dark glasses', the CIO officers, as well as the imposing figures of three soldiers in red berets. On the right of the three soldiers, almost outside of the scene, are two crouching 'dissidents' with machine guns, covered by a curtain of blood (see Figure 8.3).

To promote discussion of the atrocities among his public, Maseko also painted statements uttered by key ZANU-PF government officials during the *Gukurahundi* on the walls, drawn from *Breaking the Silence*. This included Emmerson Mnangagwa's infamous words at a 1983 rally in Matabeleland North: 'Blessed are they who follow the path of the government laws, for their days on earth shall be increased. But woe unto those who will choose the path of collaboration with dissidents for we will certainly shorten their stay on earth.'[13] A day

---

[13] In CCJP and LRF, *Breaking the Silence*, p. 54. See also, Eppel, *Owen Maseko and the Gukurahundi*.

after his exhibition opened, Maseko was arrested and taken to Bulawayo Central Police Station.

In this chapter, I elaborate on the events following Maseko's arrest, which resonate with the experiences of individuals accused of political offences in Harare as discussed in earlier chapters, that is, laws were amended, Maseko's identity as an artist and a legitimate citizen deserving of dignified treatment was threatened, the case met severe delays and legal procedures were flouted as the prosecution attempted to perform its political arguments in court.

Following Maseko's arrest, his exhibition was closed and subsequently banned under the Censorship and Entertainment Control Act, an Act dating back to Rhodesian Front rule. To ban the exhibition the Censorship Control Act had to be altered, in effect to cover a loophole in the act relating to art. Echoing many who were accused of political offences in Zimbabwe, Maseko picked up on ZANU-PF's contradictory attitude towards, and use of, the rule of law. He noted that, 'they can amend laws overnight in Zimbabwe, I was so surprised ... they have to keep amending the law in order to adhere to it'.[14] Under the ban his exhibition remained closed to the public and was covered up with newspapers until its dismantling in 2015 (see Figure 8.4).

Maseko was kept in police custody for five nights. Police officers in Bulawayo Central Police Station's Law and Order division first discussed whether there were grounds on which to deport Maseko. He explained that because of his 'Malawian surname' the police 'were hoping that I wasn't Zimbabwean enough'. Like many of the people I spoke to about their encounters with the police, Maseko wanted to maintain his composure, and his sense of humour, in these exchanges. He informed the police that he had 'never been to Malawi', but would prefer to 'be close to Lake Malawi, just send me somewhere nice'.[15] The police then shifted to questioning him about being a British spy. As Maseko's wife Sian was British, and his case received international publicity at the time of his arrest, the police inquired into his political affiliation, whether he was an MDC activist, whether he had any connections to foreign intelligence services and whether his exhibition received British funding.

---

[14] Interview, Owen Maseko, visual artist, Bulawayo, 8 January 2012.   [15] Ibid.

Figure 8.4 Covered windows in the National Gallery
Source: Robin Hammond, *New York Times*, 2011, in Owen Maseko, *Trials and Tribulations of an Artist*. Copyright © Robin Hammond/Panos Pictures

For Maseko this kind of questioning was a 'sad attempt by the government to make me look like a criminal, not an artist', and indicated to him that the police were reluctant to challenge him on the specific content of his exhibition. He explained:

They did ask all sort of questions and so on because they were more interested in my background than what was actually happening, you know. But only to discover that I just did art on canvas, it was simple as that. I don't have a history of any political activism in that sense. So I think that that was really terribly disappointing for them, I would say.[16]

The police could find no grounds on which to prosecute Maseko, other than his exhibition. To his amusement, Maseko then observed the police debate what to charge him with:

You know it was this whole thing, we were sitting in the charge office, and they were saying 'what about treason' 'ah no, we can't do that', perusing through ... in front of me ... the penal code, [and] we were all eating

[16] Ibid.

lunch ... they were like 'treason', 'ah no, not treason', 'undermining the authority of the president', 'ah of course, definitely that one'.[17]

Indicative of widespread experiences of Bulawayo's political subordination to Harare, as discussed in Chapter 7, Maseko understood this debate among the police both as a sign of their general professional incompetence, and as a first indication that they were 'wait[ing] for a particular phone call from Harare' to receive 'all the instructions'.[18] His initial suspicion was confirmed, Maseko continued, when a prosecutor from Harare turned up at his trial. By appointing Tawanda Zvekare, described by ZLHR as 'one of [the attorney general's] senior law officers famous for persecuting human rights defenders',[19] to try the case, ZANU-PF was signalling its ability and willingness to deploy civil servants committed to carrying out their orders – the 'good boys' – from Harare to maintain order in Bulawayo.

Five days after his arrest Maseko appeared in Bulawayo's Magistrates' Courts to apply to be released on bail. He was first charged under Section 42 of the Criminal Law (Codification and Reform) Act for 'causing offence to persons of a particular race [or] tribe',[20] with an alternative charge of contravening Section 33, 'undermining authority of or insulting the President'.[21] During his bail hearing Maseko was represented by Kucaca Phulu, Abammeli's founder, introduced in Chapter 7, who told SW Radio Africa that 'these charges are mere figments of the imagination of the powers that be'. The exhibition, he continued, did not contain any material that was offensive to either the president or to a race or tribe. The remand magistrate, Victor Mpofu, told the courtroom that because the sentences for these charges tended to be fines, rather than incarceration, it was in the interest of justice that Maseko be released.[22] His bail conditions, however, were strict, and included weekly reporting at Bulawayo Central Police Station. Maseko further noted that he was harassed at

[17] Ibid.   [18] Ibid.
[19] ZLHR, 'State Ropes in Zvekare to Persecute Maseko', *Legal Monitor*, edition 62, 13 September 2010, p. 1.
[20] Government of Zimbabwe, *Criminal Law (Codification and Reform) Act* (Government Printer, Harare, 2005), s. 42(2).
[21] Government of Zimbabwe, *Criminal Law Act*, s. 33.
[22] Lindie Whiz, 'Gukurahundi Exhibit Artist Gets Bail', *New Zimbabwe*, 31 March 2010, accessed on at www.newzimbabwe.com/news-2142-Gukurahundi+exhibit+artist+gets+bail/news.aspx.

the police station and followed around by the 'men in dark glasses', the same imposing figures from the CIO as those he had painted in the backdrop of his *Unity Accord* installation.[23]

Following months of reporting Maseko appeared in front of magistrate Ntombizodwa Mazhandu at Bulawayo's Magistrates' Courts in September 2010. In the following two sections, I show that during his brief trial the defence lawyers and prosecution narrated distinct claims about the relationship between history, law and state authority in their courtroom performances. Maseko's defence team relied heavily on 'rule-based play'[24] in their fight for his freedom of expression. By following legal procedures, and reminding the state of these procedures in court, they intended to 'embarrass' the prosecutor for his 'acting as if, because he was the State, he had the prerogative to behave as he saw fit'.[25] Such rule-bound performances reminded the trial's audience of civil society actors, independent media, police and representatives from the president's office of the possibility that a full trial against the artist would necessitate putting ZANU-PF's historical human rights abuses on record. In this manner, Maseko and his defence team performed their understanding that the legitimacy of law, and the authority of the state, were bound up in the 'professional' delivery of 'substantive justice'.

In stark contrast, by bringing this violent history to the public's attention again the prosecution told a story that placed the interests of the government and the nation above the law. It took the case as an opportunity to remind Zimbabwean citizens, through the state's courtroom narratives, that history could repeat itself. Through Maseko's harassment in arrest and detention, and through the prolonged closure of his exhibition, ZANU-PF demonstrated that, as it had in the past, it maintained control both over coercive force and over the public articulation and visual representation of historical narratives. In the creation of this narrative the state echoed the tactics it used in other trials and which were explored in Chapters 6 and 7. By portraying the exhibition as a 'national security threat', however, the prosecution used language which held particular meaning for Matabeleland's citizens. The state's narrative echoed the accusations made against ZAPU supporters and

---

[23] Interview, Owen Maseko, visual artist, Bulawayo, 8 January 2012.
[24] For the distinction between 'rule-based play' and 'improvisation' in legal performances see: Rogers, 'Violence and Play'.
[25] Jeremiah Bamu, in personal correspondence with author, 25 August 2013.

civilians during the *Gukurahundi* to stress the 'dangers' of talking
about the repression of the era. In effect the prosecution's performance
served as a blatant reminder that anyone critical of the party's rule
could be subjected to violence and so 'silenced' once more.

Defending Owen Maseko in the Magistrates' Courts

On 13 September 2010, Owen Maseko's trial began before magistrate
Mazhandu. He was represented by three human rights lawyers, one of
whom, Jeremiah Bamu, had come down from ZLHR's Harare office to
assist Lizwe Jamela and Nosimilo Chanayiwa on the case. I discussed
Jamela's refusal to represent the MLF members in Chapter 7. Although
Maseko was also making a statement about the region's violent history, Jamela took the case because he saw Maseko as 'an artist whose
human rights need protection'.[26] Jamela explained that he needed both
his colleagues to attend the trial for two reasons. First, he worked with
Chanayiwa and Bamu to 'try to strategise, to make avenues to see how
we're going to tackle it', as the case was 'the main case that has been
keeping [him] busy' and 'disturbing' him.[27] This strategising, Jamela
continued, was important in his courtroom performance as the mark
of a 'good lawyer' was 'one who knows the law. ... If you're not so
sure about something, you can always read, ask around and consult
colleagues, rather than embarrassing yourself assuming that you know
everything.' In addition, he continued, the presence of multiple human
rights lawyers in the courtroom sent a public message that 'this is a
serious case, and we will not be distracted or harassed in the process'.[28]
As in the Gwisai trial, discussed in Chapter 6, prominent human rights
lawyer Alec Muchadehama's explanation that human rights lawyers
should not 'stand out alone', applied. Muchadehama continued that by
working as a group, lawyers were able 'not to be distracted by those
sideshows [of lawyers' harassment and arrest] and we will then be able
to concentrate on our cases'.[29]

Jeremiah Bamu noted that such tactics were particularly important
in Maseko's trial as the prosecution's actions at the start of the case
demonstrated how the 'political instructions' from Harare would set

[26] Interview, Lizwe Jamela, human rights lawyer, Harare, 6 September 2010.
[27] Ibid.   [28] Ibid.
[29] Interview, Alec Muchadehama, human rights lawyer, Harare, 12 January 2012.

the tone for the state's performance as the trial progressed.[30] During the first hearing on 13 September 2010, Zvekare read the charges to the court and accused Maseko of contravening not Section 42 but Section 31 of the Criminal Law Act, that is, 'publishing or communicating false statements prejudicial to the State'.[31] Under the new, more serious charge, Maseko faced a maximum sentence of twenty years in prison, as opposed to the one year maximum sentence on the previous charge.

These new charges took Maseko and his defence team by surprise. While they could point to other examples within the arts sector of artists who had suffered arrest and detention by the police, or who had been taken through the motions of a trial in ZANU-PF's efforts to obstruct their work on politically motivated violence, the government's response was more heavy-handed in Maseko's case.[32] This is evident when looking at several examples of similar arrests. In March and April 2010, for instance, Okay Machisa, the executive chairperson for Zimbabwe Human Rights Association (ZimRights), and other staff members including Olivia Gumbo and Joel Hita were arrested when they organised a photo exhibition, *Reflections*, on the political violence surrounding the 2008 elections. On 26 April 2010, Joel Hita was charged under POSA for organising a public meeting without notifying the police authorities, which carries a fine. The same charges were brought against ZimRights as an organisation in August of the same year. Magistrate Dorothy Mwanyisa in Masvingo's Magistrates' Courts acquitted both ZimRights and Hita on 23 January 2012.[33]

In March 2011, Styx Mhlanga, a Bulawayo-based playwright and director, commented that he would have liked to see more references to the liberation war heroes from Matabeleland in a poem displayed at

---

[30] Interview, Jeremiah Bamu, human rights lawyer, Harare, 28 September 2010.

[31] Government of Zimbabwe, *Criminal Law Act*, s. 31. See also, ZLHR, 'State Forced to Drop Charges against Maseko', *ZLHR News*, 13 September 2010, accessed on 15 March 2013 from http://archive.kubatana.net/html/archive/hr/100913zlhr1.asp?sector=ARTCUL&year=2010&range_start=1.

[32] Interviews with human rights lawyers, Lizwe Jamela, Harare, 6 September 2010 and Jeremiah Bamu, Harare, 28 September 2010.

[33] 'Acquittal of Mr. Joel Hita and ZimRights – ZWE 001/0210/OBS 023.4', *FIDH*, 26 January 2012, accessed on 17 August 2013 at www.fidh.org/en/africa/Zimbabwe,204/Acquittal-of-Mr-Joel-Hita-and; Zimbwa Hamunyari, 'Masvingo, Bulawayo Judgements Shame ZRP', *ChangeZimbabwe*, 23 January 2012, accessed on 17 August 2013 at http://changezimbabwe.com/index.php/news-mainmenu-2/1-latest/3803-masvingo-bulawayo-judgements-shame-zrp.

the National Gallery. Mhlanga explained that he made this comment
'because poems should unite people and not divide them along tribal
lines'. He was arrested and, like Maseko's initial charge, charged under
Section 42 of the Criminal Law (Codification and Reform) Act for
'causing offence to persons of a particular tribe', but was subsequently
released.[34]

In January 2011, ten members of the Rooftop Promotions team were
arrested at the Nedziwa Business Centre in Cashel Valley, Manicaland.
Rooftop Promotions, a Harare-based theatre company, was touring
with their performance of *Rituals*, a play about the impact of the
political violence surrounding the 2008 elections, and possibilities for
healing within communities following the violence.[35] That same
month, Chief Superintendent Rita Nomsa Masina banned the play in
Bulawayo, but magistrate Rose Dube overturned this ban in February
2011.[36] Although the Censorship Board had approved the play, the
Rooftop Promotions team was charged under Section 46 of the
Criminal Law Act for causing criminal nuisance.[37] For this charge
the maximum sentence was a fine, and/or six months' imprisonment.[38]
Magistrate Nickson Mangoti in Mutare acquitted them on 22 March
2011. In this instance the public prosecutor Fletcher Karombe con-
curred during the trial that the evidence against the cast and crew of
Rooftop Promotions was insufficient, and pressed the court to
acquit them.

In Maseko's case, Zvekare justified the switch to the heavier charges
by arguing that the police had misjudged the gravity of the case. The

---

[34] Government of Zimbabwe, *Criminal Law Act*; 'Mhlanga Charged with Tribe
Hate Crime', *New Zimbabwe*, 7 March 2011, accessed on 4 September 2013 at
www.newzimbabwe.com/news/news.aspx?newsID=4624; Sithandekile
Mhlanga, 'Zimbabwe Police Arrest Bulawayo Writer in Literary-Political
Criticism Row', *VOA Zimbabwe*, 9 March 2011, accessed on 4 September
2013 at http://m.voazimbabwe.com/a/1456981.html; 'Styx Mhlanga Released!',
Byo24NEWS, 10 March 2011, accessed on 4 September 2013 at http://
bulawayo24.com/index-id-news-sc-local-byo-1928-article-Styx+Mhlanga
+released+!.html.

[35] 'Rituals Actors Arrested on Stage', *The Standard*, 10 January 2011, accessed on
17 August 2013 at www.thestandard.co.zw/2011/01/10/rituals-actors-arrested-
on-stage/.

[36] ZLHR, 'Victory as Magistrate Overturns Police Ban', *Legal Monitor*, edition 79,
7 February 2011, p. 3.

[37] 'Rituals Team Charged with Beating Drums', *The Zimbabwean*, 17 March
2011, accessed on 18 August 2013 at www.thezimbabwean.co/articles/38141.

[38] Government of Zimbabwe, *Criminal Law Act*, s. 46.

prosecution argued that, given the exhibition's focus on the *Gukurahundi*, its content was 'insulting to the President' and posed a threat to the nation's security.[39] The government, he reminded the public in court, took such threats very seriously. Therefore, his office in Harare altered the charges upon review. Maseko, he argued:

published to the public visual images with accompanying legends which incited or promoted public disorder or public violence or endangered public safety. The visual images and accompanying explanatory legends were materially false, rabidly tribalistic and divisive to the nation of Zimbabwe and therefore prejudicial to the State.[40]

The alternative charge of violating Section 33 (insulting or undermining the authority of the president) was maintained.[41]

The defence lawyers' responded by using the courtroom as a stage on which to perform an understanding of law in which politically motivated prosecutions failed to mobilise law as a 'language of stateness' able to legitimise ZANU-PF's rule. The defence team critiqued the state's knowledge of legal proceedings, arguing that the charge against Maseko could not simply be altered in court, and that Zvekare was not using 'the proper legal procedures'.[42] The state's behaviour, the defence argued, 'was calculated to prejudice and embarrass [Maseko]'.[43] Reflecting the language of shame and embarrassment used by 'rebel' prosecutors such as John and David in Chapter 2, however, Maseko and his lawyers continued that the state's tactics were ultimately unsuccessful. Instead, the lawyers 'embarrassed' Zvekare by reminding him how the state should go about opening a new record against Maseko.[44]

Through such performances the defence demonstrated their knowledge of legal procedure, and reminded the state that, in their view, it must play by the rules to successfully capitalise on the authority of law. As I showed in Chapter 3, citizens' invocations of the law in this

---

[39] Summary Jurisdiction, C.R. 553/03/2010, p. 1.

[40] Outline of the State Case C.R. 553/03/2010, p. 1; interview, Owen Maseko, visual artist, Bulawayo, 8 January 2012.

[41] ZLHR, 'State Forced to Drop Charges against Maseko'; also in 'State's Bid for Charges against Maseko Foiled', *MISA-Zimbabwe*, 14 September 2010, accessed on 15 March 2013 at www.swradioafrica.com/pages/maseko140910.htm.

[42] ZLHR, 'State Forced to Drop Charges against Maseko'. [43] Ibid.

[44] Interview, Owen Maseko, visual artist, Bulawayo, 8 January 2012.

manner worked in part because they played to a divided state, staffed with police officers or judicial officials who were viewed as either complying with ZANU-PF's orders, or as remaining 'professional', impartial and ethical in their interpretation of the law. Although Maseko and his defence team could not be certain how magistrate Mazhandu would respond, they remained committed to performing in this manner. Jeremiah Bamu recalled that they were 'lucky' as magistrate Mazhandu was 'very professional and independent. She would pick on the legal issues and dispute and address those.'[45] Despite the prosecutor's protests over the 'sensitive' content of Maseko's exhibition, and the threat his work posed to national security, she argued that the initial charges against Maseko should be withdrawn. Maseko was duly brought to the police station to record a new warned and cautioned statement before the trial continued with the new charges.[46]

In line with their effort to draw attention to the limits that law could place on the state's ability to 'silence' the artist, at Maseko's next court appearance his defence lawyers applied for the case to be referred to the Supreme Court. In their application the three defence lawyers presented their argument in terms of Maseko's constitutional rights, asking the court to determine whether Maseko's freedoms of expression and conscience were infringed upon by criminalising his art. They argued that art was open to interpretation and that there was need to examine the constitutionality of the charges as the visual artist had 'only translated his thoughts (because he had the freedom of thought under the constitution) into a visible form (because he had the freedom of expression). Like any artist, Maseko opened himself to legitimate comment and criticism.'[47] He had not opened himself up to arrest, detention or trial.

Before she could make her decision, magistrate Mazhandu argued it was necessary to see the images that the prosecution alleged were 'insulting' and 'dangerous'. After visiting the National Gallery, magistrate Mazhandu granted the defence application, referring the case to the Supreme Court. In her ruling she stated that 'it is no secret that *Gukurahundi* did happen. That it happened in Matabeleland is not a secret. I don't see how the application before me is frivolous and

---

[45] Interview, Jeremiah Bamu, human rights lawyer, Harare, 28 September 2010.
[46] ZLHR, 'State Forced to Drop Charges against Maseko'.
[47] ZLHR, 'Victory: Gukurahundi Picture Case Goes to Supreme Court', *Legal Monitor*, edition 63, 20 September 2010, p. 1.

neither is it vexatious.'[48] For Maseko, magistrate Mazhandu's ruling was 'very significant'. While she had not made a favourable initial impression on him, as he was convinced 'she was asleep the whole time', Maseko characterised the referral of his case to the Supreme Court as a 'win-win situation'.[49] He explained that, if the Supreme Court were to decide that his arrest and prosecution were unconstitutional, he would be freed and have grounds to reopen the exhibition. If the court were to rule against him, his case would go to trial, in which case the *Gukurahundi* would be central to his evidence. Maseko explained:

Basically what that means is we're putting the *Gukurahundi* on trial. So we call 400 witnesses, of people who have experienced everything that was written on those walls ... because now the onus is on the state to prove that the statements are false. They have to prove that what Emmerson Mnangagwa [whose words were in Maseko's graffiti] said during that time was false.[50]

Reflecting not only the widespread perception of courts as record keepers, but also the hope this would ensure that those responsible for the *Gukurahundi* abuses would be held accountable in the future, the human rights lawyers agreed that magistrate Mazhandu's ruling was significant in this regard.[51]

In addition to her willingness to assess the case on its legal merits, rather than responding to political influence, Jeremiah Bamu was impressed by the magistrate's ability to stand up to Tawanda Zvekare. He recalled that when Zvekare 'was making long-winded arguments, magistrate Mazhandu ended up telling him "you are now wasting the court's time, this is your argument, I've recorded it, if you have anything else to say, let it be in your argument"'. In a context where members of the judiciary who critiqued ZANU-PF's 'good boys' came under attack, Bamu thought this was especially 'brave and bold

---

[48] ZLHR, 'Victory: Gukurahundi Picture Case Goes to Supreme Court'; also in Ruling, CRB 3133/10 and ZLHR, 'Magistrate Refers Maseko's Application to Supreme Court', *ZLHR*, 18 September 2010, accessed on 15 March 2013 at www.swradioafrica.com/pages/magistrates200910.htm.

[49] Interview, Owen Maseko, Bulawayo, visual artist, 8 December 2011.

[50] Ibid.

[51] Interview, Jeremiah Bamu, human rights lawyer, Harare, 28 September 2010; discussion with Lizwe Jamela, human rights lawyer, Bulawayo 25 November 2011, recorded in field notes.

on her part'. He knew Zvekare to be one of 'the trusted lieutenants of the AG [attorney general]', a member of the notorious 'clique' of prosecutors discussed in Chapter 2, who 'worked under political instructions' and would 'never run short of arguments, no matter how stupid these arguments are'.[52]

Over the course of the trial, Maseko and his lawyers argued, it became increasingly apparent that the prosecutor could only sustain 'a political argument, not a legal argument'.[53] Zvekare, Bamu explained, 'tried his best to argue based on the law, but his constant point of emphasis was more on the politics of the day'.[54] As we saw in the Gwisai and MLF cases, ZANU-PF was able to use courtroom narratives to express the forms of political engagement that it authorised. As in the MLF case, during Maseko's trial Zvekare's courtroom performance emphasised the alternative forms of authority that ZANU-PF relied upon to maintain its power, playing both on the manner in which *Gukurahundi* was justified by government officials and the media in the 1980s, and on the continued conflation of ethnicity and party political belonging in the Ndebele-speaking population's 'tribal' threat to ZANU-PF's rule. In doing so he tried to send a political message that ZANU-PF remained capable of orchestrating widespread violence to repress its opposition. In the following section, I examine the key arguments Zvekare put forward to make his case against Maseko.

Gukurahundi as Strategy: Narrating Violence and Conditional Citizenship

As I have shown, in the 1980s government officials argued for maintaining the repressive emergency powers of the Rhodesian era to ensure national security, the preservation of law and order and the protection of citizens' rights.[55] The violence of the *Gukurahundi* was justified in legal language, as ZANU-PF played up regional ethnic differences to portray ZAPU 'as a treasonous, Ndebele party' threatening the security

---

[52] Interview, Jeremiah Bamu, human rights lawyer, Harare, 28 September 2010. Magistrate Ntombizodwa Mazhandu was herself arrested in February 2012 for not following proper bail procedure.
[53] Interview, Jeremiah Bamu, human rights lawyer, Harare, 28 September 2010.
[54] Ibid.   [55] Karekwaivanane, *The Struggle over State Power.*

of the newly established nation.[56] In Maseko's case, Zvekare proposed
to curtail his rights because Maseko's exhibition could 'perpetuate
tribal tensions and conflict', and have 'a destabilizing effect on the
State of Zimbabwe which enjoys hard won peace, love, and har-
mony'.[57] Zvekare justified incarcerating Maseko for his art, and shutting down his exhibition to maintain a 'silence' around the events of
the *Gukurahundi*, by arguing that he was acting in the interest of
safeguarding peace and security in Matabeleland, and Zimbabwe
more broadly.

Maseko and his lawyers recalled that the state's narrative tactics
were evident throughout the trial. Bamu, for example, explained how
the prosecution invoked arguments that had been used by the state to
call for a ban on Maseko's exhibition at the National Gallery,[58]
namely 'that the *Gukurahundi* would be a tribal-based thing, because
it occurred in Matabeleland, and it should not come into the public
domain'.[59] Zvekare had first brought forward this argument when the
defence objected to altering the charges brought against Maseko in
court without following the correct procedures.[60] In his response to the
defence, Zvekare spoke for approximately three hours to construct a
narrative that Maseko's case was of 'sensitive nature', warning the
court that the exhibition (mis)represented the *Gukurahundi* as a
'tribal-based event' that would incite the people of Matabeleland to
rise up against the Shona.[61]

To sustain his argument that the exhibition 'had the real risk or
possibility of causing hatred', Zvekare drew the court's attention to the
Unity Accord installation in Maseko's exhibition (Figure 8.3). The
installation, he argued, 'suggested that the President through bloodshed forced then ZAPU political party to sign the Unity Accord with
ZANU'.[62] Zvekare further told the court that, by placing President
Robert Mugabe and Joshua Nkomo side by side, the latter with a knife
in his back, Maseko had implied that 'the President is a rabid tribalist

---

[56] Alexander and Mcgregor, 'Elections, Land and the Politics of Opposition in
   Matabeleland', p. 513.
[57] Outline of the State Case C.R. 553/03/2010, p. 2.
[58] Government of Zimbabwe, 'General Notice 236 of 2010', *Government Gazette*,
   27 August 2010; ZLHR, 'State Forced to Drop Charges against Maseko'.
[59] Interview, Jeremiah Bamu, human rights lawyer, Harare, 28 September 2010.
[60] Interview, Owen Maseko, visual artist, Bulawayo, 8 January 2012.
[61] Interview, Jeremiah Bamu, human rights lawyer, Harare, 28 September 2010.
[62] Outline of the State Case C.R. 553/03/2010, p. 2.

who desires the decimation of the Ndebele people'.[63] Zvekare continued that, through his art, Maseko aimed 'to mock and ridicule the Unity Accord signed in 1987 between the then main political parties ZANU and ZAPU'.[64] In addition, he argued, Maseko's installation had failed to portray the ways that the Unity Accord 'led to the peace and stability that the country enjoys today'.[65]

Through this line of argument, Zvekare cleverly drew the public's attention to two possible associations with the Unity Accord. Sabelo Ndlovu-Gatsheni and Wendy Willems illustrate how ZANU-PF's strategy of 'cultural nationalism' combined the state, nation, ruling party and president 'into one symbol of national sovereignty that needed to be jealously guarded'.[66] When expressing this understanding of nationalism in Bulawayo after 2000, ZANU-PF drew on the Unity Accord both as a symbol for aspirations for peace and security in the country, and as a threatening reminder of the party's capacity for violence. As a symbol, ZANU-PF attempted to garner support in Matabeleland by conflating Joshua Nkomo, ZAPU president at the signing of the Unity Accord, with an ideal of Zimbabwean 'unity' that it argued was under threat from the MDC. As a result of the violence that preceded the accord, however, the mention of 'unity' was strongly, and often negatively, entangled with memories of the *Gukurahundi*. As a threat, the Unity Accord primarily 'served to remind citizens about the potential consequences of not supporting the ruling party', and how that had authorised the use of state violence against them.[67]

By narrating a script in court that echoed the criminalising language the government had used to justify its violent actions in the 1980s, and that played on symbolic reminders of the lack of recognition for, and the possibility of the resurgence of this violence to date, Zvekare played on the fear attached to memories of *Gukurahundi*. Many civil society members, political activists, lawyers and artists I spoke to in Bulawayo observed how the region lived 'in a constant state of fear'.[68] This

---

[63] Ibid., p. 1.   [64] Ibid., p. 2.   [65] Ibid., p. 2.

[66] Ndlovu-Gatsheni and Willems, 'Making Sense of Cultural Nationalism', pp. 952–3.

[67] Ibid., p. 964.

[68] In interviews with Vumani Ndlovu, Bulawayo Agenda, Bulawayo, 10 November 2011; Jenni Williams, Women of Zimbabwe Arise, Bulawayo, 27 November 2011, Effie Ncube, political analyst, Bulawayo, 12 January 2012.

sentiment was captured in the *Breaking the Silence* report in 1997, which commented that:

While there is indeed peace in the rural areas of Matabeleland in the 1990s, beneath this there remains both a 'feeling of alienation from the national body politic', and a firm perception that Matabeleland continues to be neglected in terms of development. There is also a belief that a 5 Brigade-type onslaught could happen again at any time. 'We can still be eliminated at any time ... This wound is huge and deep'.[69]

When Zvekare drew the public's attention to the dangers that Maseko's exhibition posed to the peace and security of the nation, he did so in order to highlight how, as in the past, the government's responsibility to safeguard the nation could and would trump the safety of a subset of its citizens. After the defence had listed Maseko's rights under the constitution, for instance, Zvekare responded that 'the rights in question were not absolute', and could be 'waived' to protect national security.[70] Zvekare concluded that, in fact, 'the accused had no right whatsoever' to publish his exhibition, and should thus prepare to face the consequences of displaying his work.[71]

Similar to the narratives it presented in the Gwisai and MLF treason trials, the prosecution articulated a conceptualisation of conditional citizenship in court. Only citizens who were deemed to support ZANU-PF and its efforts to maintain the safety and security of the Zimbabwean nation were accorded protection under the law. Nonetheless, Maseko and his defence lawyers maintained their commitment to fighting against this depiction of citizenship through the law. In their application to refer the case to the Supreme Court, for example, the defence lawyers reminded the courts that Maseko was a 'full citizen' of Zimbabwe, and so entitled to live his life in a 'dignified' manner.[72] For this, his rights to practice as an artist needed to be defended. The defence concluded that:

The net effect of these violations has a negative bearing on the Applicant's future expression of his freedoms of conscience (thought) and expression.

---

[69] CCJP and LRF, *Breaking the Silence*, p. 60.
[70] Zenzele Ndebele, 'Maseko Release: Victory for Gukurahundi Artist', *Zimbabwe Netzwerk*, 18 September 2010, accessed on 17 February 2012 at: www.zimbabwenetzwerk.de/Aktuelles/20100918/.
[71] Outline of the State Case C.R. 553/03/2010, p. 2.
[72] Jeremiah Bamu, in personal correspondence with author, 25 August 2013.

His livelihood is based on his works of art. If such works of art can be willy nilly made subjects of criminal prosecutions, simply because certain functionaries of the state do not approve of what they perceive to be the meaning of that work of art, it would mean that before [the] Applicant develops his thought into a visible form of art, he first has to second guess how the state would interpret that thought, before translating it into visible form. There is no guarantee that he will ever guess correctly what the State's attitude will be in respect of each of his pieces of art and this would make it impossible for him to produce any further work of art as the State may construe it to be an offence and see his prosecution. Uncertainty will breed in the law, and as a result of such uncertainty, he will be curtailed from practising his trade in art, which is the very essence of his survival [73]

On 18 September 2010, magistrate Mazhandu granted the defence application and referred the case to the Supreme Court. In a display of its ability to maintain control over the artists' life, however, the prosecution stalled the process for almost three years, burdening Maseko with 'the prospect of being imprisoned at any time'. On 6 November 2013, he won his case in the Supreme Court. His exhibition remained closed down, however, until he was ordered to dismantle it in 2015.

Conclusion

In this chapter, I have examined how Owen Maseko, his defence lawyers, state prosecutor Tawanda Zvekare and magistrate Mazhandu used and understood the law when confronted with Zimbabwe's violent 1980s history and its legacies in the courtroom. By banning *Sibathontisele*, arresting and detaining Owen Maseko, and placing him on trial, ZANU-PF asserted the state's coercive capacity. Working through certain individuals within the attorney general's office willing to follow political 'instructions', the party demonstrated its willingness to alter the law to repress citizens who expressed their opposition to the manner in which the country had been governed in the past, or continued to be ruled in the present. While Maseko and his defence team relied on 'proper legal procedure' to 'embarrass' the public prosecutor and to fight for Maseko's right to express himself through his art, the prosecution invoked language that echoed

---

[73] Application for referral to Supreme Court, pp. 6–7.

justifications of the *Gukurahundi* violence in the 1980s. In his court-room performances, Zvekare highlighted the ongoing efficacy of ZANU-PF's *Gukurahundi* narrative as a method through which to assert the party's power and its control over instruments of coercion. The different roles attributed to the law through the courtroom per-formances in the Maseko trial not only served to draw attention to the *Gukurahundi* as a violent historical event that had, and continued to have, a deep effect on how citizens within the region negotiated their citizenship and interactions with the Zimbabwean state. These strat-egies were also indicative of interactions between history, the law and state authority that have come up throughout this book. Through their rule-bound behaviour, for instance, Maseko's defence team echoed widely held and long-standing notions of professional conduct to advocating for Maseko's rights as an artist, and as a citizen deserving of 'substantive justice'.

Conclusion

'Government Is a Legal Fiction' – Performing Law, the State, Citizenship and Politics

Zim is a land of silent silence,
where they edit expression on final cut pro
with police whips and guns and prisons
people living hand to mouth,
famished for rights, for freedom,
for the sound of their own true voices
see us walk like zombies in Zim, like
paralyzed by fear of the state in Zim
we could flee our shadows in Zim,
we see nothing, we hear nothing in Zim
let them silence us, beat us in Zim, like
what does freedom matter in Zim?[1]

I think the law is fundamental. Law guarantees freedom. For any state to function in a proper manner or for it to maintain itself, you need law. Law protects our basic human freedoms ... and for me the law becomes the nexus that governs my conduct or my relation with another fellow citizen. So how can we live together harmoniously, or without any problems? It has to be with law. ... Have no faith in a politician. But have faith in God, and in good laws.[2]

On 24 January 2020, High Court Judge Christopher Dube-Banda ruled that Vice President Constantino Chiwenga was acting in a manner that had 'the potential to ... bring the standing of the status of the rule of law in Zimbabwe in serious disrepute'.[3] Embroiled in an

---

[1] NoViolet Bulawayo, 'For Owen', quoted in 'Clarity', in Lavina Greenlaw (ed.) *1914, Goodbye to All That: Writers on the Conflict between Life and Art* (London, Pushkin Press, 2014), np.

[2] Interview, Tamuka Chirimambowa, student and political activist, Harare, 4 January 2012.

[3] From Judgment HH 74-20, p. 4 (issued on 24 January 2020 by Justice Dube-Banda in *Marry Mubaiwa-Chiwenga v. Constantino Guvheya Dominic Nyikadzino Chiwenga*).

acrimonious divorce, the vice president and former army general had enlisted the support of the military to bar his wife, Marry Mubaiwa-Chiwenga, from seeking access to her three minor children and to their home. Marry had applied for an urgent order to regain this access, an order that Justice Dube-Banda granted while arguing that no person in Zimbabwe was above the law. In his twenty-one-page judgement, Justice Dube-Banda observed that Vice President Chiwenga was in fact 'no ordinary citizen, and his conduct is particularly objectionable as he has taken an oath to uphold the laws of Zimbabwe'.[4] He further argued that the aim of the court was to 'do justice between litigants', something it could only achieve if it did 'not allow itself to be swayed by technical objections and failures which do not go to the root of the matter'.[5] He concluded: 'Let the rule of law reign supreme'.[6]

The independent media celebrated Justice Dube-Banda's decision for highlighting the judiciary's continued commitment to 'substantive justice', despite persistent political challenges to this commitment.[7] Justice Dube-Banda's comments critiqued the actions of Zimbabwe's vice president, a man who had taken up this position following the military coup in November 2017 which ousted then President Robert Mugabe from power after thirty-seven years. The coup too was a matter that came to the High Court, as on 24 November 2017 Justice George Chiweshe ruled the coup to be constitutional,[8] a ruling in line with the ZANU-PF government's pattern of legalising politically contentious actions after the fact. Mugabe was replaced by former vice president and minister of justice, Emmerson Mnangagwa, who vowed to fight 'corruption' and 'criminality' within the state. To date, however, the regime continues to rely on the deep-rooted and well-established tactics discussed throughout this book, tactics to target its uses of law against a select part of the country's population.[9]

---

[4] Ibid., p. 4.   [5] Ibid., p. 19.   [6] Ibid., p. 20.

[7] Tim E. Ndoro, 'High Court Roasts VP Chiwenga for Using Military in Domestic Matters', *iHarare*, 25 January 2020, accessed on 25 January 2020 at: https://iharare.com/high-court-roasts-vp-chiwenga-for-using-military-in-domestic-matters/; Paidamoyo Muzulu, 'How Many Justices Dube-Banda Does Zim Have?' *Newsday*, 29 January 2020, accessed on 30 January 2020 at: www.newsday.co.zw/2020/01/how-many-justices-dube-banda-does-zim-have/

[8] From Judgment HC 10820/17 (issued on 24 November 2017 by Chiweshe in *Sibanda and Chikoma v. Mugabe and others*).

[9] For more details on the changes and continuities in the place of law since the coup, see Susanne Verheul, 'From "Defending Sovereignty" to "Fighting

In July of 2020, for example, journalist Hopewell Chin'ono was arrested after working to expose extensive corruption within President Mnangagwa's government.

Contradiction and complexity thus continue to mark debates on the place of law in Zimbabwe. This was also evident in the discussions over Chiwenga's case when, on 25 June 2020, the Supreme Court overturned Justice Dube-Banda's ruling, arguing that the judge had gone 'on a frolic' and had 'misdirected himself'.[10] Disputing Justice Dube-Banda's decision to draw attention to the vice president's position as someone who took an oath to uphold the rule of law, the Supreme Court argued that it was the judge who had not acted in a manner that upheld justice, and concluded that:

> it appears that the learned judge *a quo* was overwhelmed by the status of the appellant as Vice President of the country and the intensity of the conflict. His vision was apparently clouded by the dust of the conflict, prompting him to wade into its murky waters in aid of the respondent [Marry Mubaiwa-Chiwenga], and granting her relief that she had not asked for. Such conduct was injudicious and an affront to the time-honoured tenets of justice, fairness and equality before the courts. In the absence of any evidence of abuse of office, the appellant ought to have been treated like any other citizen before the court *a quo*.[11]

I introduced this book by looking at a case review published in 2001 by High Court Judge Michael Gillespie, in which he tied his resignation from the bench to the fact that he was no longer able to practice professionally, and consciably, due to political interference within Zimbabwe's judiciary. Justice Gillespie's decision, and the public debates on his judgement, were significant because they suggested that judicial institutions, practitioners and ideas about the law played an essential role in Zimbabwe's political debate and action. This recognition motivated my study of the law in Zimbabwe, a study which pushed me to move us beyond the accepted notion that law is a façade or a mask for political repression. In this book I have worked to explore the constitutive facets of law for understandings of the state,

Corruption": The Political Place of Law in Zimbabwe after November 2017', *Journal of Asian and African Studies*, 56, 2, 2021, pp. 189–203.
[10] From Judgment SC 86/20, p. 15 (issued on 25 June 2020 by Justice Gwuanza, Justice Garwe, and Justice Bhunu in *Constantine Guvheya Dominic Chiwenga v. Marry Mubaiwa*).
[11] Ibid., pp. 21–2.

and of citizenship, through the lens of the trials of individuals accused of political offences in Harare's and Bulawayo's Magistrates' Courts between 2000 and 2012. The brief discussion of the circumstances and debates surrounding Justice Dube-Banda's ruling above demonstrates that the law continues to occupy a central position in Zimbabwean politics. By way of conclusion I therefore want to highlight what a study of trials as political performances can teach us about the role of law in establishing, maintaining and contesting state authority, and in defining, creating and debating citizenship within postcolonial regimes.

To do so I again return to the Introduction to reflect on the quote this book opened with, from a human rights lawyer, Tawanda Zhuwarara, who argued that 'government itself is a legal fiction'.[12] I interpret this statement in three ways. The first aligns most closely with Zhuwarara's original line of argument. Zhuwarara maintained that, through its verbal and physical attacks on the law and the courts after 2000, the ZANU-PF government had damaged its claims to legitimacy. The ruling party's attack on the law, he explained, was fundamentally an attack on itself.[13] Interpreted in this manner, the notion that 'government is a legal fiction' pushes us to examine who held which understandings of law, which were considered as legitimate, and whether, how and to what effect these understandings shaped the authority of judicial institutions, and the ZANU-PF-led government. In a second interpretation, I connect Zhuwarara's statement directly to his position as a human rights lawyer and a Zimbabwean, to ask what his view can tell us about the ways in which law is tied to expressions of a particular kind of citizenship. Finally, I narrow the focus down to the conceptualisation of a 'legal fiction', to argue that we can read Zhuwarara's statement as one which highlights the ways legal encounters produce historical and political narratives.

In arguing that 'government is a legal fiction', Tawanda Zhuwarara proposed that, through its attacks on the judiciary, ZANU-PF was undermining its legitimacy to rule. The period between 2000 and 2012 was indeed a time of intense political contestation and rapid economic decline, during which negotiations through and over the law took place in a context where legal processes were widely used

---

[12] Interview, Tawanda Zhuwarara, human rights lawyer, Harare, 7 September 2010.
[13] Ibid.

to violently arrest members of civil society organisations and political opponents of ZANU-PF. At the same time, Zimbabwean citizens consistently framed their criticisms of the ZANU-PF government in rights-based language, reported crimes to the police and engaged a growing number of human rights lawyers in litigation against the state.

This book has shown that while law in Zimbabwe after 2000 appeared to be a double-edged sword, the judiciary remained a productive site for public contestation. The judiciary remained as this site for contestation because, contrary to much literature on the place of law in postcolonial repressive or authoritarian regimes,[14] Zimbabwean citizens and civil servants did not merely understand law as inherently double-edged. Instead, within their political imaginations, Zimbabweans allowed for repression and resistance to coexist. To affirm this understanding of law they also, and importantly, required the judiciary to *work* in such a manner that, occasionally, justice was seen to be done. In other words, certain Zimbabwean legal professionals and citizens subscribed to E. P. Thompson's seminal conclusion that law's legitimacy stems from the possibility of justice.[15]

In order to locate law's legitimacy in the judiciary's ability to provide occasionally 'just' outcomes, we need to understand how legitimacy was established through law's fragmented hegemony,[16] better understood as an ideology,[17] which captured citizens' consciousness.[18] In Zimbabwe the authority law granted the state was tied both to the ways citizens engaged with the law, their 'legal consciousness',[19] and to understandings and expectations of the state that were held both by citizens and civil servants, their 'state consciousness'. In this manner, this study builds both on the manner in which socio-legal studies scholars have focused on everyday interactions with law among citizens,[20] and on anthropological research which takes seriously how governance is performed within African politics.[21] This scholarship,

---

[14] C.f. Comaroff and Comaroff, *Law and Discourse in the Postcolony*; Ginsburg and Moustafa, *Rule by Law*.
[15] Thompson, *Whigs and Hunters*.   [16] Merry, 'Courts as Performances'.
[17] Comaroff and Comaroff, *Of Revelation and Revolution*.
[18] Benton, *Law and Colonial Cultures*. See also, Hirsch and Lazarus-Black, 'Introduction'.
[19] Merry, *Getting Justice and Getting Even*.
[20] C.f. Merry, *Getting Justice and Getting Even*; Feldman, 'Difficult Distinctions'; McKay, 'Afterlives'; Sundar, 'The Rule of Law and Citizenship in Central India'.
[21] Bierschenk and Olivier de Sardan, *States at Work*; Lund, 'Twilight Institutions'.

however, often does not take the state as its starting point, or locates governance as working outside of, or beyond, formal state structures. I argue that, in order to engage with citizens' understandings of law, we first need to look at how law is mobilised, understood and debated *within* 'the state' as an idea and a set of institutions separated from the political party in power.

In Zimbabwe, state institutions were staffed by judicial officials and civil servants who were divided in their approaches to, and uses of, law, reflecting divergent understandings of how law grants the state authority. This meant that law's legitimacy could be performed through invocations of alternative nationalist and anti-colonialist claims to authority, through debates over 'professionalism' and 'justice' and through practices of rule-bound behaviour which sat side by side with attempts to co-opt legal institutions to coerce and repress political opposition. While Zhuwarara argued that ZANU-PF's attacks on the judiciary threatened their legitimacy, in exploring such attacks the versatility of political performance through law comes to light, demonstrating how these performances might also mobilise alternative political and jurisprudential claims to authority, and allow law itself to work as multiple 'languages of stateness'.[22]

Here I build on Thomas Hansen and Finn Stepputat's ethnographic explorations of the postcolonial state. While Hansen and Stepputat allow for law to work as one of multiple 'languages of stateness', law often remains unexplored as a multifaceted language itself. By combining E. P. Thompson's understanding of the effect of occasional 'just' outcomes in legal institutions on state authority[23] with Lauren Benton's recognition of the manner in which citizens can express their expectations of the state through the language and practice of law,[24] and taking this combined approach into the postcolonial setting, the versatility of law's languages is exposed.

When recognising that law is a versatile language of stateness, it becomes important to ask not just what understanding of law is performed by specific peoples, and within specific spaces, but also to ask what is at stake within these performances. In contrast to studies which examine invocations of the law as acts of resistance by marginalised or informal orders seeking inclusion in dominant, state-bound

---

[22] C.f. Hansen and Stepputat, *States of Imagination.*
[23] Thompson, *Whigs and Hunters.*   [24] Benton, *Law and Colonial Cultures.*

rule,[25] I argue that law was invoked not for incorporation *within*, but for recognition *of*, this rule-bound ordering. Put differently, these were not demands for a narrow, legal citizenship. Rather, at stake in these performances was a claim to definitions of what constitutes a 'good citizen', and what makes a 'good state'. In this sense, Zhuwarara's assertion that a government that did not follow the law was undermining its own legitimacy can also be read as a critique of ZANU-PF's governance, and an attempt to 'expose' its shortcomings. This critique reflected his position as a human rights lawyer and his understanding of himself as a Zimbabwean claiming a particular, richly elaborated citizenship.

Zhuwarara was joined by certain judicial officials, civil servants, activists, artists, teachers, clergy and human rights lawyers in claiming this richly elaborated citizenship. In part, this citizenship was rights-based, in as much as they demanded that the Zimbabwean state accord them with basic human, social, economic and political rights. It was, however, also a citizenship that recognised a personal obligation or responsibility to behaving in a moral, dignified, civil and humane manner towards fellow Zimbabweans. These personal responsibilities remained tied to the idea of a state as a set of institutions that could, and should, safeguard these values. Only a state that was staffed by 'good' Zimbabwean citizens who adhered to a moral code, and therefore behaved in a professional, ethical and impartial manner within their work, could foster a 'good' society.

Performances of moral citizenship were thus rooted in an imagination of a state that was held partly responsible for upholding it. This was the state that could be granted authority. It was, however, also an aspirational state, as activists understood the ZANU-PF government to be manipulating state institutions to retain political control. In this context a 'good citizen' was not only expected to act in a moral, dignified manner. A 'good citizen' was also tasked with the role of 'exposing' the government for failing to provide the 'proper state'.

As morally and politically engaged citizens, activists saw it as their role to 'expose' their treatment at the hands of the police, the conditions they endured in the detention cells and the lack of legal foundation for their trials. In the political trials that took place in Zimbabwe's Magistrates' Courts, for example, lawyers' performances drew

---

[25] Comaroff, 'Colonialism, Culture and the Law: A Foreword'.

attention to sensory and physical evidence of the maltreatment of activists in police detention, such as bruises, cuts, blood and the 'smell of decay' in order to criticise the ZANU-PF government for undermining the law by torturing activists, and by extension threatening the standing of the state as the guarantor of 'justice' and the protector of 'moral citizenship'.

In refusing to accept that their treatment was legitimate, that it could grant ZANU-PF authority or that it was acceptable within Zimbabwean society, activists also rejected the manner in which political trials confronted them with an alternative conceptualisation of their citizenship. We saw, for example, that through their arrest, detention and trial, activists were cast as 'hooligans' or 'criminals' and as a danger to Zimbabwean society and the nation. By threatening their position as 'good citizens', activists' pervasive, often violent interactions with the security and judicial services had the power to humiliate them in the eyes of their families. In addition to the public or private humiliations that played out on the stages of arrest, detention and trial, understandings of citizenship were further influenced by regional dynamics. Specifically, in the regions of Zimbabwe which remained very much alive to their *Gukurahundi* history, claims to belonging within the Zimbabwean nation were shaped not merely by present-day exclusions, but by a history of 'silence' and experiences of neglect.

Claims to citizenship and political belonging in Zimbabwe were thus far from straightforward demands. The complexity of such interactions did not, however, undermine or diminish activists' commitment to performing 'good citizenship' and of demanding the 'proper state'. Distinguishing between the techniques of governance relied upon by ruling parties and peoples' diverse imaginations of the state that the law authorises – their state consciousness – provides us with a new and more nuanced perspective on how constructions of citizen–state relations can impact the place of law in postcolonial regimes.

When we recognise that law is not merely 'deployed', but shapes and is shaped by norms and political subjectivities, then what happens within the space between the rule-bound state that is available to, and the rule-bound state that is demanded by, Zimbabwean activists remains an important question. To reflect on this we need to consider how, and to what effect, narratives were constructed both within and about the courts. This will push us to identify the ways these narratives and their interactions 'write' and 'perform' the disjuncture between the reality and imagination of postcolonial states.

In a third interpretation of Zhuwarara's comments, his conceptualisation of government as a 'legal fiction' draws our attention to the role of law and the courts in 'writing the state'. Through the production of legal narratives, courts legitimise a particular interpretation of 'truth'.[26] In their efforts to 'expose' their physical maltreatment and the material decline of certain state institutions within the courtroom, for example, activists and human rights lawyers considered courts to be record keepers,[27] writing the ZANU-PF government's violent excesses into a record that might allow a new regime to guarantee justice in the future. Drawing on an alternative interpretation of the legitimacy of law, politically 'instructed' prosecutors also presented narratives within the courtroom. Often portrayed as mere emblems of the power of law, I have argued for recognising a far wider set of roles that prosecutors might play. In politically motivated trials, prosecutors stepped outside the law, and the authority this granted to citizens' ideal of the state, to perform narratives that portrayed the defendants (and often their lawyers too) as threats to the security of the nation and the ideals of liberation that ZANU-PF claimed to embody. In this way the prosecutors' courtroom narratives were aimed at inscribing a state authority that was built around the articulation of which forms of political engagement and citizenship it deemed permissible.

By framing political contestations through and over the law in Zimbabwe within the binary of repression and resistance, we obscure the diverse and productive ways that the legitimacy of the law, and its relation to state authority, were publicly contested after 2000. By situating the notion of government as a 'legal fiction' alongside the arguments made across this book, three such sites of contestation emerged. In the first, the dynamics *within* state institutions were shown to shape legal consciousness. In the second, the relationship between legal consciousness and particular imaginations of citizenship proved to be fertile ground for the articulation of critiques of the government in ways that remained embedded in expectations and ideals of the law.

---

[26] Scheppele, 'Foreword'. See also, Sarat and Kearns, *History, Memory and the Law*; Barak-Erez, 'Collective Memory and Judicial Legitimacy'.
[27] Falk-Moore, 'Systematic Judicial and Extra-Judicial Injustice'.

In the third, we saw how the interactions between different actors' legal and state consciousness within the courtroom produced narratives that articulated contradictory claims to state authority.

Taken together, the approach this book has taken shows us the significant ways in which the judiciary remained a productive site for public contestation. In the case of Zimbabwe between 2000 and 2012, it has revealed that for citizens and civil servants alike, the law, as both a set of institutions and practices and as a political ideal, continued to be central to expressions of a particular kind of citizenship tied to notions of humanity, dignity and morality, and to the making of state authority, rooted in rule-bound, ethical and 'professional' conduct and able to deliver 'substantive justice'. If, henceforth, we take seriously the constitutive place of law in the making of states and citizenship, then one last, and stimulating, question remains: What dynamics and sites of contestation might be revealed not only in Zimbabwe after 2012, but across a range (post)colonial countries and cases?

Bibliography

Interviews

Tinoziva Bere, human rights lawyer, in email to author, 23 June 2010.

George, student activist, Harare, 10 and 20 July 2010.

Philip, student activists, Harare, 21 July 2010.

Sarah, former magistrate, Harare, 5 August 2010.

David Hofisi, human rights lawyer, Harare, 12 August 2010.

Faith, student activist, Harare, 12 August 2010.

Jason, student activist, Harare, 12 August 2010.

Peter, student activist, Harare, 12 August 2010.

Grace, former prosecutor, Harare, 16 August 2010.

Sizwe, former prosecutor, Harare, 16 August 2010.

Alec Muchadehama, human rights lawyer, Harare, 19 August 2010 and 12 January 2012.

Kumbirai, MDC activist, Mbare, 20 August 2010.

Tasimba, MDC activist, Mbare, 20 August 2010.

Rex Shana, Deputy Secretary of the Judicial College, Harare, 24 August 2010.

Jabusile, student activist, civil society leader, Harare, 25 August 2010.

Jeremy, political activist, 25 August 2010.

Obert Gutu, Deputy Minister of Justice, Harare, 1 September 2010.

Pishai Muchauraya, MDC MP, Harare, 2 September 2010.

Lizwe Jamela, human rights lawyer, Harare, 6 September 2010.

Tawanda Zhuwarara, human rights lawyer, Harare, 7 September 2010.

Belinda Chinowawa, human rights lawyer, Harare, 8 September 2010.

George, student activist, Harare, 9 September 2010.

John and David, prosecutors, Harare, 10 September 2010.

Otto Saki, former human rights lawyer, Harare, 14 September 2010.

Rose Hanzi, human rights lawyer, Harare, 14 September 2010.

Madock Chivasa, student and political activist, 15 September 2010.

Marshall, student activist, civil society leader, Harare, 15 September 2010.

Henry, student activist, Harare, 16 September 2010.

Tafadzwa Mugabe, human rights lawyer, Harare, 21 July and 18 September 2010.

238

Darlington, civil society leader, Harare, 21 September 2010.

Hilary, student activist, Harare, 22 September 2010.

Edward Mapara, executive secretary, Law Society of Zimbabwe, Harare, 22 September 2010.

Malcolm, political activist, Harare, 27 September 2010.

Samsung, student activist, Harare, 27 September 2010.

Jeremiah Bamu, human rights lawyer, Harare, 28 September 2010.

Vumani Ndlovu, Bulawayo Agenda, Bulawayo, 10 November 2011.

Victor, civil society member, Bulawayo, 10 November 2011.

Florence Ndlovu, ZimRights paralegal officer, Bulawayo, 11 November 2011.

Mbuso Fuzwayo, Ibhetshu-Likazulu member, Bulawayo, 14 November 2011.

Percy Mcijo, Zimbabwe Congress of Trade Unions, Bulawayo, 15 November 2011.

Gerald, lawyer, Christian Legal Assistance, Bulawayo, 16 November 2011.

Sibusiso, human rights lawyers, lawyer, Bulawayo, 22 November 2011.

Magodonga Mahlangu, Women of Zimbabwe Arise activist, Bulawayo, 27 November 2011.

Jenni Williams, Women of Zimbabwe Arise activist, Bulawayo, 27 November 2011.

Matshobana Ncube, human rights lawyer, Bulawayo, 29 November 2011.

Kucaca Phulu, human rights lawyer, Bulawayo, 29 November 2011.

Father Marko Mkandla, priest, Hwange, 30 November 2011.

Wisdom, MDC supporter, Bulawayo, 5 December 2011.

Effie Ncube, political analyst, Bulawayo, 12 December 2011.

Mkhokheli, political activist and MDC-T member, Bulawayo, 13 December 2011.

Sheunesu, student activist, Bulawayo, 13 December 2011.

Bhekizwe, student activist, Bulawayo, 14 December 2011.

Tamuka Chirimambowa, student and political activist, Harare, 4 January 2012.

Blessing Vava, student activist, Harare, 4 January 2012.

Clever Bere, student activist, Harare, 5 January 2012.

Cleto Manjova, ZINASU and Heal Zimbabwe, Harare, 5 January 2012.

Owen Maseko, visual artist, Bulawayo, 8 January 2012.

John Makumbe, University of Zimbabwe lecturer and political analyst, Harare, 11 January 2012.

Greg Linington, University of Zimbabwe lecturer, Harare, 18 January 2012.

Eddson Chakuma, labour activist, Harare, 18 January 2012.

Bryant Elliot, human rights lawyer, Harare, 20 January 2012.

Patrick, teacher, Harare, 20 January 2012.

Andrew Makoni, human rights lawyer, Harare, 23 January 2012.

Lovemore Madhuku, political activist and University of Zimbabwe lecturer, Harare, 23 January 2012.
Tony Reeler, political analyst, Harare, 23 January 2012.
Promise Mkwananzi, student activist, Harare, 28 January 2012.
Simba, student activist, Harare, 1 February 2012.
Alec Muchadehama, in personal correspondence with author, 25 March 2012.
Jeremiah Bamu, in personal correspondence with author, 25 August 2013.
Hopewell Gumbo, student activist, Harare, 29 September 2015.
Matshobana Ncube, in personal correspondence with author, 19 December 2016.

Human Rights Reports

Amnesty International, *Zimbabwe: Continued Clamp Down on Dissent* (New York, Amnesty International, March 2011).
Bar Human Rights Committee (BHRC), *'A Place in the Sun', Zimbabwe: A Report of the State of the Rule of Law in Zimbabwe after the Global Political Agreement of September 2008* (London, BHRC, June 2008).
Catholic Commission for Justice and Peace (CCJP) and Legal Resources Foundation (LRF), *Breaking the Silence, Building True Peace: A Report into the Disturbances in Matabeleland and the Midlands 1980–1988* (Harare, CCJP and LRF, 1997).
Human Rights Watch (HRW). *Fast Track Land Reform in Zimbabwe.* (New York, HRW, 2002).
    'You Will Be Thoroughly Beaten': The Brutal Suppression of Dissent in Zimbabwe (New York, HRW, November 2006).
    Bashing Dissent: Escalating Violence and State Repression in Zimbabwe (New York, HRW, May 2007).
    'Bullets for Each of You': State-Sponsored Violence since Zimbabwe's March 29 Elections (New York, HRW, June 2008).
    'Our Hands Are Tied': Erosion of the Rule of Law in Zimbabwe (New York, HRW, November 2008).
    False Dawn: The Zimbabwe Power-Sharing Government's Failure to Deliver Human Rights Improvements (New York, HRW, August 2009).
Institute of Justice and Reconciliation and Solidarity Peace Trust, *'Policing the State': An Evaluation of 1,981 Political Arrests in Zimbabwe 2000–2005* (Johannesburg, Solidarity Peace Trust, December 2006).
International Bar Association (IBA), *Report of IBA Zimbabwe Mission 2001* (London, IBA, 2001).

International Bar Association Human Rights Institute (IBAHRI), *Partisan Policing: An Obstacle to Human Rights and Democracy in Zimbabwe* (London, IBA, October 2007).

Zimbabwe: Time for a New Approach (London, IBA, September 2011).

Legal Resources Foundation (LRF), *Justice in Zimbabwe* (Harare, LRF, September 2002).

Progressive Teachers Union Zimbabwe (PTUZ), *Every School Has a Story to Tell: A Study into Teacher's Experiences with Elections in Zimbabwe* (Harare, PTUZ, 2011).

Progressive Teachers Union Zimbabwe (PTUZ) and Research and Advocacy Unit (RAU), *Political Violence and Intimidation against Teachers in Zimbabwe* (Harare, PTUZ and RAU, 2012).

Sokwanele, '*I Can Arrest You': The Zimbabwe Republic Police and Your Rights* (Harare, Sokwanele, July 2012).

Solidarity Peace Trust (SPT), '*Subverting Justice': The Role of the Judiciary in Denying the Will of the Zimbabwean Electorate since 2000* (Johannesburg, SPT, March 2005).

Punishing Dissent, Silencing Citizens: The Zimbabwe Elections 2008 (Durban, SPT, May 2008).

Walking a Thin Line: The Political and Humanitarian Challenges Facing Zimbabwe's GPA Leadership – and Its Ordinary Citizens (Johannesburg, SPT, June 2009).

The Hard Road to Reform (Durban, SPT, April 2011).

Hard Times in Matabeleland: Urban Deindustrialization and Rural Hunger (Durban, SPT, 2011).

The REDRESS Trust, *The Case of Henry Dowa: The United Nations and Zimbabwe under the Spotlight* (Harare, REDRESS, January 2004).

Transparency International, *Johannes Tomana's Reign as Attorney General of Zimbabwe: A Trail of Questionable Decisions* (Harare, Transparency International, 2011).

Zimbabwe Human Rights NGO Forum, *Teaching Them a Lesson: A Report on the Attack on Zimbabwean Teachers* (Harare, Zimbabwe Human Rights NGO Forum, 2002).

Zimbabwe Republic Police (ZRP), *Opposition Forces in Zimbabwe: A Trail of Violence* (Harare, ZRP, March 2007).

Court Documents

Judgment HH 148-2001 (issued on 26 September 2001 by Justice Gillespie in *State v. Humbarume*).

Judgment HH 169-2004 (issued on 15 October 2004 by Justice Garwe in *State v. Tsvangirai*).

Outline of the State Case C.R. 553/03/2010.

Judgment HB 53/11 (issued on 24 March 2011 by Justice Ndou in *Thomas, Gazi and Siwela v. State*).

Appeal Judgment HB 59/11 (issued on 31 March 2011 by Justice Ndou in *Thomas, Gazi and Siwela v. Attorney General*).

Decision on State Appeal in Stave v. Gwisai and Others, 13-HH-020 (issued on 16 January 2013 by Justice Hungwe).

Judgment HC 10820/17 (issued on 24 November 2017 by Justice Chiweshe in *Sibanda and Chikoma v. Mugabe and others*).

Judgment HH 74-20 (issued on 24 January 2020 by Justice Dube Bundu in *Marry Mubaiwa-Chiwenga v. Constantino Guvheya Dominic Nyikadzino Chiwenga*).

Judgment SC 86/20 (issued on 25 June 2020 by Justice Gwuanza, Justice Garwe and Justice Bhunu in *Constantine Guvheya Dominic Chiwenga v. Marry Mubaiwa*).

Printed Secondary Sources

Abrams, P. 'Notes on the Difficulty of Studying the State', *Journal of Historical Sociology*, 1, 1, 1988, pp. 58–89.

Alexander, J. 'Dissident Perspectives on Zimbabwe's Post-independence War', *African: Journal of the International African Institute*, 68, 2, 1998, pp. 151–82.

'Legacies of Violence in Matabeleland, Zimbabwe', in Preben Kaarsholm (ed.), *Violence, Political Culture and Development in Africa* (Oxford, James Currey, 2006), pp. 105–21.

The Unsettled Land: State-Making and Politics of Land in Zimbabwe 1893–2003 (Oxford, James Currey, 2006).

'The Political Imaginaries and Social Lives of Political Prisoners in Post 2000 Zimbabwe', *Journal of Southern African Studies*, 36, 2, 2010, pp. 483–503.

'Nationalism and Self-Government in Rhodesian Detention: Gonakudzingwa, 1964–1974', *Journal of Southern African Studies*, 37, 3, 2011, pp. 551–69.

'Rethinking the State and Political Opposition Through the Prism of the Prison', *Critical African Studies*, 4, 6, 2011, pp. 69–83.

Alexander, J. and McGregor, J. 'Elections, Land and the Politics of Opposition in Matabeleland', *Journal of Agrarian Change*, 1, 4, 2001, pp. 510–33.

Alexander, J., McGregor, J. and Ranger, T. *Violence and Memory: One Hundred Years in the 'Dark Forests' of Matabeleland* (Oxford, James Currey, 2000).

Alexander, P. 'Zimbabwean Workers, the MDC and the 2000 Election', *Review of African Political Economy*, 27, 85, 2000, pp. 385–406.

Anderson, D. 'Punishment, Race and "The Raw Native": Settler Society and Kenya's Flogging Scandals, 1895–1930', *Journal of Southern African Studies*, 37, 3, 2011, pp. 479–98.

Ball, M. 'All the Law's a Stage', *Law and Literature*, 11, 2, 1999, pp. 215–21.

Barak-Erez, D. 'Collective Memory and Judicial Legitimacy: The Historical Narrative of the Israeli Supreme Court', *Canadian Journal of Law and Society*, 16, 1, April 2001, pp. 93–112.

Barnes, T. 'Politics of the Mind and Body: Gender and Institutional Culture in African Universities', *Feminist Africa*, 8, 2007, pp. 8–25.

Baron, J. B. and Epstein, J. 'Is Law Narrative?', *Buffalo Law Review*, 45, 1997, pp. 141–87.

Bens, J. 'The Courtroom as an Affective Arrangement: Analysing Atmospheres in Courtroom Ethnography', *The Journal of Legal Pluralism and Unofficial Law*, 50, 3, 2018, pp. 336–55.

Benson, K. and Chadya, J. M. 'Ukubhinya: Gender and Sexual Violence in Bulawayo, Colonial Zimbabwe, 1946–1956', *Journal of Southern African Studies*, 31, 3, 2005, pp. 587–610.

Benton, L. *Law and Colonial Cultures: Legal Regimes in World History, 1400–1900* (Cambridge, Cambridge University Press, 2002).

Bhebe, N. and Ranger, T. (eds), *The Historical Dimensions of Democracy and Human Rights in Zimbabwe. Volume One: Pre-colonial and Colonial Legacies* (Harare, University of Zimbabwe Publications, 2001).

Bierschenk, T. and Olivier de Sardan, J.-P. 'Powers in the Village: Rural Benin between Democratisation and Decentralisation', *Africa: Journal of the International African Institute*, 73, 2, 2003, pp. 145–73.

Bierschenk, T. and Olivier de Sardan, J.-P. (eds), *States at Work: Dynamics of African Bureaucracies* (Boston, Brill, 2014).

Bourbon, A. de, 'Zimbabwe: Human Rights and the Independent Bar', *Advocate*, December 2002, pp. 18–20.

Bourdieu, P. 'The Force of Law: Towards a Sociology of the Juridical Field', *Hastings Law Journal*, 38, 1987, pp. 805–53.

Brooks, V. 'Interrupting the Courtroom Organism: Screaming Bodies, Material Affects and the Theatre of Cruelty', *Law, Culture and the Humanities*, 2014, pp. 1–20.

Bulawayo, N. 'For Owen', quoted in 'Clarity', in Greenlaw, L. (ed.) *1914, Goodbye to All That: Writers on the Conflict between Life and Art* (London, Pushkin Press, 2014).

Butler, J. *Gender Trouble: Feminism and the Subversion of Identity* (New York, Routledge, 1990).

   Bodies That Matter: On the Discursive Limits of 'Sex' (New York, Routledge, 1993).

   Excitable Speech: A Politics of the Performance (New York, Routledge, 1997).

Cabantingan, L. 'Fashioning the Legal Subject: Popular Justice and Courtroom Attire in the Caribbean', *Political and Legal Anthropology Review*, 41, 1, 2018, pp. 68–84.

Caillois, R. *Man, Play, and Games* (Urbana, University of Illinois Press, 2001) [Translation of *Les Jeux et Les Hommes*, 1961, by Meyer Barash].

Cammiss, S. '"He Goes Off and I Think He Took the Child": Narrative (Re) Production in the Courtroom', *King's Law Journal*, 17, 1, 2006, pp. 71–95.

Chanock, M. *Law, Custom and Social Order: The Colonial Experience in Malawi and Zambia* (Cambridge, Cambridge University Press, 1985).

   'Writing South African Legal History: A Prospectus', *Journal of African History*, 30, 2, 1989, pp. 265–88.

Chaumba, J., Scoones, I. and Wolmer, W. 'From *Jambanja* to Planning: The Reassertion of Technocracy in Land Reform in South-Eastern Zimbabwe?', *Journal of Modern African Studies*, 41, 4, 2003, pp. 533–54.

Clarke, K. M. and Goodale, M. (eds), *Mirrors of Justice: Law and Power in the Post Cold War Era* (Cambridge, Cambridge University Press, 2010).

Comaroff, J. and Comaroff, J. L. *Of Revelation and Revolution: Christianity, Colonialism and Consciousness in South Africa* (London, University of Chicago Press, 1991).

   'Criminal Justice, Cultural Justice: The Limits of Liberalism and the Pragmatics of Difference in the New South Africa', *American Ethnologist*, 31, 2, 2004, pp. 188–204.

   (eds), *Law and Disorder in the Postcolony* (London, University of Chicago Press, 2006).

Comaroff, J. L. 'Colonialism, Culture and the Law: A Foreword', *Law and Social Inquiry*, 26, 2, 2001, pp. 305–14.

Conquergood, D. 'Lethal Theatre: Performance, Punishment and the Death Penalty', *Theatre Journal*, 54, 3, 2002, pp. 339–67.

Coutin, S. 'The Chicago Seven and the Sanctuary Eleven: Conspiracy and Spectacle in U.S. Courts', *Political and Legal Anthropology Review*, 16, 3, 1993, pp. 1–28.

Deutsch, J.-G. 'Celebrating Power in Everyday Life: The Administration of the Law and the Public Sphere in Colonial Tanzania, 1890–1914', *Journal of African Cultural Studies*, 15, 2002, pp. 93–103.

Dorman, S. R. *Understanding Zimbabwe: From Liberation to Authoritarianism* (London, Hurst & Company, 2016).

Dumbutshena, E. 'Address to the Harare Magistrates and Prosecutors Forum, 15 September 1989', *Legal Forum*, 1, 6, 1989.

Eltringham, N. 'Spectators to the Spectacle of Law: The Formation of a "Validating Public" at the International Criminal Tribunal for Rwanda', *Ethnos*, 77, 3, 2012, pp. 425–45.

Feldman, I. 'Difficult Distinctions: Refugee Law, Humanitarian Practice, and Political Identification in Gaza', *Cultural Anthropology*, 22, 1, 2007, pp. 129–69.

Ferguson, R. A. 'The Judicial Opinion as Literary Genre', *Yale Journal of Law & the Humanities*, 2, 1, 1990, pp. 201–19.

Fontein, J. 'Anticipating the *Tsunami*: Rumours, Planning and the Arbitrary State in Zimbabwe', *Africa*, 79, 3, 2009, pp. 369–98.

Foucault, M. *Discipline and Punish: The Birth of the Prison* (New York, Vintage Books, 1979).

Garfinkel, H. 'Conditions of Successful Degradation Ceremonies', *American Journal of Sociology*, 61, 5, 1956, pp. 420–4.

Geller, L. and Hemenway, P. 'Argument and Courtroom Theatrics', *National Association of Administrative Law Judges*, 16, 2, 1996, pp. 175–84.

Gillespie, J. 'Theatrical Justice (Criminal Trial as a Morality Play)', *Northern Ireland Legal Quarterly*, 31, 1, 1980, pp. 67–72.

Ginsburg, T. and Moustafa T. (eds), *Rule by Law: The Politics of Courts in Authoritarian Regimes* (Cambridge, Cambridge University Press, 2008).

Goffman, E. *The Presentation of Self in Everyday Life* (New York, Anchor Books, 1959).

Asylums: Essays on the Social Situation of Mental Patients and Other Inmates (Chicago, Aldine Publishers, 1962).

Goodale, M. *Anthropology and Law: A Critical Introduction* (New York, New York University Press, 2017).

Government of Zimbabwe, *Transitional National Development Plan: 1982/ 3–1984–5, Volume One* (Harare, Government Printer, 1982).

Criminal Law (Codification and Reform) Act (Harare, Government Printer, 2005).

Gready, P. 'Autobiography and the "Power of Writing": Political Prison Writing in the Apartheid Era', *Journal of Southern African Studies*, 19, 3, 1993, pp. 489–523.

Greenberg, A. 'Selecting a Courtroom Design', *Judicature*, 59, 9, 1976, pp. 422–8.

Gregory, M. *From Rhodesia to Zimbabwe: An Analysis of the 1980 Elections and an Assessment of the Prospects* (Johannesburg, South African Institute of International Affairs, 1980).

Hansen, T. B. and Stepputat F. *States of Imagination: Ethnographic Explorations of the Postcolonial State* (London, Duke University Press, 2001).

Hancon, J. 'The Architecture of Justice. Iconography and Space Configuration in the English Law Court Building', *Architectural Research Quarterly*, 1, 4, 1996, pp. 50–9.

Harbinger, R. 'Trial by Drama', *Judicature 55*, 3, 1971, pp. 122–8.

Hatchard, J. 'The Right to Legal Representation Must Be Upheld', *MOTO*, December 1984–January 1985.

Hodgkinson, D. 'The "Hardcore" Student Activist: The Zimbabwe National Students Union (ZINASU), State Violence, and Frustrated Masculinity, 2000–2008', *Journal of Southern African Studies*, 39, 4, 2013, pp. 863–83.

Hornberger, J. '"My Police – Your Police": The Informal Privatisation of the Police in the Inner City of Johannesburg', *African Studies*, 63, 2, 2004, pp. 213–30.

Hynd, S. 'Deadlier than the Male? Women and the Death Penalty in Colonial Kenya and Nyasaland, c. 1920–57', *Stichproben*, 12, 2007, pp. 13–33.

Jackson, B. S. 'Narrative Theories and Legal Discourse', in Nash, C. (ed.), *Narrative in Culture: The Uses of Storytelling in the Sciences, Philosophy, and Literature* (London and New York, Routledge, 1994).

Jeater, D. *Law, Language and Science: The Invention of the "Native Mind" in Southern Rhodesia, 1890–1930* (Portsmouth, Heinemann, 2007).

Jones, J. 'Freeze! Movement, Narrative and the Disciplining of Price in Hyperinflationary Zimbabwe', *Social Dynamics*, 36, 2, 2010, pp. 338–51.

Karekwaivanane, G. H. *The Struggle over State Power in Zimbabwe: Law and Politics since 1950* (Cambridge, Cambridge University Press, 2017).

Killingray, D. 'Punishment to Fit the Crime? Penal Policy and Practice in British Colonial Africa', in Florence Bernault (ed.), *A History of Prison and Confinement in Africa* (Portsmouth, Heinemann, 2003), pp. 97–118.

Kriger, N. *Guerrilla Veterans in Post-War Zimbabwe: Symbolic and Violent Politics, 1980–1987* (Cambridge, Cambridge University Press, 2003).

Lazarus-Black, M. and Hirsch, S. F. (eds), *Contested States: Law, Hegemony and Resistance* (London, Routledge, 1994).

LeBas, A. *From Protest to Parties: Party-Building and Democratization in Africa* (Oxford, Oxford University Press, 2013).

Lebert, T. 'An Introduction to Land and Agrarian Reform in Zimbabwe', in P. Rosset, R. Patel and M. Courville (eds), *Promised Land: Competing Visions of Agrarian Reform* (New York, Institute for Food and Development Policy, 2006), pp. 40–56.

Lund, C. 'Twilight Institutions: Public Authority and Local Politics in Africa', *Development and Change*, 37, 4, 2006, pp. 685–705.

Madhuku, L. 'Law, Politics and the Land Reform Process in Zimbabwe', in M. Masiiwa (ed.), *Post-independence Land Reform in Zimbabwe: Controversies and Impact on the Economy* (Harare, Friedrich Ebert Stiftung and Institute of Development Studies & University of Zimbabwe, 2004), pp. 124–47.

An *Introduction to Zimbabwean Law* (Harare, Weaver Press and Friedrich Ebert-Stiftung, 2010).

Mann K. and Roberts R. (eds), *Law in Colonial Africa* (London, James Currey, 1991).

Masunungure, E. V. *Defying the Winds of Change: Zimbabwe's 2008 Elections* (Harare, Weaver Press, 2008).

Mazarire, G. C. 'Discipline and Punishment in ZANLA: 1964 – 1979', *Journal of Southern African Studies*, 37, 3, 2011, pp. 571–91.

McCandless, E. *Polarization and Transformation in Zimbabwe: Social Movements, Strategy Dilemmas, and Change* (Plymouth, Lexington Books, 2011).

McCulloch, J. *Black Peril, White Virtue: Sexual Crime in Southern Rhodesia, 1902–1935* (Bloomington, Indiana University Press, 2000).

McKay, R. 'Afterlives: Humanitarian Histories and Critical Subjects in Mozambique', *Cultural Anthropology*, 27, 2, 2012, pp. 286–309.

Merry, S. E. 'Everyday Understandings of the Law in Working-Class America', *American Ethnologist*, 13, 2, 1986, pp. 253–70.

'Legal Pluralism', *Law and Society Review*, 22, 5, 1988, pp. 869–96.

Getting Justice and Getting Even: Legal Consciousness Among Working Class Americans (London, University of Chicago Press, 1990).

'Courts as Performances: Domestic Violence Hearings in a Hawai'i Family Court', in Lazarus-Black, M. and Hirsch, S. (eds), *Contested States: Law, Hegemony, and Resistance* (London, Routledge, 1994).

Milstein, M. I. and Bernstein, L. R. 'Trial as Theater', *Trial*, 33, 10, 1997, pp. 64–9.

Ministry of Information, Posts, and Telecommunications, *A Chronicle of Dissidency in Zimbabwe* (Harare, Government Printer, August 1984).

Mitchell, T. 'Society, Economy and the State Effect', in G. Steinmetz (ed.), *State/Culture: State-Formation after the Cultural Turn* (London, Cornell University Press, 1999), pp. 76–97.

Moore, S. F. *Social Facts and Fabrications: Customary Law on Kilimanjaro, 1880–1980* (Cambridge, Cambridge University Press, 1986).

'Systematic Judicial and Extra-judicial Injustice: Preparations for Future Accountability', in R. P. Werbner (ed.), *Memory and the Postcolony: African Anthropology and the Critique of Power* (London, Zed Books, 1998), pp. 126–51.

Moyo, S. 'The Political Economy of Land Acquisition and Redistribution in Zimbabwe, 1990–1999', *Journal of Southern African Studies*, 26, 1, 2000, pp. 5–20.

Mthwakazi Liberation Front (MLF), *Free Mthwakazi: Why Should Mthwakazi Secede from Zimbabwe?* (Bulawayo, MLF, 2014).

Mukoko, J. *The Abduction and Trial of Jestina Mukoko: The Fight for Human Rights in Zimbabwe* (Sandton, KMM Review Publishing, 2016).

Mulcahy, L. *Legal Architecture: Justice, Due Process and the Place of Law* (Oxford, Routledge, 2011).

'Putting the Defendant in Their Place: Why Do We Still Use the Dock in Criminal Proceedings?' *British Journal of Criminology*, 53, 2013, pp. 1139–56.

Munochiveyi, M. *Prisoners of Rhodesia: Inmates and Detainees in the Struggle for Zimbabwean Liberation 1960–1980* (Basingstoke, Palgrave Macmillan, 2014).

Murphy, P. '"There's No Business Like . . . ?", Some Thoughts on the Ethics of Acting in the Courtroom', *South Texas Law Review*, 44, 1, 2002, pp. 111–25.

Muzondidya, J. 'From Buoyancy to Crisis: 1980–1997', in Raftopoulos, B. and Mlambo, A. (eds), *Becoming Zimbabwe: A History from the Pre-colonial Period to 2008* (Harare, Weaver Press, 2009), pp. 167–200.

Naldi, G. J. 'Land Reform in Zimbabwe: Some Legal Aspects', *The Journal of Modern African Studies*, 31, 4, 1993, pp. 588.

'Constitutional Challenge to Land Reform in Zimbabwe', *Comparative and International Law Journal of Southern Africa*, 1998, pp. 78–91.

Ncube, W. 'Constitutionalism, Democracy and Political Practice in Zimbabwe', in Mandaza, I. and Sachikonye, L. (eds), *The One-Party State and Democracy* (Harare, SAPES Trust, 1991).

'Controlling Public Power: The Role of the Constitution and the Legislature', *Legal Forum*, 9, 6, 1997, pp. 12–22.

'The Courts of Law in Rhodesia and Zimbabwe: Guardians of Civilisation, Human Rights and Justice or Purveyors of Repression', in

Bhebe, N. and Ranger, T. (eds), *The Historical Dimensions of Democracy and Human Rights in Zimbabwe. Volume One: Pre-Colonial and Colonial Legacies* (Harare, University of Zimbabwe Publications, 2001), pp. 99–123.

Ndakaripa, M. 'Ethnicity, Narrative, and the 1980s Violence in the Matabeleland and Midlands Provinces of Zimbabwe', *Oral History Forum d'Histoire Orale*, 34, 2014, pp. 2–47.

Ndlovu-Gatsheni S. 'Who Ruled by the Spear? Rethinking the Form of Governance in the Ndebele State', *African Studies Quarterly*, 10, 2–3, 2008, pp. 71–94.

'Rethinking *Chimurenga* and *Gukurahundi* in Zimbabwe: A Critique of Partisan National History', *African Studies Review*, 55, 3, 2012, pp. 1–26.

Ndlovu-Gatsheni, S. and Willems, W. 'Making Sense of Cultural Nationalism and the Politics of Commemoration under the Third Chimurenga in Zimbabwe', *Journal of Southern African Studies*, 35, 4, 2009, pp. 945–65.

Neveu, C. 'Discussion: Anthropology and Citizenship', *Social Anthropology*, 13, 2, 2005, pp. 199–202.

Oomen, B. 'Vigilantism or Alternative Citizenship? The Rise of Mapogo a Mathamaga', *African Studies*, 63, 2, 2004, pp. 153–71.

Palley, C. 'Law and the Unequal Society: Discriminatory Legislation in Rhodesia under the Rhodesian Front from 1963 to 1969', *Race*, 12, 1, 1970, pp. 15–47.

Parush, A. 'The Courtroom as a Theater and the Theater as Courtroom in Ancient Athens', *Israeli Law Review*, 35, 2001, pp. 118–37.

Peterson, D. R. 'Morality Plays, Marriage, Church Courts and Colonial Agency in Central Tanganyika, ca. 1876–1928', *American Historical Review*, 111, 4, 2006, pp. 983 –1010.

Philippopoulos-Mihalopoulos, A. 'Flesh of the Law: Material Legal Metaphors', *Journal of Law and Society*, 43, 1, 2016, pp. 45–65.

Pirie, F. *The Anthropology of Law* (Oxford, Oxford University Press, 2013).

Raftopoulos, B. and Phimister, I. R. *Keep on Knocking: A History of the Labour Movement in Zimbabwe* (Harare, Baobab, 1997).

Raftopoulos, B. and Mlambo, A. (eds), *Becoming Zimbabwe: A History from the Pre-colonial Period to 2008* (Harare, Weaver Press, 2009).

Ranger, T. 'Tradition and Travesty: Chiefs and the Administration in Makoni District, Zimbabwe, 1960–1980', *Africa*, 52, 3, 1982, pp. 20–41.

'Matabeleland since the Amnesty', *African Affairs*, 88, 351, 1989, pp. 161–73.

Voices from the Rocks: Nature, Culture and History in the Matopos Hills of Zimbabwe (Oxford, James Currey, 1999).

'Democracy and Traditional Political Structures in Zimbabwe, 1890–1999', in Bhebe, N. and Ranger, T. (eds), *The Historical Dimensions of Democracy and Human Rights in Zimbabwe. Volume One: Pre-Colonial and Colonial Legacies* (Harare, University of Zimbabwe Publications, 2001), pp. 31–52.

'Nationalist Historiography, Patriotic History and the History of the Nation: The Struggle over the Past in Zimbabwe', *Journal of Southern African Studies*, 30, 2, 2004, pp. 215–34.

Rogers, N. 'Violence and Play in Saddam's Trial', *Melbourne Journal of International Law*, 8, 2, 2007, pp. 428–42.

Sachikonye, L. '"From Growth with Equity" to "Fast-Track" Reform: Zimbabwe's Land Question', *Review of African Political Economy*, 96, 2003, pp. 227–40.

Sarat, A. *When the State Kills: Capital Punishment and the American Condition* (Princeton, Princeton University Press, 2001).

Sarat, A. and Kearns, T. R. (eds), *History, Memory, and the Law* (Ann Arbor, University of Michigan Press, 1999).

Schechner, R. *Performance Theory* (New York, Drama Books Specialists, 1988).

Scheppele, K. L. 'Foreword: Telling Stories', *Michigan Law Review*, 87, 8, 1989, pp. 2073–98.

Schmidt, E. 'Negotiated Spaces and Contested Terrain: Men, Women, and the Law in Colonial Zimbabwe, 1890–1939', *Journal of Southern African Studies*, 16, 4, 1990, pp. 622–48.

Shutt, A. K. '"The Natives Are Getting out of Hand": Legislating Manners, Insolence and Contemptuous Behaviour in Southern Rhodesia, c. 1910–1963', *Journal of Southern African Studies*, 33, 3, 2007, pp. 653–72.

Stone Peters, J. 'Theatricality, Legalism and the Scenography of Suffering: The Trial of Warren Hastings and Richard Brinsley Seridan's "Pizarro"', *Law and Literature*, 18, 1, 2006, pp. 15–45.

'Penitentiary Performances Spectators, Affecting Scenes, and Terrible Apparitions in the Nineteenth-Century Model Prison', in Sarat, A., L. Douglas and M. Merrill Umphrey (eds), *Law and Performance* (Boston, University of Massachusetts Press, 2018), pp. 18–67.

Sundar, N. 'The Rule of Law and Citizenship in Central India: Post-colonial Dilemmas', *Citizenship Studies* 15, 3–4, 2011, pp. 419–32.

Tendi, B. M. *Making History in Mugabe's Zimbabwe: Politics, Intellectuals and the Media* (Oxford, Peter Lang, 2010).

Thompson, E. P. *Whigs and Hunters: The Origin of the Black Act* (New York, Pantheon Books, 1975).

Tow, A. 'Teaching Trial Practice and Dramatic Technique', *Journal of Paralegal Education and Practice*, 13, 1, 1997, pp. 59–96.

Tredgold, R. *The Rhodesia That Was My Life* (London, George Allen and Unwin, 1968).

Tsunga, A. 'The Professional Trajectory of a Human Rights Lawyer in Zimbabwe between 2000 and 2008', *Journal of Southern African Studies*, 35, 4, 2009, pp. 977–91.

Turner, V. *The Anthropology of Performance* (New York, PAJ Publications, 1986).

Verheul, S. '"Rebels" and "Good Boys": Patronage, Intimidation, and Resistance in Zimbabwe's Attorney General's Office Post-2000', *Journal of Southern African Studies*, 39, 4, 2013, pp. 765–82.

'"Zimbabweans Are Foolishly Litigious": Exploring the Internal Logics for Appeals to a Politicised Legal System', *Africa*, 86, 1, 2016, pp. 78–97.

'"Rotten Row Is Rotten to the Core": The Material and Sensory Politics of Harare's Magistrates Courts after 2000', *PoLAR: Political and Legal Anthropology Review*, 43, 2, 2020, pp. 262–79.

'From "Defending Sovereignty" to "Fighting Corruption": The Political Place of Law in Zimbabwe after November 2017', *Journal of Asian and African Studies*, 56, 2, 2021, pp. 189–203.

Weitzer, R. *Transforming Settler States: Communal Conflict and Internal Security in Northern Ireland and Zimbabwe* (Oxford, University of California Press, 1990).

Werbner, R. 'In Memory: A Heritage of War in Southwestern Zimbabwe', in Bhebe, N. and Ranger, T. (eds), *Society in Zimbabwe's Liberation War* (Oxford, James Currey, 1996), pp. 192–205.

'Smoke from the Barrel of a Gun: Postwars of the Dead, Memory and Reinscription in Zimbabwe', in *Memory and the Postcolony: African Anthropology and the Critique of Power* (London, Zed Books, 1998).

Zeilig, L. '"Increasing My Value Proposition to the Struggle": Arthur Mutambara and Student Politics in Zimbabwe', *African Sociological Review*, 10, 2, 2006, pp. 94–115.

Zimbabwe Law Reports (ZLR), *Davies and Others v Minister of Lands, Agriculture and Water Development* (Harare, ZLR, 1994).

Zimudzi, T. B. 'African Women, Violent Crime and the Criminal Law in Colonial Zimbabwe, 1900–1952', *Journal of Southern African Studies*, 30, 3, 2004, pp. 499–518.

Zvakanyorwa Wilbert Sadomba, *War Veterans in Zimbabwe's Revolution: Challenging Neo-Colonialism and Settler and International Capital* (Oxford, James Currey, 2011).

Unpublished Sources

Backman, A. *Courtroom Atmospheres: Affective Dynamics in Courts Sessions of Criminal Matter in Vienna* (Masters' thesis, Stockholm University, 2017).

Feltoe, G 'Law, Ideology and Coercion in Southern Rhodesia' (M.Phil dissertation, Kent University, 1978).

Gubbay, A. 'The Plight of Successive Chief Justices of Zimbabwe in Seeking to Protect Human Rights and the Rule of Law', *Rothschild Lecture* (unpublished lecture, 2001), accessed on 11 March 2012 at www .rothschildfostertrust.com/materials/lecture_gubbay.pdf

'The Progressive Erosion of the Rule of Law in Independent Zimbabwe', *International Rule of Law Lecture* (unpublished lecture, December 2009).

Karekwaivanane, G. H. *Legal Encounters: Law, State and Society in Zimbabwe, c. 1950 –1980* (D.Phil thesis, University of Oxford, 2012).

Online Sources

Anonymous. 'Acquittal of Mr. Joel Hita and ZimRights – ZWE 001/0210/ OBS 023.4', *FIDH*, 26 January 2012, retrieved from www.fidh.org/.

'Ardent Mugabe Supporter Now AG', *Zimbabwe Times*, 18 December 2008, retrieved from www.zimbabwesituation.com/.

'Bulawayo's New Party Organising Secretary Arrested', *Radio VOP*, 17 February 2011, retrieved from www.radiovop.com/.

'Chinotimba Sues Minister for US 19 Million for Loss of Business', *The Insider*, 2 December 2011, retrieved from www.insiderzim.com/.

'Chipinge Man Jailed for Insulting Mugabe', *Radio VOP*, 3 September 2010, retrieved from www.radiovop.com.

'Cop in MLF Trial Admits Some Exhibits Not in Court', 26 April 2012, retrieved from www.chronicle.co.zw/.

'Court Quashes Gwisai's Application', *The Herald*, 15 September 2011, retrieved from http://allafrica.com/.

'Court Watch 1/2013 [Supreme Court and High Court Judges and Labour and Administrative Court Presidents]', *Veritas*, 25 January 2013, retrieved from http://archive.kubatana.net/.

'Demonstrations in Zimbabwe Will Be Crushed: Mnangagwa', *RadioVOP*, 7 February 2011, retrieved from www.radiovop.com.

'Free at Last', *NewsDay*, 16 March 2011, retrieved from www.newsday .co.zw/.

'Gukurahundi Exhibition Pulled Down', *New Zimbabwe*, 9 April 2015, retrieved from www.newzimbabwe.com/.

'Gwisai Sentencing Set for Today', *The Herald*, 20 March 2012, retrieved from www.herald.co.zw/.

'MDC-T Violence Threats a Fantasy: ZRP', *Zimbabwe Broadcasting Corporation*, 3 February 2011, retrieved from www.zbc.co.zw/.

'Mhlanga Charged with Tribe Hate Crime', *New Zimbabwe*, 7 March 2011, retrieved from www.newzimbabwe.com/.

'MLF Leaders Still in Police Custody', *Radio VOP*, 5 March 2011, retrieved from www.zimbabwesituation.com/.

'MLF Leaders' Trial Opens, Key Witness Rebuffs Police Claims', *Radio VOP*, 20 March 2012, retrieved from www.zimbabwesituation.com/.

'MLF Members in Hiding, Four More Arrested', *Radio VOP*, 12 March 2011, retrieved from www.zimbabwesituation.com/.

'MLF Pair Released on Bail', *NewsDay*, 7 April 2011, retrieved from www.newsday.co.zw/.

'Mthwakazi Leaders Have a Case to Answer – Magistrate', *Radio VOP*, 11 March 2011, retrieved from www.zimbabwesituation.com/.

'Mthwakazi Trio's Case Splits Lawyers', *New Zimbabwe*, 16 March 2011, retrieved from www.newzimbabwe.com/.

'Mthwakazi Liberation Leaders Re-arrested', *Radio VOP*, 20 January 2012, retrieved from www.zimbabwesituation.com/.

'Mthwakazi Treason Trio Seek Discharge', *New Zimbabwe*, 1 November 2012, retrieved from www.newzimbabwe.com/.

'New Zimbabwe Opposition Party Launched', *Radio VOP*, 29 December 2010, retrieved from www.radiovop.com/.

'Police Ordered to Crackdown on Matland Secessionists', *Radio VOP*, 26 January 2011, retrieved from www.radiovop.com/.

'Police Recant Testimony in Siwela Trial', *New Zimbabwe*, 20 March 2012, retrieved from www.zimbabwesituation.com/.

'Retired Magistrate Takes over Chinamasa Trial', *New Zimbabwe*, 4 August 2006, retrieved from www.zimbabwesituation.com/.

'Rituals Actors Arrested on Stage', *The Standard*, 10 January 2011, retrieved from www.thestandard.co.zw/.

'Rituals Team Charged with Beating Drums', *The Zimbabwean*, 17 March 2011, retrieved from www.thezimbabwean.co/.

'Secessionists Pile Pressure on Mugabe', *The Standard*, 26 February 2011, retrieved from www.thestandard.co.zw/.

'Siwela's Condition Worsens in Prison', *Radio VOP*, 25 May 2011, retrieved from www.zimbabwesituation.com/.

'Siwela Suffers New Bail Blow', *New Zimbabwe*, 10 May 2011, retrieved from www.newzimbabwe.com/.

'Staff at AG's Office Expose External Intervention', *Zimbabwe Times*, 8 March 2009, retrieved from www.zimbabwesituation.com/.

'State's Bid for Charges against Maseko Foiled', *MISA-Zimbabwe*, 14 September 2010, retrieved from www.swradioafrica.com/.

'State Blocks Mthwakazi Leaders' Release', *Radio VOP*, 24 March 2011, retrieved from www.zimbabwesituation.com/.

'State v Munyaradzi Gwisai and Others: Application for Discharge – Court Watch 2/2012', 2 February 2012, *VERITAS*, retrieved from http://archive.kubatana.net/.

'Styx Mhlanga Released!', *Byo24NEWS*, 10 March 2011, retrieved from http://bulawayo24.com/.

'Top Former Judge Says Mugabe "Engineered Lawlessness"', *Deutsche Presse-Agentur*, October 6 2011, retrieved from www.iol.co.za/.

'Tsvangirai's Utterances Expose Penchant for Violence', *The Herald*, 31 January 2011, retrieved from www.herald.co.zw/.

'Weekly Media Update', *Media Monitoring Project Zimbabwe* (November 2002), retrieved from www.mmpz.org/.

'Zimbabwe: Police Arrest Attorney General Gula-Ndebele', *Financial Gazette*, 8 November 2007, retrieved from www.zimbabwesituation .com/.

'Zimbabwe State Prosecutor Refuses to Handle Treason Case after Threats from Security Agents', *Zim Online*, 13 March 2006, retrieved from www.zimbabwesituation.com/.

'Zanu PF's Final Blow on Judiciary?', *Financial Gazette*, 21 November 2002, retrieved from www.zimbabwesituation.com/.

'Zim Police Investigates Fliers to Topple Mugabe', *Radio VOP*, 15 August 2011, retrieved from www.zimbabwesituation.com/.

Abammeli Human Rights Lawyers Network, 'Statement by Abammeli', *Abammeli*, 16 March 2011, retrieved from http://zimdiaspora.com/.

Abammeli Human Rights Lawyers Network, 'Who We Are?' and 'Mission', *Abammeli*, retrieved from www.abammelilawyers.com/.

Chimakure, C. and Muleya, D. 'Gula-Ndebele Tangled in Succession War', *Zimbabwe Independent*, 23 November 2007, retrieved from www .thestandard.co.zw/.

Chinembiri, T. 'Paul Siwela Poses a National Security Threat', *Bulawayo24*, 25 April 2016, retrieved from http://bulawayo24.com/.

Chitemba, B. 'Jailed Siwela Left in Dilemma', *The Zimbabwe Independent*, 27 May 2011, retrieved from www.zimbabwesituation.com/.

Crisis in Zimbabwe Coalition, 'Court Finds Gwisai, 5 Others Guilty', *CRISIS*, 20 March 2012, retrieved from http://archive.kubatana.net/.

Dube, J. 'Nkomo's Ghost Rises to Fight Land Grab', *IOL*, 6 May 2000, retrieved from www.iol.co.za/.

Dube, P. 'Mugabe Will Rule Zimbabwe Forever: Mnangagwa', *Daily News*, 25 March 2011, retrieved from http://archive.kubatana.net/.

Eppel, J. *Owen Maseko and the Gukurahundi*, 5 April 2010, retrieved from http://archive.kubatana.net/.

Gonda, V. 'Magistrate's Conflict of Interest Exposed in Land Case', *SW Radio Africa*, 1 February 2010, retrieved from www.zimbabwesituation.com/.

Government of Zimbabwe, 'General Notice 236 of 2010', *Government Gazette*, 27 August 2010, retrieved from www.zimlii.org/.

Guma, L. 'Chikafu Case Highlights Intimidation of the Judiciary', *SW Radio Africa*, 25 April 2007, retrieved from www.zimbabwesituation.com/.

'Kucaca Phulu: Behind the Headlines', *SW Radio Africa*, 24 March 2011, retrieved from www.zimbabwesituation.com/.

'High Court Orders Release of Mthwakazi Duo, Siwela Still Held', *SW Radio Africa*, 31 March 2011, retrieved from http://allafrica.com/.

'Munyaradzi Gwisai on Question Time: Part 1', *SW Radio Africa*, 20 April 2011, retrieved from http://archive.kubatana.net/.

'Nehanda Radio Speaks to Paul Siwela', *Nehanda Radio*, 6 January 2014, retrieved from http://nehandaradio.com/.

Gumbo, H. 'I Wish to Thank You All for the Overwhelming Solidarity during Our Trial', 7 March 2012, retrieved from http://archive.kubatana.net/.

Hamunyari, Z. 'Masvingo, Bulawayo Judgements Shame ZRP', *ChangeZimbabwe*, 23 January 2012, retrieved from http://changezimbabwe.com/.

ISO(Z), 'Update on Arrests and Detention', *ISO(Z)*, 24 February 2011, retrieved from http://archive.kubatana.net/.

'Bail Hearing: Gwisai and 5 Others Granted Bail', *ISO(Z)*, 17 March 2011, retrieved from http://archive.kubatana.net/.

'Update on Zimbabwean Socialists' Treason Trial', *ISO(Z)*, 18 July 2011, retrieved from http://archive.kubatana.net/.

Karimakwenda, T. 'Siwela Awaits Release after Granting of Bail', *SW Radio Africa*, 1 June 2011, retrieved from www.zimbabwesituation.com/.

'Siwela Release Not Confirmed', *SW Radio Africa*, 1 June 2011, retrieved from www.zimbabwesituation.com/.

Kunene, T. 'Released Secessionist Leader Siwela Fears for His Life', *RNW*, 8 June 2011, retrieved from www.zimbabwesituation.com/.

Kuwana, F. 'Gono Splashes US$1M in Bribes Ahead of Presidential Bid', *ZimDiaspora*, 24 January 2009, retrieved from www.zimbabwesituation.com/.

Lupande, F. 'Xmas Crimes Keep Court Busy', *The Herald*, 27 December 2014, retrieved from www.herald.co.zw/.

Madongo, I. 'Paul Siwela Wife Hunted down by Secret Police', *SW Radio Africa*, 21 March 2011, retrieved from www.zimbabwesituation.com/.

'Mangoma, Paul Siwela Trials Drag on', *SW Radio Africa*, 17 May 2011, retrieved from http://allafrica.com/.

Maduna, T. *Toilet Democracy*, 12 July 2005, retrieved from http://swradioafrica.com/.

Makombe, L. 'Mubarak, Mugabe Regimes: So Many Parallels to Draw', *Zimbabwe Independent*, 25 February 2011, retrieved from http://allafrica.com/.

Mangwende, B. 'Chigovera Forced to Retire', *Daily News*, 17 April 2003, retrieved from www.zimbabwesituation.com/.

Manyukwe, C. 'Chinamasa off the Hook', *Financial Gazette*, 16 February 2006, retrieved from www.zimbabwesituation.com/.

'Chinamasa Under Probe', *Zimbabwe Independent*, 28 April 2006, retrieved from www.zimbabwesituation.com/.

'Chinamasa Trial in Doubt', *Zimbabwe Independent*, 30 June 2006, retrieved from www.zimbabwesituation.com/.

'Chinamasa Set to Deny Charges', *Zimbabwe Independent*, 28 July 2006, retrieved from www.zimbabwesituation.com/.

'No Way Out for Chinamasa, Says AG's Office', *Zimbabwe Independent*, 29 September 2006, retrieved from www.zimbabwesituation.com/.

'Prosecutor in Chinamasa Case Resigns', *Zimbabwe Independent*, 13 October 2006, retrieved from www.zimbabwesituation.com/.

'Hands-off, AG Warns Chihuri', *Financial Gazette*, 14 December 2007, retrieved from www.zimbabwesituation.com/.

Maphosa, T. 'Zimbabwe Justice Minister's Trial Finally under Way', *Voice of America*, 9 August 2006, retrieved from www.zimbabwesituation.com/.

Maseko, O. 'So I Went … ', *The 1980 Alliance*, no date, retrieved from http://the1980.org/.

Trials and Tribulations of an Artist, 17 July 2011, retrieved from www.osisa.org/.

Presentation at the Oslo Freedom Forum, 15 May 2013, retrieved from www.youtube.com/.

Matabele Liberation Organization, *About Us*, 2011, retrieved from www.matabeleliberation.org/.

Mhlanga, S. 'Zimbabwe Police Arrest Bulawayo Writer in Literary-Political Criticism Row', *VOA Zimbabwe*, 9 March 2011, retrieved from http://m.voazimbabwe.com/.

Mlotshwa, K. 'New Radical Matabeleland Political Party on the Cards', *Zimbabwe Mail*, 26 December 2010, retrieved from www.zimbabwesituation.com/.

'Government Cracks Whip on Secessionists', *The Standard*, 7 March 2011, retrieved from www.zimbabwesituation.com/.

Moyo, J. 'Zimbabwe: Bid to Dilute Sovereignty Slammed', *The Herald*, 18 April 2002, retrieved from http://allafrica.com/.

Mthwakazi Liberation Front (MLF), 'Open Letter to His Excellency President Robert Gabriel Mugabe', *MLF*, 24 February 2011, retrieved from www.mthwakaziliberationfront.org/.

Munyoro, F. 'Judges Get Vehicles, Goods', *The Herald*, 1 August 2008, retrieved from www.zimbabwesituation.com/.

Muzulu, P. 'How Many Justices Dube-Banda Does Zim Have?' *Newsday*, 29 January 2020, retrieved from www.newsday.co.zw.

Ncube, M. 'Chihuri Crushes New Party', *The Zimbabwean*, 15 March 2011, retrieved from www.zimbabwesituation.com/.

Ncube, N. 'More Woes for AG', *Financial Gazette*, 15 November 2007, retrieved from www.zimbabwesituation.com/.

Ndebele, Z. 'Maseko Release: Victory for Gukurahundi Artist', *Zimbabwe Netzwerk*, 18 September 2010, retrieved from www.zimbabwenetzwerk.de/.

Ndoro, T. E. 'High Court Roasts VP Chiwenga for Using Military in Domestic Matters', *iHarare*, 25 January 2020, retrieved from hhtp://iharare.com.

Nemukuyu, D. 'Zimbabwe: Rotten Row Courts in a Mess', *The Herald*, 26 March 2009, retrieved from http://allafrica.com/.

Nkala, S. 'Bereaved Siwela Sneaks Back', *The Standard*, 1 December 2019, retrieved from www.thestandard.co.zw/.

Nkatazo, L. 'AG Appeals against Chinamasa Acquittal', *New Zimbabwe*, 23 September 2006, retrieved from www.zimbabwesituation.com/.

'Zimbabwe's Top Prosecutor Removed from Post', *New Zimbabwe*, 11 December 2009, retrieved from www.newzimbabwe.com/.

Nyangove, P. 'Siwela Critically Ill', *The Standard*, 29 May 2011, retrieved from www.zimbabwesituation.com/.

Nyathi, K. 'New Radical Movements Expose Tribal Fault Lines', *The Standard*, 15 January 2011, retrieved from www.thestandard.co.zw/.

Petras, I. 'Statement by ZLHR on Formation of Abammeli Human Rights Lawyers', in 'Behind the Headlines', *SW Radio Africa*, 24 March 2011, retrieved from www.zimbabwesituation.com/.

Raftopoulos, B. 'Lest We Forget: From LOMA to POSA', address at public meeting commemorating the 1960 protests, 24 July 2003, retrieved from http://archive.kubatana.net/.

Rupapa, T. 'State Says Gwisai Has Case to Answer', *The Herald*, 6 March 2011, accessed on 3 July 2011 at www.herald.co.zw/.

'Community Service for Gwisai', *The Herald*, 21 March 2012, retrieved from www.herald.co.zw/.

Saki, O. and Chiware, T. *The Law in Zimbabwe*, GlobalLex, February 2007, available at www.nyulawglobal.org/globalex/Zimbabwe.html.

Sema, T. 'Zim Activists in Danger of Unlawful Prison Sentences: Release Them Now!' *SAMWU Press Statement*, 14 March 2012, retrieved from www.zimbabwesituation.com/.

Sibanda, T. 'MDC Decries Appointment of Johannes Tomana as Attorney-General', *SW Radio Africa*, 18 December 2008, retrieved from www.zimbabwesituation.com/.

'Bail Hearing for 29 MDC-t Activists Postponed for 7th Time', *SW Radio Africa*, 19 March 2012, retrieved from www.zimbabwesituation.com/.

'Prosecution Case against MLF Leaders "Shaky"', *SW Radio Africa*, 23 March 2012, retrieved from www.zimbabwesituation.com/.

'Treason Trial against MLF Leaders Resumes in Bulawayo', *SW Radio Africa*, 23 April 2012, retrieved from http://allafrica.com/.

Sokwanele, 'Compromised Judgement: Magistrate Samuel Zuze's Offer Letter', *ThisisZimbabwe Blog*, 30 January 2010, retrieved from www.zimbabwesituation.com/.

Verheul, S. 'Land, Law, and the Courts in Zimbabwe' in Alexander, J., McGregor, J. and Tendi, M. (eds), *Handbook of Zimbabwean Politics*, July 2020, retrieved from https://www.oxfordhandbooks.com/view/10.1093/oxfordhb/9780198805472.001.0001/oxfordhb-9780198 805472-e-4.

Veritas, 'Court Watch 8/2012 [Prosecutors' Record of Abuse of Power to Delay Bail]', *Veritas*, 25 April 2012, retrieved from http://archive.kubatana.net/.

Whiz, L. 'Gukurahundi Exhibit Artist Gets Bail', *New Zimbabwe*, 31 March 2010, retrieved from www.newzimbabwe.com/.

Zikhali, M. 'Gagged: Owen Maseko's Art in Zimbabwe', 23 May 2010, retrieved from www.dispatchesinternational.org/.

ZLHR, 'Arrest of Magistrate, Public Prosecutor and Senior Lawyer', *Kubatana*, 10 January 2004, retrieved from http://archive.kubatana.net/.

The Legal Monitor, edition 13, 21 September 2009, retrieved from http://archive.kubatana.net/.

The Legal Monitor, edition 19, 26 October 2009, retrieved from http://archive.kubatana.net/.

'State Forced to Drop Charges against Maseko', *ZLHR News*, 13 September 2010, retrieved from http://archive.kubatana.net/.

'State Ropes in Zvekare to Persecute Maseko', *Legal Monitor*, edition 62, 13 September 2010, retrieved from http://archive.kubatana.net/.

'Magistrate Refers Maseko's Application to Supreme Court', *ZLHR*, 18 September 2010, retrieved from www.swradioafrica.com/.

'Victory as Magistrate Overturns Police Ban', *Legal Monitor*, edition 79, 7 February 2011, retrieved from http://archive.kubatana.net/.

'Labour Activist Gwisai and 45 Others Languish in Police Custody as Artists Freed on Summons', *ZLHR News*, 21 February 2011, retrieved from http://archive.kubatana.net/.

'Unidentified People Interrogate Activists as They Remain in Custody', *ZLHR News*, 22 February 2011, retrieved from http://archive.kubatana .net/.

'Gwisai Bemoans Torture as Muchadehama Challenges Placement of Activists on Remand', *ZLHR News*, 24 February 2011, retrieved from http://archive.kubatana.net/.

The Legal Monitor, edition 82, 28 February 2011, retrieved from http:// archive.kubatana.net/.

'Hard Labour and Solitary Confinement for Treason Suspects', *ZLHR News*, 7 March 2011, retrieved from http://archive.kubatana.net/.

'Charge Shopping State Water down Treason Charges against Gwisai and Five Others', *ZLHR News*, 18 July 2011, retrieved from http://archive .kubatana.net/.

The Legal Monitor, edition 136, 26 March 2012, retrieved from http:// archive.kubatana.net/.

Zulu, B. 'Terror Bases Unlawful Says Chigovera', *Zimbabwe Independent*, 8 February 2002, retrieved from http://allafrica.com/.

African Studies Series